# Visual Quicl



# WINDOWS 3.1

Webster & Associates

Peachpit Press

**Microsoft Windows 3.1 Visual QuickStart Guide**
Webster & Associates

Peachpit Press, Inc.
2414 Sixth Street
Berkeley, CA 94710
(510) 548-4393
(510) 548-5991 (fax)



## Notice of Liability:



## Trademarks:



First Edition published 1992

ISBN 0-938151-92-4

Printed and bound in the United States of America

# Why a Visual QuickStart?

Virtually no one actually reads computer books—instead, people use them as references. This series of **Visual QuickStart Guides** has made that reference easier thanks to a new approach to learning computer applications.

Conventional computer books usually teach you about a program using extensive textual explanations. A **Visual QuickStart Guide** takes a far more visual approach—pictures literally show you what to do, and text is limited to clear concise commentary. Learning is easier, because a **Visual QuickStart** familiarizes you with the look and feel of your software. Learning is also faster, because you don't have to comb through long-winded passages to find the information you need.

It's a new approach to computer learning, but it's also solidly based on experience: Webster & Associates have logged thousands of hours of classroom training, and have authored several books on desktop publishing topics.

# Acknowledgments

This book was produced by the publication department of Webster and Associates. We wish to acknowledge the effort and dedication of the following people for researching, writing and editing this book:

Jason Berman

Wayne Clark

Roger Stott

Suzie Wynn Jones

Paul Webster

Tony Webster

Jenny Hamilton

Webster and Associates also wishes to thank Matt Wagner and Bill Gladstone from Waterside Productions, as well as Ted Nace from Peachpit Press, for their valuable assistance and cooperation.

# Contents

# INTRODUCTION TO WINDOWS 1

## WHAT IS WINDOWS?

Microsoft Windows is a powerful, graphics-based operating environment for use on your personal computer. Its function is to replace MS-DOS or PC-DOS as the interface between you and the components that make up your computer system.

### *THE OPERATING SYSTEM*

All the functions that your computer system performs are controlled through its operating system.

Your IBM or compatible computer system is handled through a program called the Disk Operating System, or simply DOS.

When you turn on your computer system, the DOS program is loaded automatically. The devices that make up your computer system—disk drives, monitor, keyboard, printers, memory chips, even the processor—are all controlled through DOS.

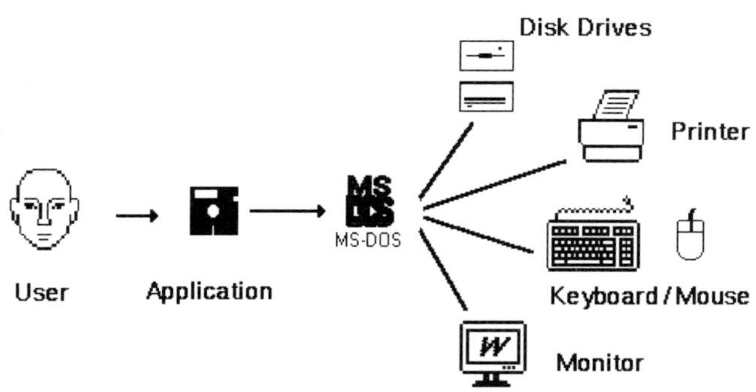


**Figure 1.** When you type commands into your computer, DOS translates them into electronic signals that drive the components of your computer system. When you run a computer program, the program interacts with DOS, then DOS communicates with your hardware.

Most of the commands you issue directly to DOS deal with disk files. Typically, you copy files between disks, organize them into directories, delete old files, and select program files to execute.

```
Microsoft(R) MS-DOS(R) Version 5.01
             (C)Copyright Microsoft Corp 1981-1988

C:\>dir

 Volume in drive C is A
 Volume Serial Number is 363C-1DE0
 Directory of  C:\

BIN          <DIR>      10-03-90  10:43p
DOS          <DIR>      10-03-90  10:38p
MENU         <DIR>      10-04-90  10:49a
SYS          <DIR>      10-03-90  10:51p
WIN2         <DIR>      06-03-91   9:59a
WINDOWS      <DIR>      05-28-91   6:08p
AUTOEXEC BAT        422 04-05-91   2:28p
COMMAND  COM      37557 11-30-88  12:00a
CONFIG   SYS         82 04-04-91   5:29p
HIMEM    SYS      11304 05-01-90   3:00a
       10 File(s)    3776512 bytes free

C:\>
```

**Figure 2.** In DOS, command words are typed in through the keyboard and appear on the screen as alphabetic or numeric characters. Feedback from DOS takes the form of messages or data displayed on the screen, also as alphanumeric characters.

Thus, because it uses only alphanumeric characters as it interacts with users, DOS is said to be a text-based operating system.

## MICROSOFT WINDOWS GRAPHIC USER INTERFACE

Microsoft Windows, like all other programs on your PC, operates through DOS.

However, instead of serving as a specialized application, like a word processor or spreadsheet program, Windows gives you an easier and more effective way to issue commands to do the same kinds of tasks you would otherwise do directly through DOS.

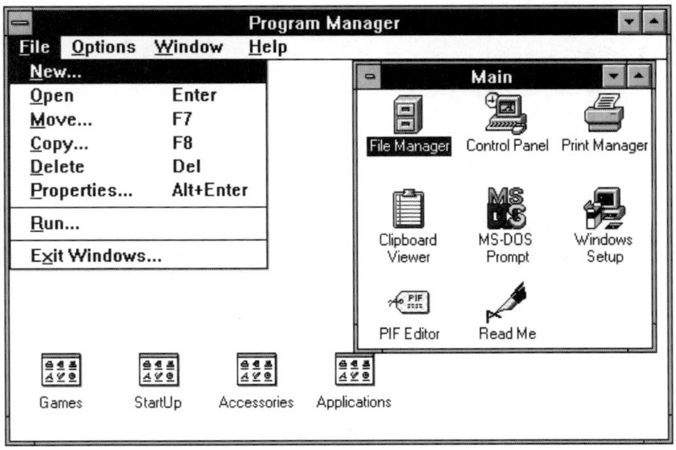


**Figure 3.** Where DOS is a text-based system, the Windows display is composed of graphic images. You type DOS commands using the keyboard, but you can issue Windows commands to select objects using a pointer on the screen.

Because it relies on graphics rather than text, Windows is said to have a graphical user interface, or GUI.

The idea behind the graphical user interface concept is that it is easier to interact with the computer through a visual medium than through a written one.

It is easier, and more intuitive, to use a pointer to choose an action than it is to type in commands that you must memorize.

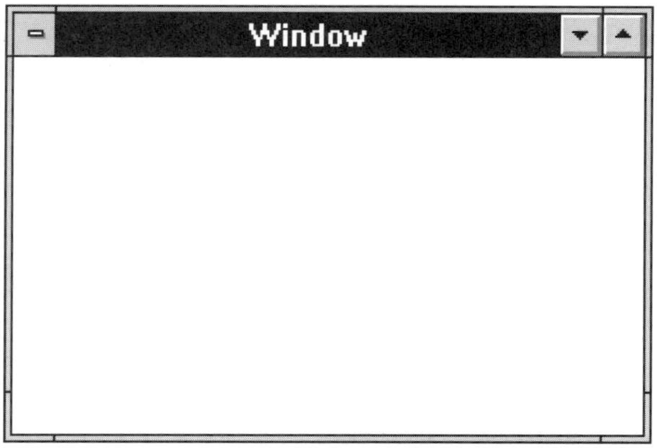


## WINDOWS

**Figure 4.** In Windows, the screen is organized into graphically drawn boxes called—as you might expect—windows. These windows serve to separate different programs and utilities within the Windows GUI.

A window can be expanded on the screen, allowing you to concentrate on its contents. Similarly, you can make windows smaller, and even tuck them out of sight, so that they do not clutter your display when your attention is on another window.

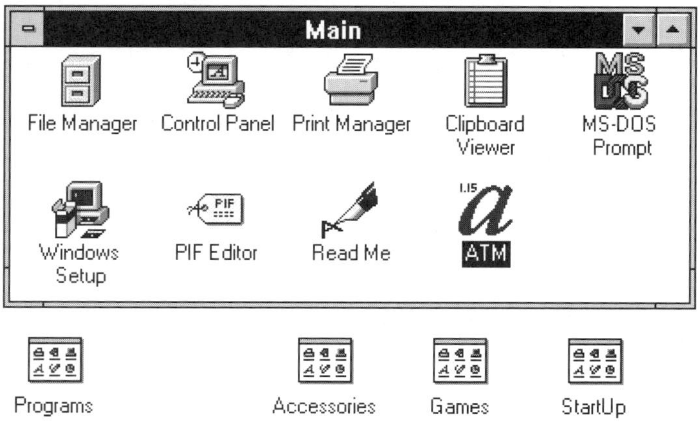


## ICONS

**Figure 5.** Within windows, graphical pictures, called icons, represent programs, groups of programs, and closed windows. An icon's design gives visual cues about its contents.

Though most icons include a written caption, you can usually identify an icon by its appearance alone.

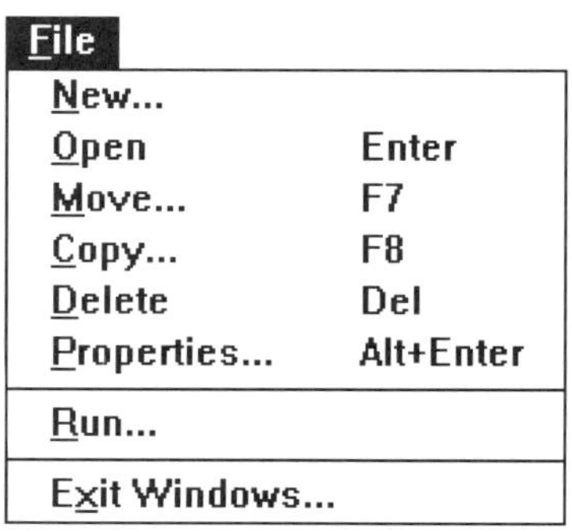


## MENUS

**Figure 6.** You never need to type in a command at the keyboard when you are using Windows. Instead, you select commands from specially organized lists called menus. Using menus, you can look at lists of available commands and choose the one you want.

## THE MOUSE

Keeping keyboard use to a minimum is central to the GUI concept. In Windows, you will use the mouse to communicate with your computer system—you can issue most Windows commands without using the keyboard at all.

As you move the mouse across your desk, a corresponding image moves across the screen. This image, which usually takes the form of a hollow arrow, is called the mouse pointer.

By positioning the mouse pointer and pressing the mouse buttons, you can signal your instructions to the Windows program without having to use the keyboard.

It is possible to use Windows without a mouse. Any kind of pointing device, like a light-pen, a track ball, or even a joystick, can be used instead.

The mouse, however, was specifically designed to let you position the pointer and press the buttons all with one hand. You will probably find the mouse the most efficient tool to communicate with Windows.

If you do not have a mouse or any other pointing device, it is still possible to use Windows through the keyboard. All of the commands that are signaled with the mouse can, if necessary, be issued from the keyboard.

However, because Windows has been designed to work as efficiently as possible with a mouse, some keyboard commands are awkward and inconvenient to use. To get the most out of Microsoft Windows, a mouse, or another pointing device, is essential.

# WHY USE WINDOWS?

In addition to the convenience of keyboard-free interaction with your personal computer, Windows offers many other advantages not available through DOS.

## *STANDARDIZED FORMAT*

In a DOS-based system, not only do you have to memorize all the DOS commands, you also have to learn the special commands, and command styles, of each application program you want to use.

Every DOS program has a unique look, as well as a unique set of commands and instructions.

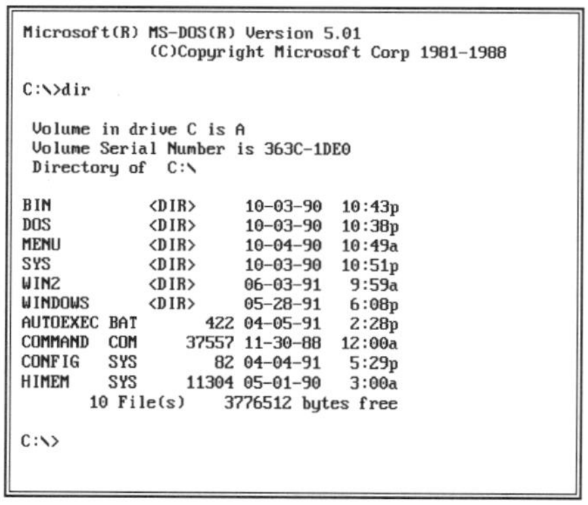


DOS

**Figure 7.** This figure compares two popular DOS programs and DOS itself. Each clearly has its own look and command style, which you must learn before you can use them.

Nothing about the appearance, or operation, of these programs ties them together.

In DOS, each application is different.

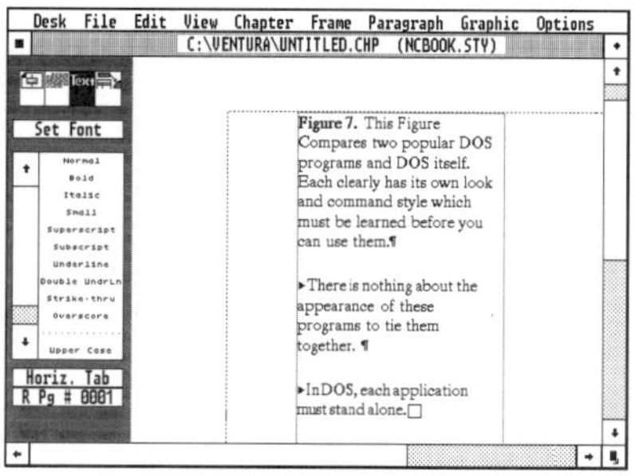


Ventura Publisher

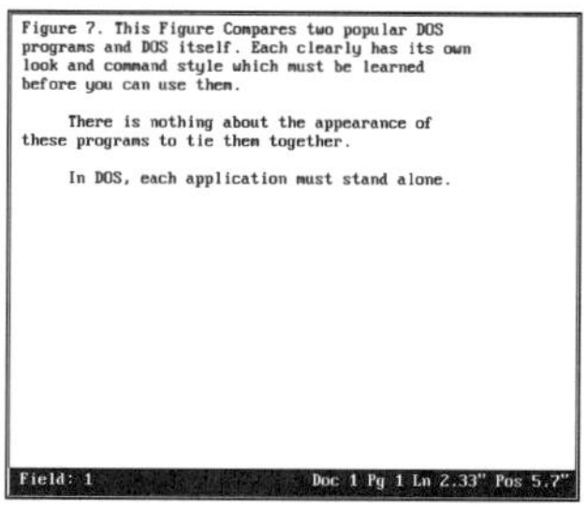


WordPerfect

Windows has developed a standardized format, using windows, icons, and menus. This format is used consistently, not only throughout Windows itself, but also in hundreds of programs specially designed to run in Windows.

**Figure 8.** Here you can compare the Windows GUI and versions of the same application programs shown in Figure 7 that are written especially for Windows.

Note the consistency in the appearance of the three programs. The windows that contain the programs are uniformly constructed, and the menus and commands are all organized along the same lines.

This similarity makes it easy to move between programs in Windows. Not having to master a new format with every new program generally makes Windows applications much easier to learn than traditional DOS programs.

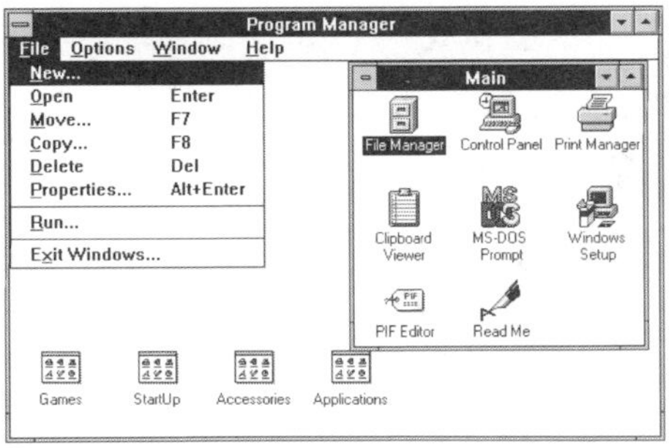


Windows

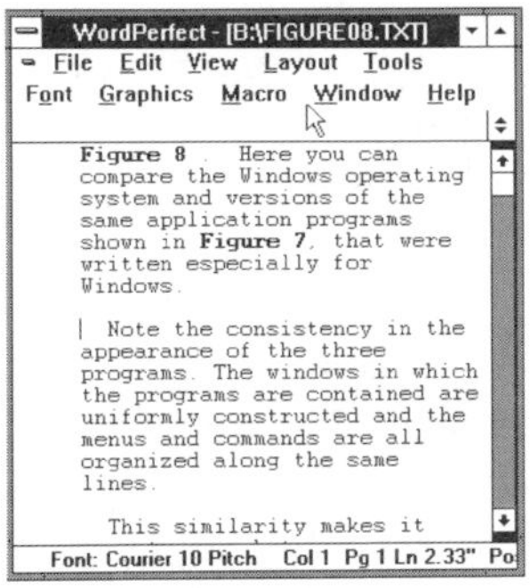


WordPerfect

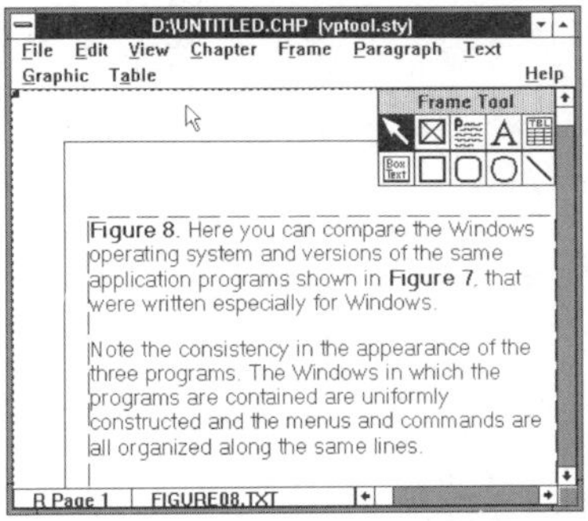


Ventura Publisher

## THE CLIPBOARD

**Figure 9.** All data-handling programs written to run under windows share a facility called the Clipboard. Using this feature, data—whether numeric, text, or graphic (where supported)—can be transferred from one program to another without requiring any conversion.

This feature is very useful in creating documents that contain a variety of data elements. Graphics, text, and numeric data can each be created using specialized applications, then transferred into a single document using the Clipboard.

## MULTIPLE APPLICATIONS

**Figure 10.** In DOS, only one program can run at a time. To switch between programs, you must exit from one and start up another. Not only is this process time consuming, but it also means that you cannot return to the original application without again exiting and restarting programs.

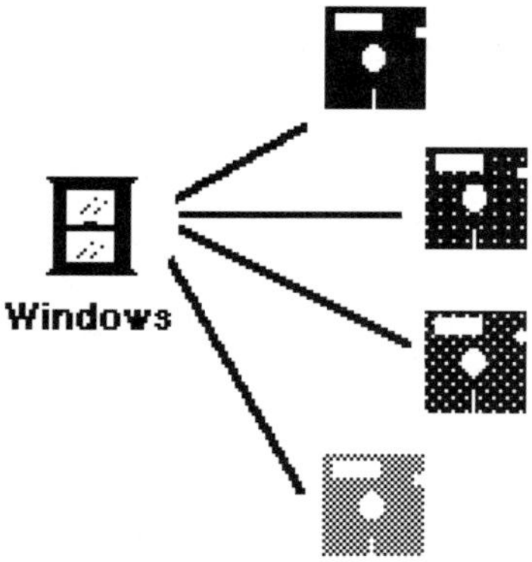


Windows allows you to start more than one program without having to exit from any of them. Each program is contained in its own window, and you can switch between windows, and therefore between programs, quickly and easily. Programs that have been started and are contained within a window are said to be opened.

The number of applications that can be open at a given time depends on the memory, disk space, and system resources available in your computer system. You can use only one program at a time, but the other programs are retained in memory and can be activated at any time.

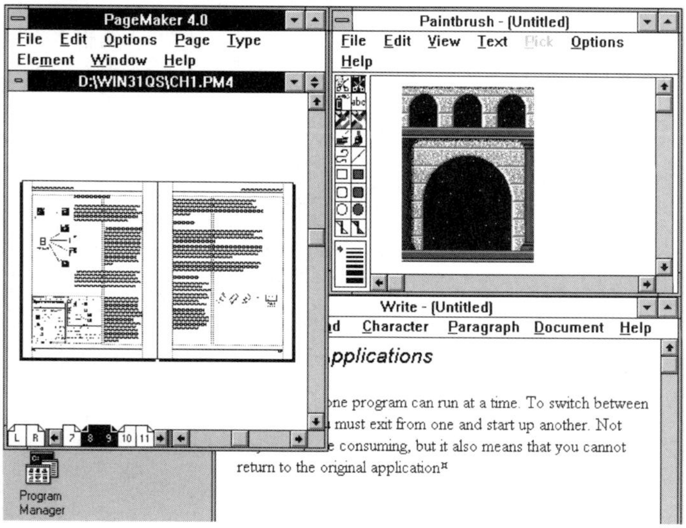


**Figure 11.** This figure shows that you can switch between a graphics program, a word processor, and a desktop publishing package. Because each program can be used to develop a different part of the same document, the ability to switch frequently between applications can improve your productivity. You don't need to show all the open applications on the screen, but you'll find that it's useful.

When several programs are open at once, the computer acts on only one program at a time. The other programs are held suspended at precisely the point you left them. When you reactivate one of these dormant programs, the application you were previously running enters the suspended state.

## MULTITASKING

If your computer has an 80386 series or higher processor, Windows will allow you to multitask several applications. When programs are multitasked, applications do not become dormant when not in use. The processor budgets its time among all the open programs.

The processor can switch its attention rapidly between the open programs. As you use one of the open applications, you will have the impression that you are receiving the uninterrupted attention of the computer processor. In fact, the processor is changing tasks many times every second.

Multitasking allows you to request a time-consuming operation from one application, such as recalculation in a large spreadsheet, and then use a second application while waiting for the first to be ready.

## VIRTUAL MEMORY

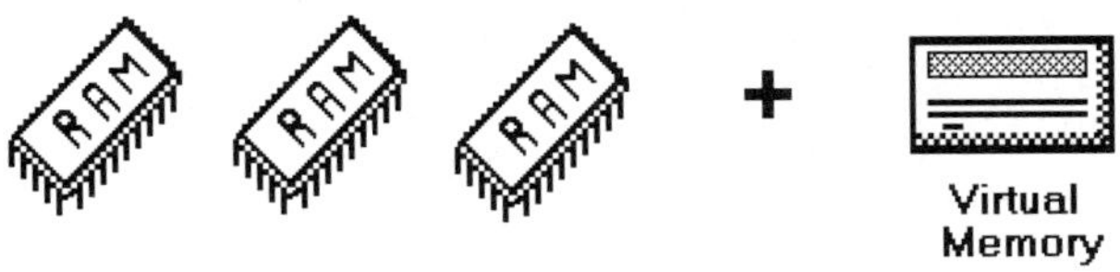


**Figure 12.** Another feature available with 80386 or higher systems is virtual memory. Windows creates a special file on your hard disk, called a swap file, where it stores information that would ordinarily be kept in memory.

Because your hard disk can store far more data than your system's real memory, the use of virtual memory greatly increases Windows' capacity to perform memory-intensive tasks.

The swap file permits you to open more applications at the same time. The increased memory provided by the swap file also allows individual applications to use far more data at once.

Because the swap file is set up by the Windows program itself, any application program you run from Windows, whether specially written for Windows or not, will benefit from the advantages of virtual memory.

## MANAGEMENT OF PERIPHERALS

When running with DOS, every application program is responsible for controlling those peripheral devices that it uses.

If your system includes a monitor, a printer, and a mouse, each program you run under DOS must include special programs, called drivers, instructing the computer on how to use these devices.

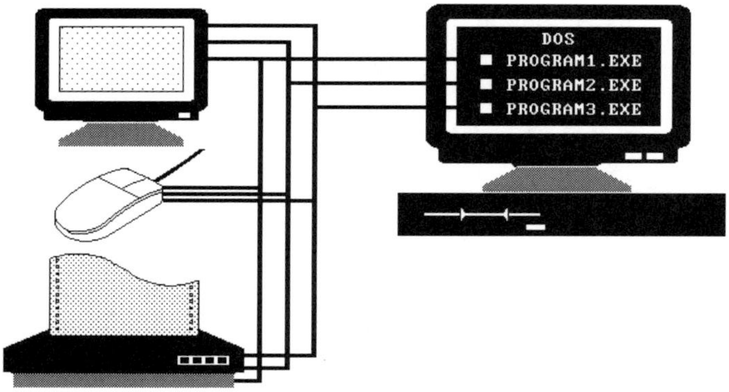


**Figure 13.** If you commonly use three application programs, each of these programs will require its own set of drivers. The three devices mentioned above would therefore require nine separate driver programs.

Many different peripherals are available for your computer system in today's marketplace. For each kind of peripheral, there are dozens, often hundreds, of different models available, each requiring a unique driver program.

Most DOS programs do not offer drivers for every available peripheral, opting instead to accommodate only the most popular models. If your system has an unusual or uncommon setup, many DOS programs may not be able to drive your equipment.

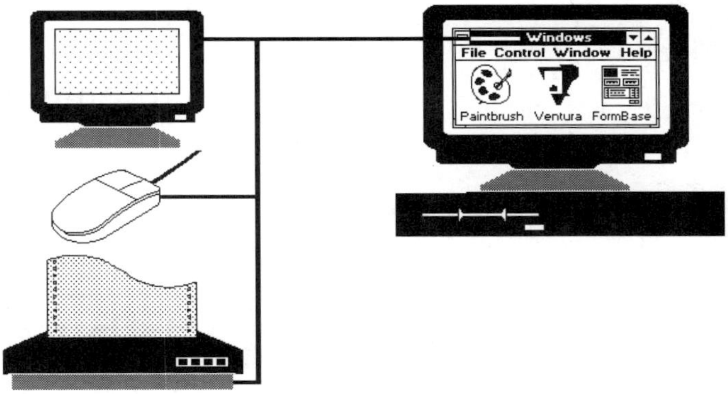


**Figure 14.** In Microsoft Windows, it is the Windows program itself that manages your computer's input and output devices. Thus, only one set of driver programs is required to handle your system's equipment. Each individual application program no longer has to supply its own drivers.

Because Microsoft, the program's writers, want to see Windows used extensively, they have taken the trouble to provide as complete a set of driver programs as possible.

Windows is thus more likely than most DOS programs to have the drivers you need for your system.

If you change your equipment, you need only change the setting once within Windows, rather than having to change the settings for each of many DOS programs.

## Windows Disadvantages

Microsoft Windows is a useful and powerful tool for your computer system, but in some situations it may be advantageous for you to stay with DOS. Some potential disadvantages of Windows are outlined below. If any of these situations apply to your system, you may want to consider running programs directly through DOS.

## RUNNING SPEED

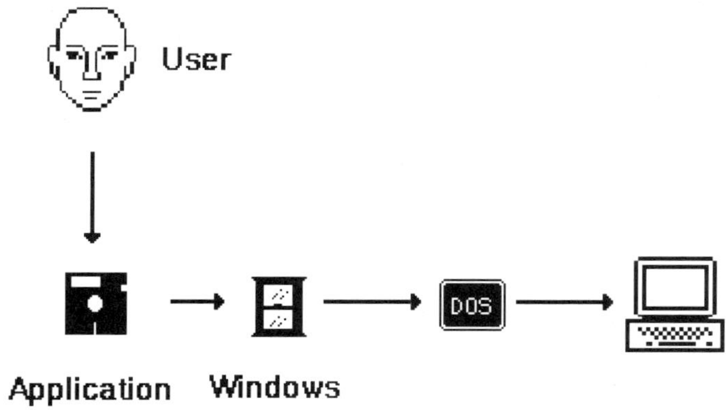


**Figure 15.** When you use Windows, you are freed from having to interact with the awkward and cumbersome DOS program. However, DOS is still present on your computer system, and while you don't have to deal with it directly any longer, Windows interacts with DOS on your behalf.

If you run an application through Windows, the application interacts with Windows, Windows interacts with DOS, and DOS operates your computer system.

Ordinarily, this interaction does not pose a problem, but some DOS applications, especially those that require a lot of disk access, will run more quickly if the Windows intermediary is eliminated.

If a DOS program you are using through Windows runs noticeably slower, you may want to run it directly from DOS. Of course, you then lose the interactive advantages of Windows.

## MEMORY USE

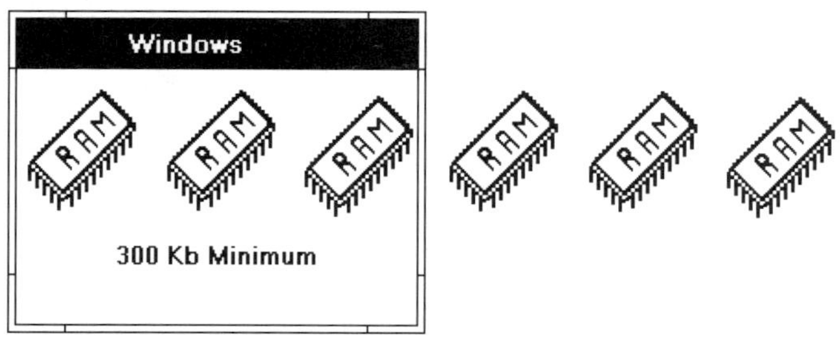


**Figure 16.** Another disadvantage of using Windows is that it takes up at least 600 kilobytes of random access memory (RAM) when running in Standard mode, and more when running in Enhanced mode.

If you run an application that requires a great deal of memory, Windows may interfere with the running of that program—especially if your computer system has only limited memory.

# Windows Running Modes

Microsoft Windows Version 3.1 can run in one of two different modes. These modes are designed to let Windows run on a wide range of computer systems and to take full advantage of each system's specifications.

The appearance and use of the Windows GUI is the same in both modes. The differences are largely transparent to you as you use Windows, but they do affect whether Windows is able to make the best use of your computer system.

The previous version of Windows, Windows 3.0, also ran in a third mode, called Real mode.

Real mode allowed Windows to run on XT computers and on systems with less than one megabyte of memory. With the recent advances in commercially available computer technology, few Windows users today would suffer from such limitations.

Real mode also permitted programs designed for version 2 of Windows to run in Windows 3.0. Because most Windows applications have now been upgraded to the Windows 3 level, this feature is no longer required.

## Standard Mode

**Figure 17.** If your computer system has an 80286, or better, processor and at least one megabyte of memory, you can run Windows in Standard mode.

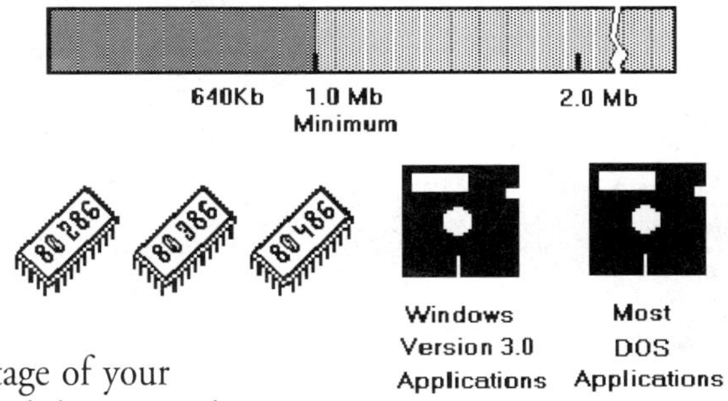


Standard mode takes maximum advantage of your computer system's memory resources and does not rely greatly on disk access. Standard mode is the most efficient of Windows' running modes.

For running individual applications that do not require large amounts of memory, Standard mode is the most efficient way to run Windows.

## 386 ENHANCED MODE

This running mode is designed to exploit the advantages of 80386 and higher level microprocessors. To use 386 Enhanced mode, your system must have an 80386 or higher processor and at least two megabytes of memory.

In Enhanced mode, Windows not only uses all available RAM, but also creates a special file on your hard disk, called a swap file, in which it stores data that would ordinarily be stored in memory.

The data in the swap file, though it is not really in the computer's RAM, is treated as though it were. The presence of this simulated memory, called virtual memory, means that the amount of memory available for application programs can actually exceed the amount of RAM on your computer.

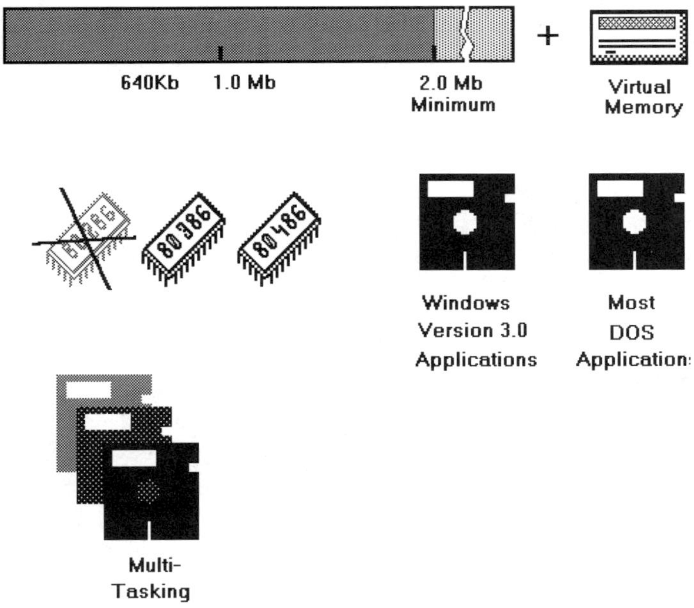


**Figure 18.** Because disk access is slower than memory access, 386 Enhanced mode is slightly less efficient than Standard mode. Some application programs will run more slowly in Enhanced mode than they do in Standard mode.

In Enhanced mode you can also make use of the multitasking feature. When multitasking, your computer system processes several applications at once. Windows directs the processor to switch its attention rapidly between the various applications, allowing you to use one program, while your computer continues to act upon the data in another application.

# Installing Microsoft Windows

The Windows installation program copies the various programs and data files that make up the Windows system onto your hard disk.

## System Requirements

**Figure 19.** Windows is a large program and will take up about five megabytes of hard disk space. Be sure that your system has the capacity to accommodate Windows' disk requirements with at least five megabytes to spare.

An additional five megabyte capacity is recommended because Windows uses your hard disk to store temporary files while it is running. If you are short on disk space, the number of applications you can open in Windows will be severely limited.

If you plan to run Windows in 386 Enhanced mode, you will want even more available disk space to accommodate the swap file. The size of your swap file, and thus the extent of virtual memory available, depends on how much hard disk space you have.

## Preparing for Installation

**Figure 20.** To install Windows, you will need to know what kinds of hardware devices make up your computer system.

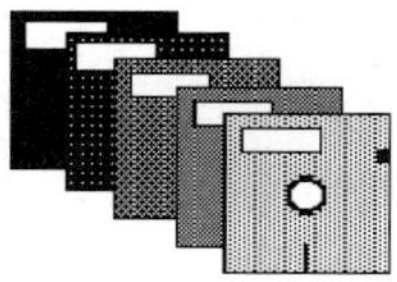

Microsoft Windows is supplied on either 5.25- or 3.5-inch diskettes. Be sure that you have all the diskettes ready before you start the installation. Part of the installation procedure asks you to identify some of the peripheral devices that make up your computer system. In particular, be sure you can identify what type of monitor, mouse, and keyboard your system uses.

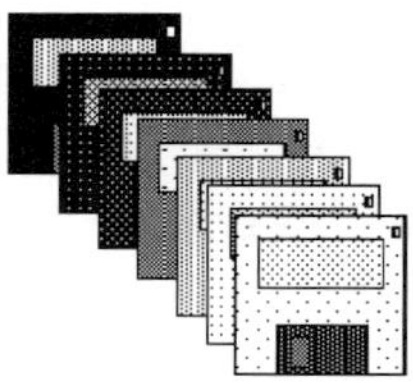

## RUNNING INSTALLATION

To install Windows on your hard disk, first turn on your computer and allow DOS to load as usual. Then place the diskette labeled Microsoft Windows Disk 1 in one of your floppy disk drives, usually drive A:. Make that drive the default drive by typing the drive letter followed by a colon, then pressing the Enter key. At the DOS prompt, type 'Setup' and press the Enter key. The Windows Setup program will then take over.

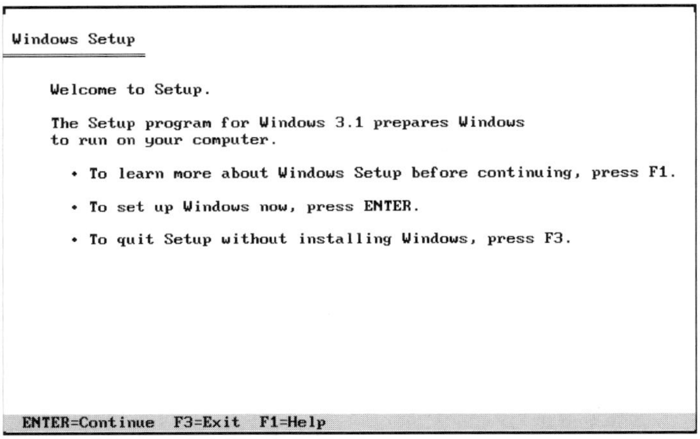


**Figure 21.** The first Setup screen appears, informing you that the Setup program is operating.

Throughout the entire Setup program, two keys, F1 and F3, serve a special purpose.

Pressing the F1 key will display Help information that explains the aspect of the Setup program that is currently running.

Pressing the F3 key will exit the Setup program and abandon the installation.

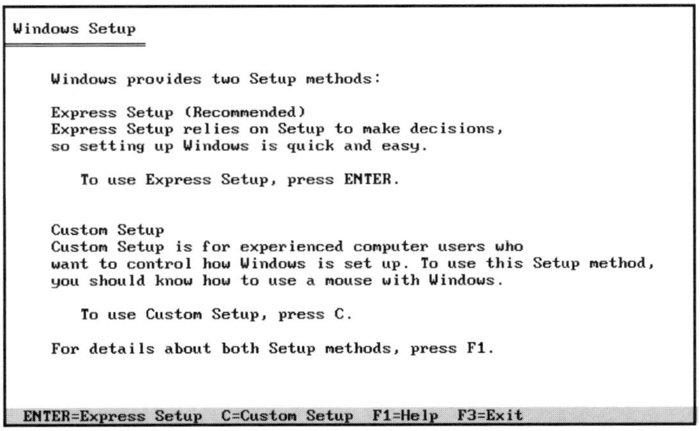


**Figure 22.** When you press the Enter key, the Setup program will ask you to select between an 'express' setup, or a 'custom' setup.

Selecting the express option allows the Setup program to install Windows automatically, based on the configuration of your computer system.

Selecting the custom option allows you to specify the details about your system.

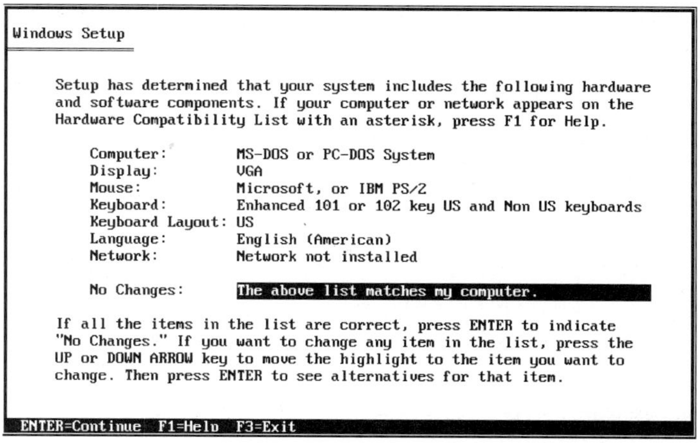


**Figure 23.** If a previous version of Windows is detected, you will be asked to enter a path for the installation. This and the following screens appear if custom setup has been chosen. This screen shows the Setup program's estimate of your equipment. If the details listed on this screen correctly describe your system's components, make sure that the phrase: *The above list matches my computer* is highlighted, as shown in this figure, and press the Enter key.

If you want to modify any of this information, use the Up and Down arrow keys on the keyboard to move the highlight bar to the detail you want to change, then press Enter. A list of choices will appear, from which you can make a new selection, also using the arrow keys.

Once your system details have been entered, the Setup program begins to copy files onto your hard disk. From time to time, a message on the screen will instruct you to insert one of the Setup disks. When the graphics-handling portions of the program have been loaded, the screen will switch from a text-based to a graphics-based display.

Once the screen has switched to a graphics-based display, you will be required to communicate with the Setup program using the standard Windows conventions, including the mouse.

At one point, you can use a special tutorial program designed to initiate new users to use of the mouse. This short tutorial introduces you to some of the basics and only takes a few minutes to run, after which you are returned to the Setup process.

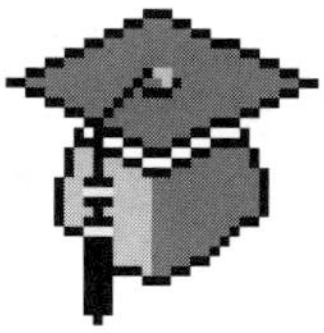

The tutorial program is also available from within Windows itself. If you do not wish to use the tutorial during the Setup process, you can run it at any time once Windows is installed.

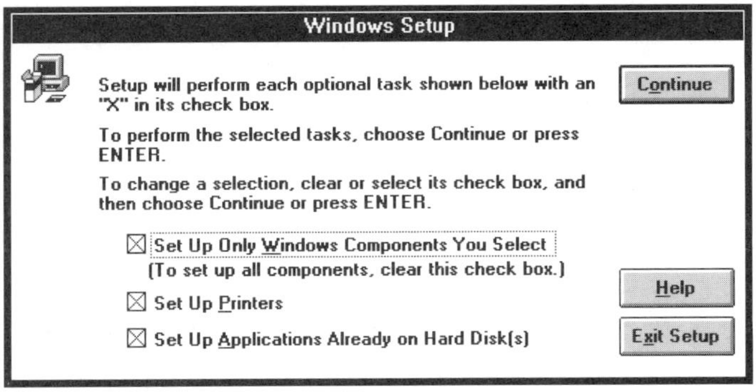


**Figure 24.** This figure shows the first Windows 3.1 dialog box you will encounter. It allows you to specify the Windows components to be installed on your computer.

Each item is displayed in this dialog box, along with a hollow box to its left. If the box contains an X, this item is selected and will be installed along with the Windows program. If the box is empty, the item has not been selected and will not be included in the Windows installation.

To select or deselect an item from this list, position the mouse pointer over the item's name (or the box to its left) and press the mouse button once. If there is no X in the box, an X will appear. If the item was already selected, this action will remove the X.

The ability to exclude parts of the Windows system from the installation is useful if Windows is being installed onto a system where hard disk space is limited.

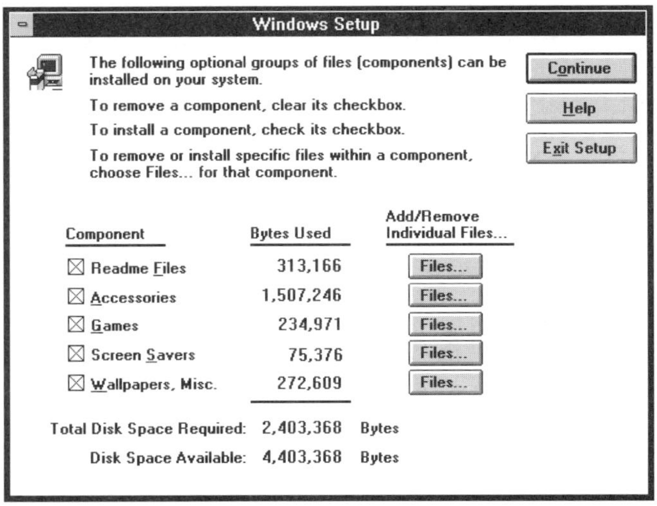


**Figure 25.** If you have sufficient space on your hard disk, it is best to install all aspects of Windows initially. You can remove any of them from the Windows system at a later date if you desire.

When the options in this dialog box have been set to your satisfaction, click the mouse button on *Continue* or press the Enter key.

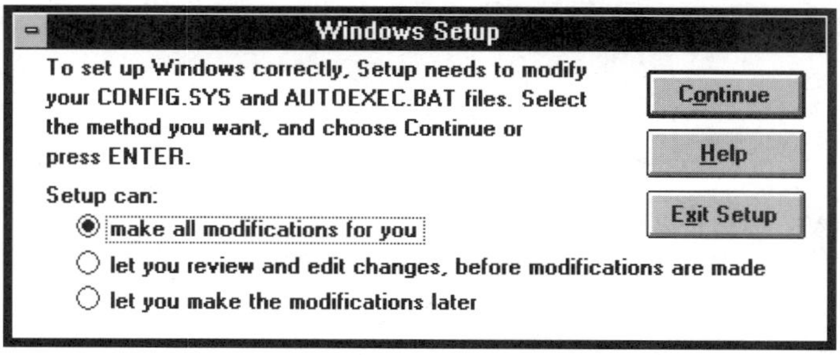


**Figure 26.** When the installation is complete, the Setup program will offer to modify two files on your hard disk.

The autoexec.bat file is a program file that is automatically run when you start your computer. It should contain a line in the form: temp=c:\temp. The directory need not read 'c:\temp', so long as a valid subdirectory is listed.

Windows creates a number of temporary files for its own use while it is running. The 'temp=' line in the autoexec.bat file indicates where those files can be safely stored.

The config.sys file lists information about your system's configuration that is read and acted upon when your computer is turned on. Some configuration items that affect Windows directly, like mouse and memory management drivers, must be present in config.sys.

The dialog box pictured in Figure 26 gives you the option of writing these two files on your own at some other time or allowing Windows to write them for you. As a compromise, you can allow Windows to write the files but give you the opportunity to edit them. Select the option best suited to your computer system by positioning the mouse pointer over its description and pressing the mouse button.

# Starting Windows

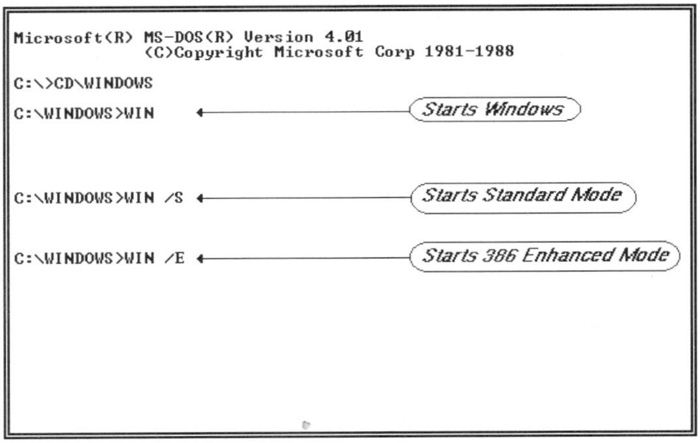


**Figure 27.** You can easily start Windows from the DOS prompt.

Simply set the default directory to the one containing Windows, then type **WIN** followed by the Enter key. This command instructs Windows to load and run in the highest of the two modes available on your computer system.

To select a specific running mode, type **WIN /x**, replacing the **x** with **S** for Standard mode, and **3** (or **E**) for 386 Enhanced mode.

# THE WINDOWS INTERFACE

2

## SOME WINDOWS DEFINITIONS

Most conventional operating systems require you to type commands at the keyboard. In Windows, operations are selected from the screen by signaling with the mouse. This newer form of interface differs greatly from the more conventional keyboard method and can best be described with its own vocabulary.

### *THE MOUSE*

As you physically move the mouse across your desktop, it causes a pointer to move across the screen. The shape of this pointer varies, depending on what commands are being executed. The mouse pointer's shape can, in fact, be used as an indicator of what Windows is doing. As we review Windows' features, we'll indicate their corresponding mouse pointer shapes.

#### BASIC MOUSE SHAPES

**Figure 1.** When Windows is waiting for instructions, no commands are in the process of being executed and the mouse pointer resembles a hollow arrow. This is the mouse pointer's usual appearance.

**Figure 2.** In situations where a command is being processed and no other instructions can be given, the mouse pointer resembles an hourglass. You can still move the mouse pointer across the screen, but you can't select any commands until the pointer is again in the shape of an arrow.

## BASIC MOUSE CONTROL

Using the mouse involves positioning the pointer on the screen and signaling an action by pressing the left mouse button. The signal can take three forms: clicking, double-clicking, and dragging.

| | |
|---|---|
| To *click:* | Position the mouse over the desired area of the screen and press, then release, the button. |
| To *double-click:* | Position the mouse over the desired area of the screen and quickly press and release the button twice. |
| To *drag:* | Position the mouse and press the button without releasing it. Then move the mouse to a new location before releasing the button. This method is generally used to move and size items on the screen. |

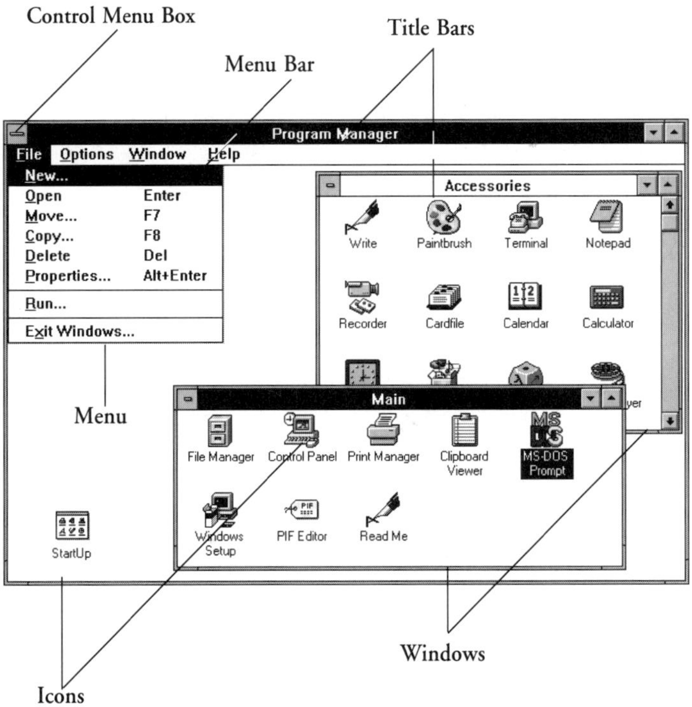


## *THE WINDOWS SCREEN*

**Figure 3.** As its name suggests, the Windows screen is organized into a number of boxes, called windows. These windows group and organize programs, dividing the screen into separate work areas.

Note that the title bar of the Accessories window is light, while the title bars of the Program Manager and Main windows are dark. The dark color indicates that the window is active. Many commands affect only active windows.

## ICONS

**Figure 4.** Icons are graphic symbols that replace written descriptions of program names. The appearance of the icon represents the function or purpose of the item for which it stands.

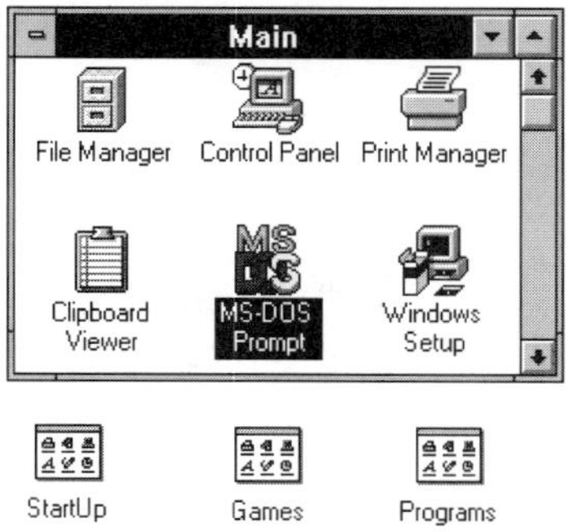


Icons also contain a description, in the form of a short caption, to help you identify their function. If this caption is highlighted, the item is said to be *selected.* You select icons by clicking them with the mouse pointer. Some commands affect only selected icons.

## MENUS

**Figure 5.** Many of the commands in Windows are issued by selection from a list of commands on the screen. Such a list is called a menu. Windows is said to be *menu driven,* because users select its commands from menus rather than type them in at the keyboard.

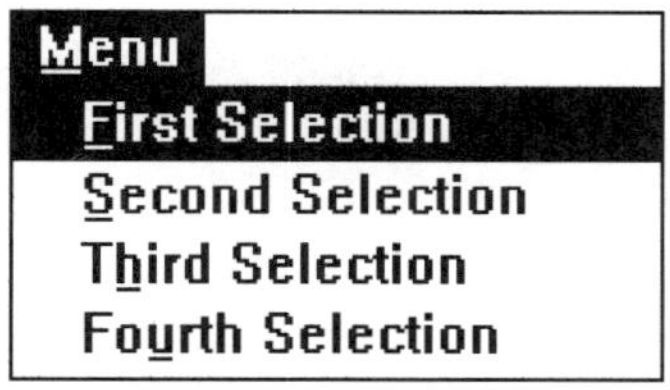


# THE PROGRAM MANAGER

**Figure 6.** The main window in the Windows interface is called the Program Manager. All the commands and functions accessible in Windows are accessed through the Program Manager.

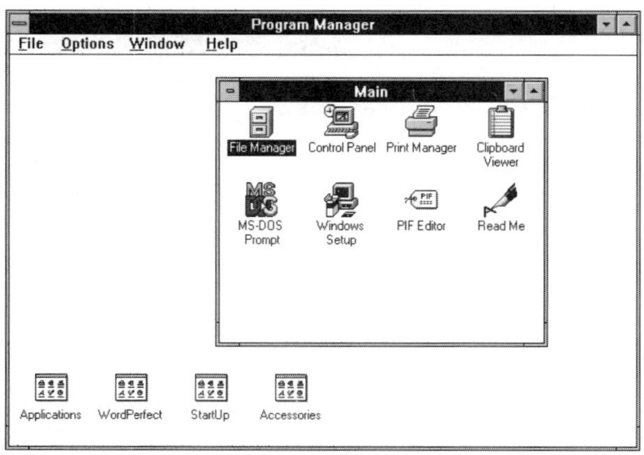


The following section explains the main features of the Program Manager.

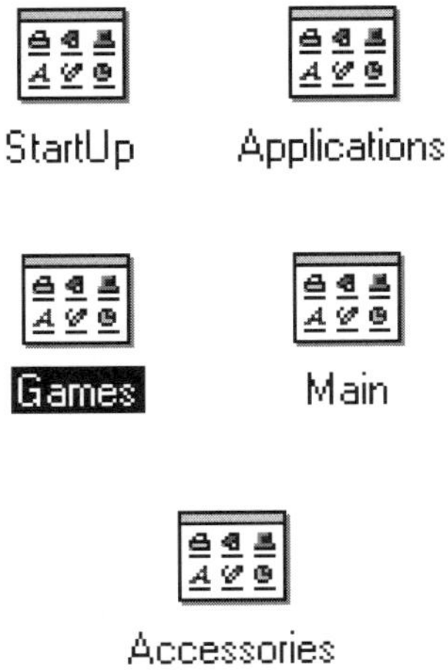


## PROGRAM GROUPS

**Figure 7.** Your computer system will include a variety of programs you will want to access through Windows, in addition to those applications included with Windows itself. These programs can be organized into program groups that separate them into logical categories and make them easier to locate.

The five program groups shown on the left are created automatically when Windows is installed. Program groups are represented by special program group icons.

Each program group can be expanded into a window containing a number of program items.

## PROGRAM ITEMS

**Figure 8.** Each application program you use through Windows is represented by a single icon within a program group, even though it may contain many DOS files. These icons are referred to as *program items.*

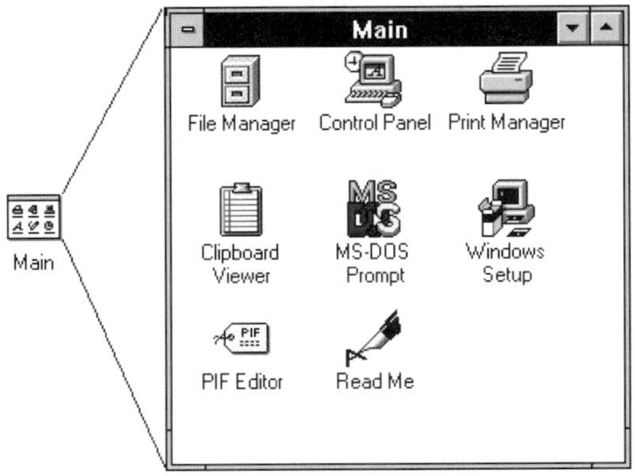


## WORK-SPACE MANIPULATION

**Figure 9.** The windows and icons on the screen are by no means fixed. The Windows screen is dynamic, and you can adjust it to suit your tastes and needs.

To open a program group icon into a window, double-click the cursor over the icon. Here the Main program group has been opened.

## RESIZING WINDOWS

**Figure 10.** The size of most windows can be adjusted. Position the mouse pointer on the window's edge and drag it across the screen until the border is in the desired position. The edge of the window you have selected is the one that will change position.

If the mouse is positioned at the window's corner, you can adjust both sides adjacent to the corner simultaneously.

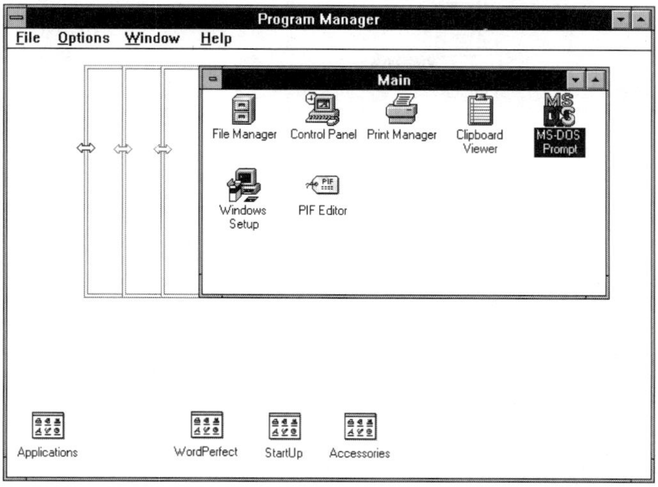


**Figure 11.** When the mouse pointer is positioned over the border of a window, it takes the shape of a two-headed arrow, indicating the directions in which you can resize the window.

**Figure 12.** To make a window fill the entire work area, click the Maximize button, represented by an arrowhead pointing up. The Maximize button is located in the upper right-hand corner of most windows.

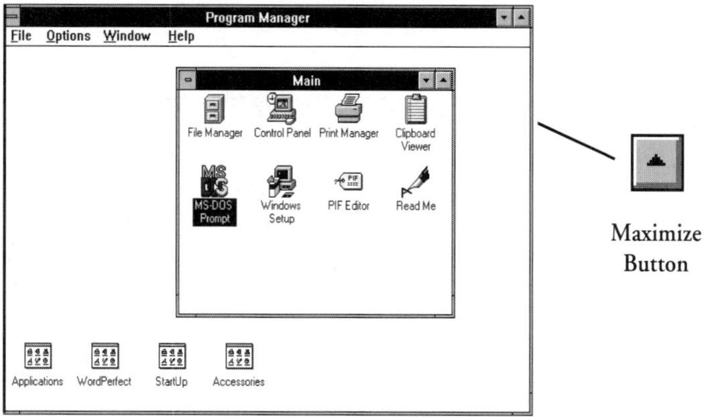

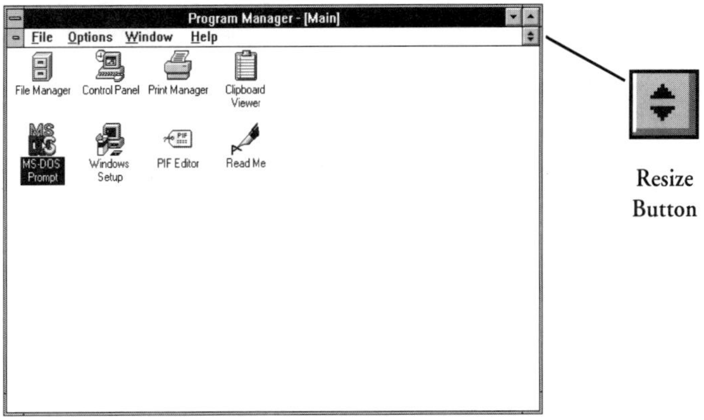


**Figure 13.** In a maximized window, the Maximize button is replaced with the Resize button, represented by two arrowheads. Clicking on the Resize button restores the window to the size and position it had on the screen before the Maximize button was used.

## SCROLLING WINDOWS

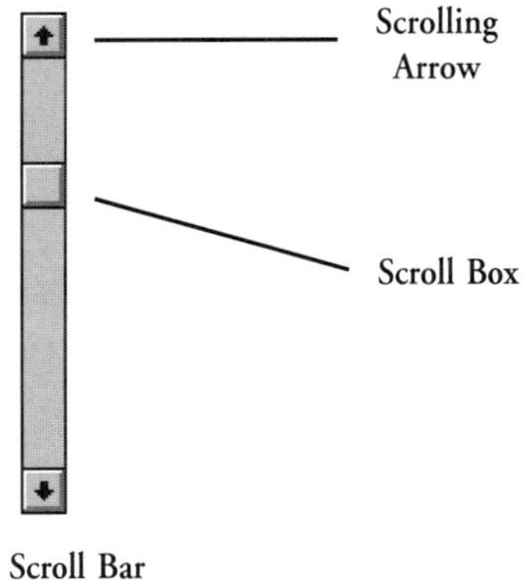


**Figure 14.** A window may not be large enough to display all of its contents at once. If so, a scroll bar will appear along either the right or bottom edge of the window.

The scroll bar consists of a shaded bar containing a scroll box, which you can move by clicking on the scrolling arrows. The scroll bar represents the window's entire contents, while the scroll box represents the section currently visible in the window.

**Figure 15.** If the scroll box is located at the top of the scroll bar, then the objects located at the top of the window are visible. Note in this figure that the program items at the bottom of the window are cut off by the window's limited size.

**Figure 16.** As you move the scroll box down the scroll bar, objects located lower in the window become visible, while items higher in the window "scroll" out of view.

You can position the scroll box quickly by dragging it within the scroll bar.

Although only some of the window's contents are visible at a time, nothing is lost or deleted when you use the scroll bars to change the window's view.

## MOVING WINDOWS

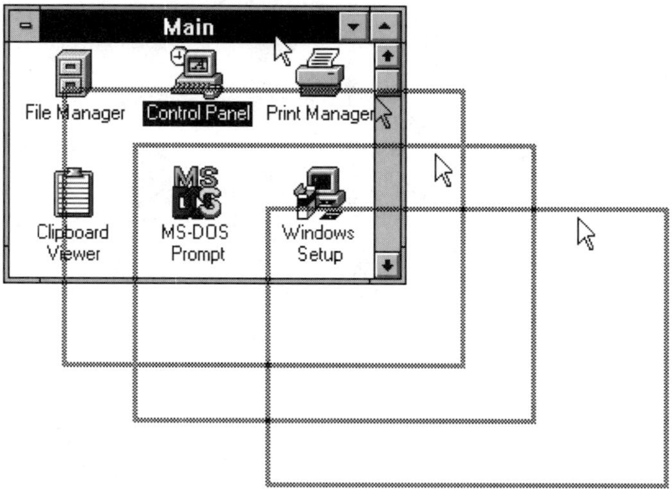


**Figure 17.** Windows can be repositioned on the screen without altering their shape or size.

To move a window, place the mouse pointer on the window's title bar and drag the window to its new location. While you are dragging, the window appears to remain stationary while a rectangle the shape and size of the window follows the mouse pointer. When you release the mouse button, the window is redrawn on the screen in its new position.

## MOVING ICONS

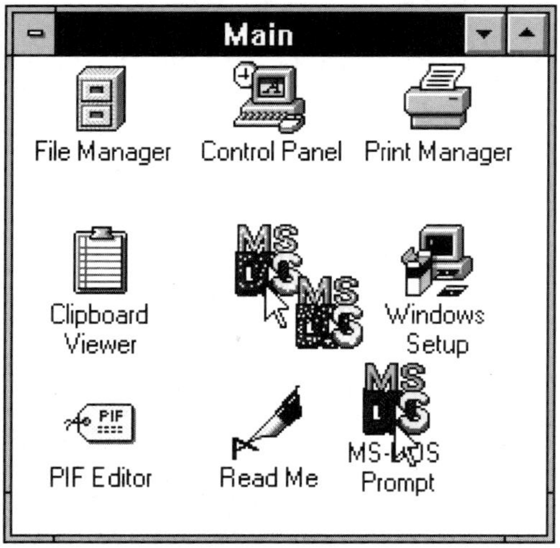


**Figure 18.** An icon's position within its window can be altered at any time. Simply select the icon with the mouse pointer and drag it to its new position. While an icon is being dragged, the mouse pointer takes the shape of the icon being positioned.

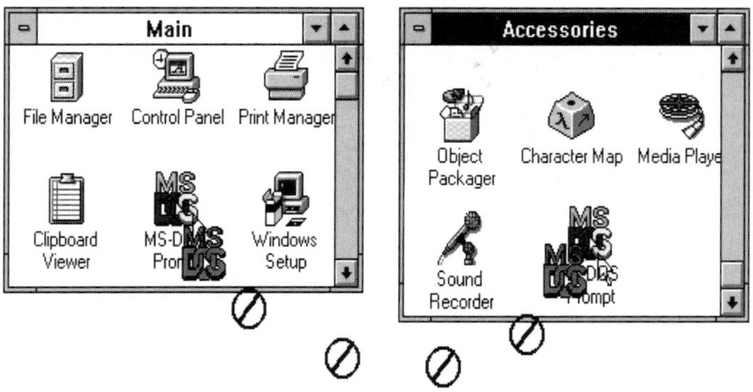


**Figure 19.** A program item icon can also be moved between program groups. This feature allows you to modify the organization of your system. To move a program item between program groups, drag the program item from its initial position until it is located within its destination window.

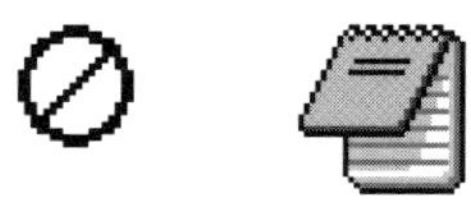

No Entry Notepad

**Figure 20.** Notice that while the item is being dragged, the mouse pointer takes the shape of the item's icon. When the icon is positioned on a part of the screen where it may not be placed, the mouse pointer takes the form of a "no entry" symbol.

## MINIMIZING WINDOWS

To prevent the screen from becoming cluttered with open windows, you can temporarily minimize a window. A minimized window is still open; any applications running within the window continue to do so. However, the window is represented as a minimized icon in the lower left-hand corner of the screen. By minimizing windows, you keep the screen display more organized without having to terminate active applications.

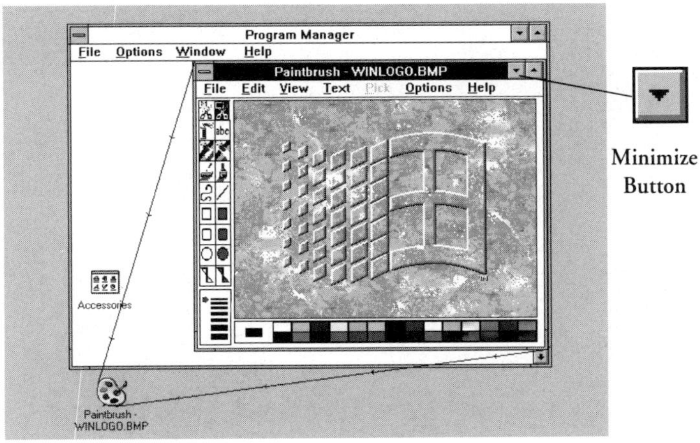


**Figure 21.** To minimize a window, click on the Minimize button, represented by an arrowhead pointing down, in the upper right corner of the frame.

A minimized window can be restored by double-clicking on the window's minimized icon.

Note that minimized icons are placed behind any active windows. If the lower left-hand side of your screen is occupied by a window, or if the Program Manager window is maximized, you will not be able to see the minimized icons. If this is the case, you must move or resize the windows that obscure the lower left corner of the screen if you want to access the minimized icons.

## CLOSING WINDOWS

**Figure 22.** To close a window, click on the control menu box, represented by a horizontal dash, in the upper left-hand corner of the screen. The window's control menu will appear.

From this menu, select the *Close* option by clicking the mouse pointer on that selection.

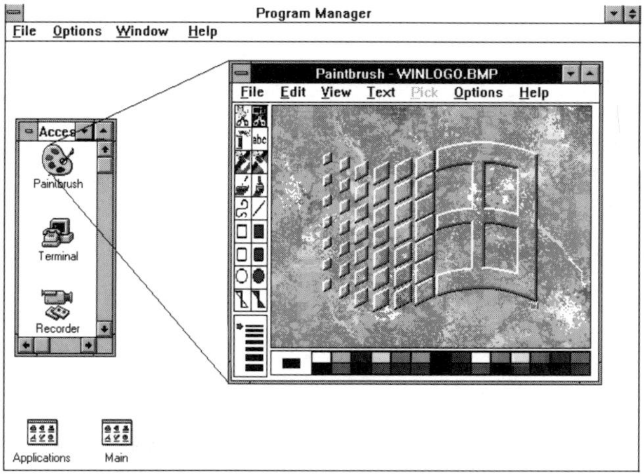


**Figure 23.** Closing a window causes it to return to the icon from which it was originally opened. Any applications running within a window are terminated when a window is closed.

For a shortcut to closing a window, double-click on the control menu box, located in the upper left-hand corner of the window. The window will close immediately.

Control Menu Box

Recall that all the programs and functions that run under Windows do so within the Program Manager window. Closing the Program Manager terminates all programs and applications running within Windows. Thus, closing the Program Manager window is equivalent to exiting from the Windows program and results in a return to DOS.

## Interacting with Windows

As a graphical interface, Windows allows you to interact with your computer system using the mouse almost exclusively. Using icons, menus, and dialog boxes, the Windows interface allows you to select the commands and operations you want without having to resort to the keyboard.

## EXECUTING APPLICATIONS

**Figure 24.** To run an application represented by a program item icon, simply double-click the mouse pointer on the desired icon.

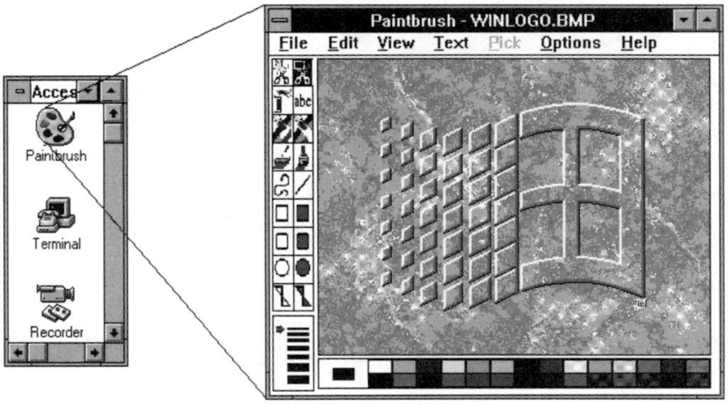


This is the most direct method of running an application. It is also possible to execute an application program through the Program Manager menu bar. This process is outlined in Chapter 3.

## THE MENU BAR

**Figure 25.** In certain windows, including the Program Manager, you will find a row of command categories located immediately below the title bar. This row is called the *menu bar.*

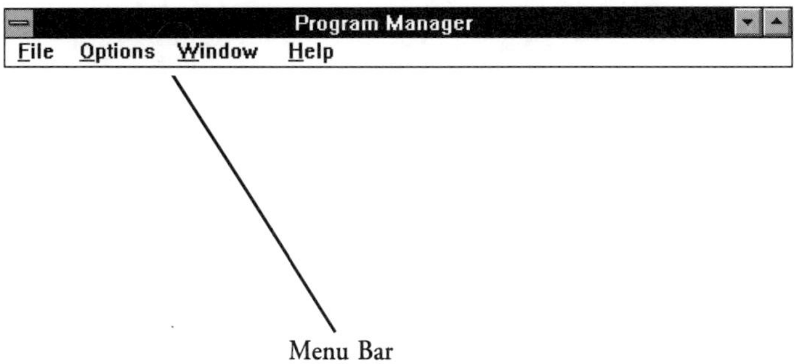


The menu bar is used in selecting commands and instructions.

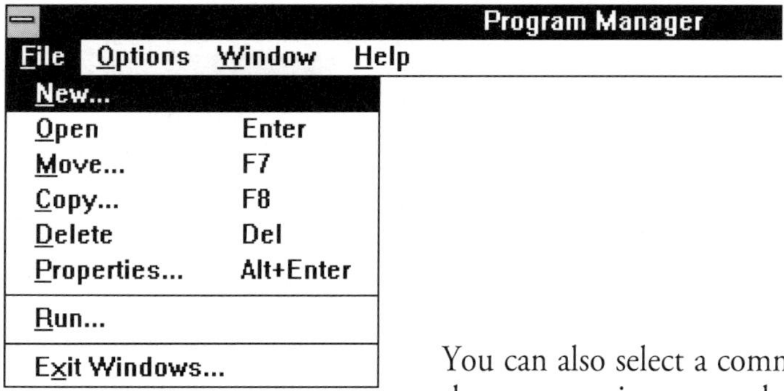


**Figure 26.** Clicking on one of the menu command categories, in this case the **File** category, will drop down a list of commands associated with that category. To carry out one of these commands, click the mouse pointer on the selected command.

You can also select a command by positioning and depressing the mouse pointer over the desired command category, dragging it down to the desired command, and then releasing the mouse button. This second method is often faster than clicking the mouse two separate times.

**Active Choice**

Inactive Choice

**Figure 27.** Most commands are listed in dark text, while a few can be written in gray. The dark commands are active and can be selected from the menu as required. The gray commands represent inactive choices that are not applicable to the current situation and are not selectable from the menu. In the right circumstances these commands will become dark and therefore selectable.

## DIALOG BOXES

Menu commands followed by an ellipsis (...) require you to provide additional information before they can be executed. The dialog boxes invoked by such commands are special windows in which you specify the details of the command you want carried out. Because Windows is a graphical interface, the methods used to collect information in the dialog boxes are designed to keep keyboard use to a minimum and mouse use to a maximum.

Dialog boxes contain a combination of different devices. A closer look, however, will show that most dialog boxes are assembled out of a few standardized interactive options.

## RADIO BUTTONS

**Figure 28.** When you must select a single item from a limited list of choices, the *radio button* will likely be used. A list of mutually exclusive options is displayed with a hollow circle beside each option.

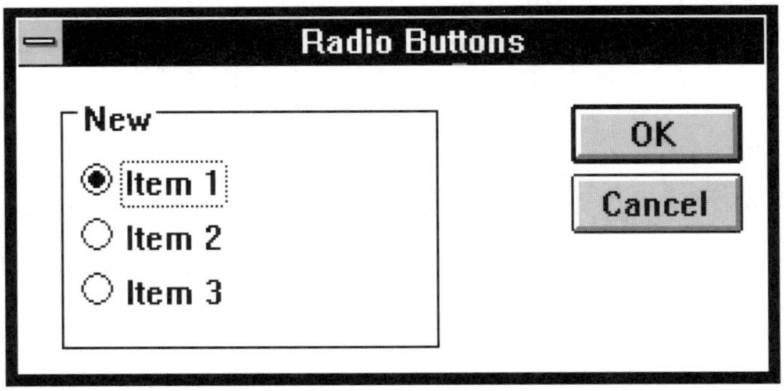


To select an option, click in its corresponding circle or on the item name itself. The selected circle will be filled in, and all the others will be hollow. Like the buttons on a car radio—after which this device is named—only one item can be selected at any time.

## CHECK BOXES

**Figure 29.** The check box device allows you to select as many or as few options from a list as you require. The various selections are listed, each with a hollow square beside it.

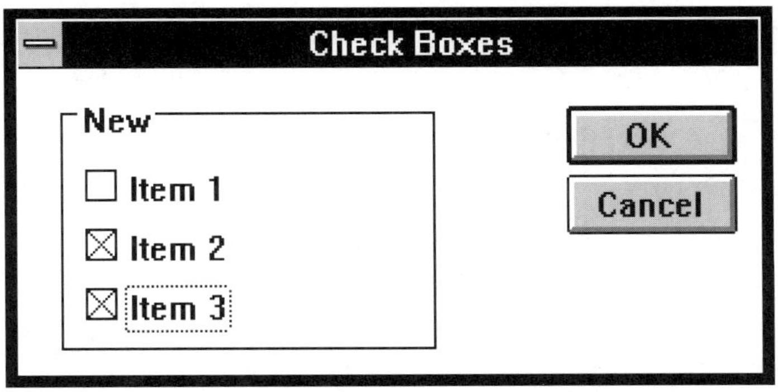


To indicate which selection you want, click in that selection's hollow box or on the item name itself, and an X will appear. Clicking an already selected box will deselect that choice, and the box will become hollow again.

## SUBMENUS

Submenus allow you to make a single choice from a relatively long list that otherwise might not fit in a dialog box.

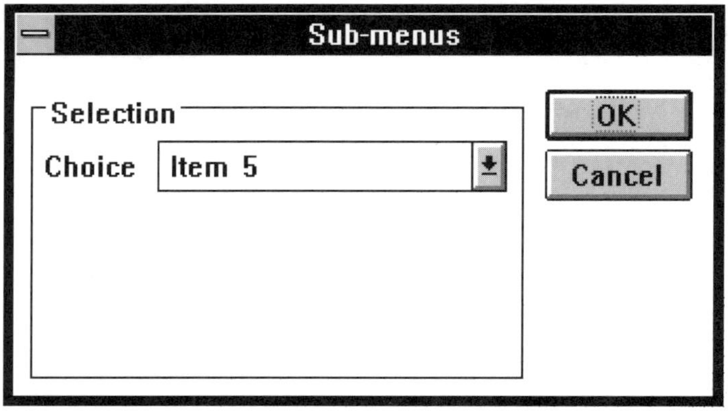


**Figure 30.** A submenu is represented in a dialog box by a single choice (the current selection) surrounded by a box with a downward-pointing arrow to its right. This arrow indicates that a submenu is available. Clicking this arrow brings the list into view.

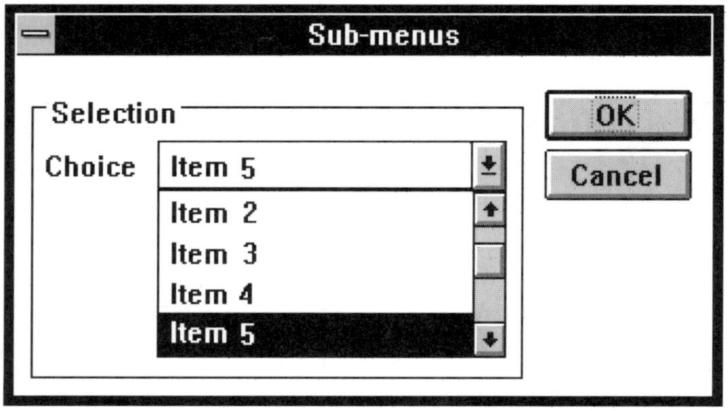


**Figure 31.** The submenu, often including a scroll bar to accommodate the number of choices, appears below the current selection, which is highlighted in the submenu.

Use the scroll bar to bring the desired selection into view and make a new selection by clicking on the desired choice.

## FILE SELECTION

Many application programs require you to select a file from the computer system. The application may read from, write to, or otherwise manipulate the file that you select. A special file selection dialog box, used by most Windows applications, will appear in such situations.

**Figure 32.** The *Open* dialog box allows you to select a file from any of your computer system's active disk drives.

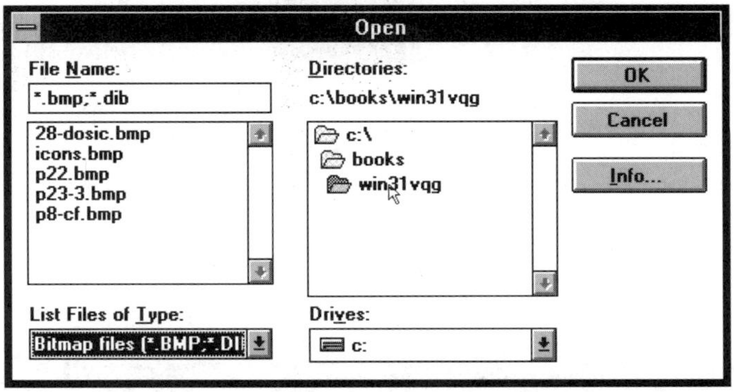


There are three important elements to every file selection dialog box: the *File Name* list box, the *Directories* list box, and the *Drives* submenu.

**Figure 33.** The *Drives* submenu contains a list of all the disk drives available on your computer system. Use this submenu to select the disk drive from which you will load the file to be selected.

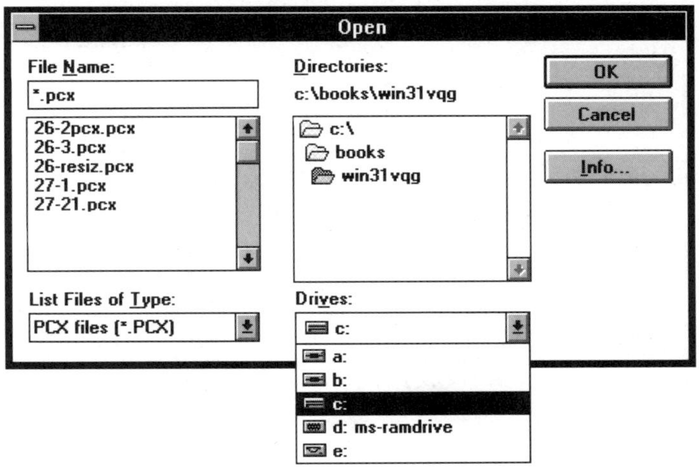


The *Directories* list box displays all the subdirectory paths that are directly accessible from the current directory.

**Figure 34.** Parent directories—subdirectories higher up in the directory tree than the current directory—are indicated by an open file folder icon.

**Figure 35.** Subdirectories lower in the tree than the current directory are indicated by a closed file folder icon.

**Figure 36.** The currently active directory—the directory from which you can select files—is indicated by an open file folder icon with a shaded interior.

The current directory path is also listed above the list box, immediately below the word *Directories.*

The *Directories* list box is used to change the current directory. To make one of the displayed subdirectory names the current directory, click once on its name, or icon, with the mouse.

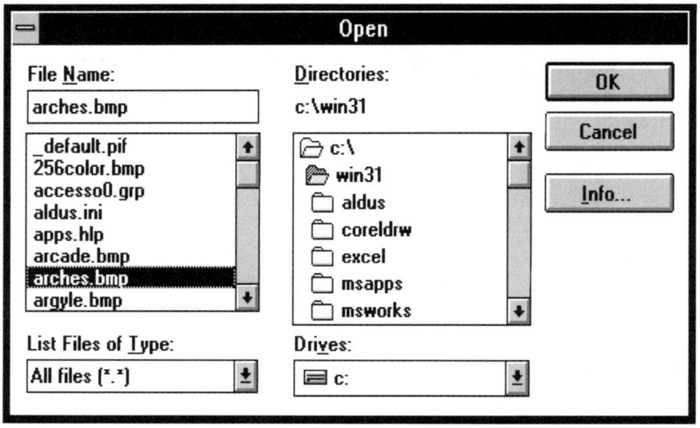


**Figure 37.** In Figure 32, the mouse pointer is shown clicking on the subdirectory win31vqg. In this figure, the current directory has been changed to c:\win31.

The *File Name* list box lists the files contained in the current directory. If the *File Name* text box at the top of this list is empty, or contains the wildcard characters *.*, all the files in the current directory are listed.

To select a file from the *File Name* list, click on the file's name once to make it appear in the *File Name* text box (as has been done with the file arches.bmp in Figure 37), then click on *OK* to confirm the selection.

As a shortcut, you can simply double-click on the name of the file to be selected.

Many file selection dialog boxes include a *List Files of Type* submenu below the *File Name* list box. This submenu allows you to select a file type from a list of file extensions commonly used by whatever program is currently running.

**Figure 38.** The extension of *.bmp has been entered into the *File Name* text box, so that only files with a .bmp extension are listed.

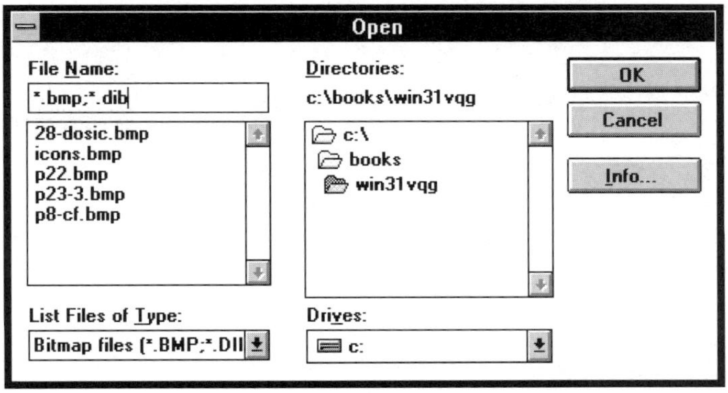


The *List Files of Type* submenu can be used to specify the extension used in the *File Name* text box.

## OK AND CANCEL

**Figure 39.** Most dialog boxes contain an *OK* button and a *Cancel* button. The use of these buttons is one of the most important features to remember about dialog boxes. Windows will not act on any of the selections made in a dialog box unless you click the *OK* button.

If you click on the Cancel button, all the selections in that dialog box will revert to the values they had before the box was activated. Any changes you have made will be ignored.

# 3 The Program Manager Menu Bar

## Menu Bar

The Windows environment is controlled through the Program Manager. All programs and applications that run under Windows run within the Program Manager window. The Program Manager menu bar contains commands to help you organize the screen and manipulate files.

To select a command from a menu bar, click the mouse pointer on the command category in the menu bar and, when the list of options appears, click again on the command of your choice.

## File Menu

**Figure 1.** The File menu contains commands for organizing the files in your Windows system. Many of these commands have shortcuts using the mouse, which may be faster for the experienced user, though a bit more difficult for the beginning or occasional user. These shortcuts will be pointed out where applicable.

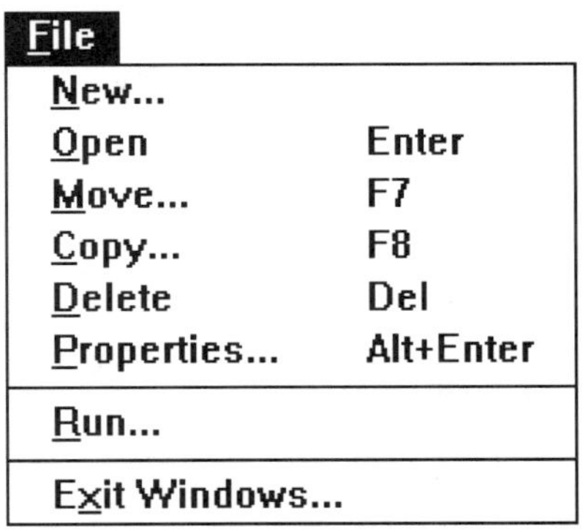

## *NEW COMMAND*

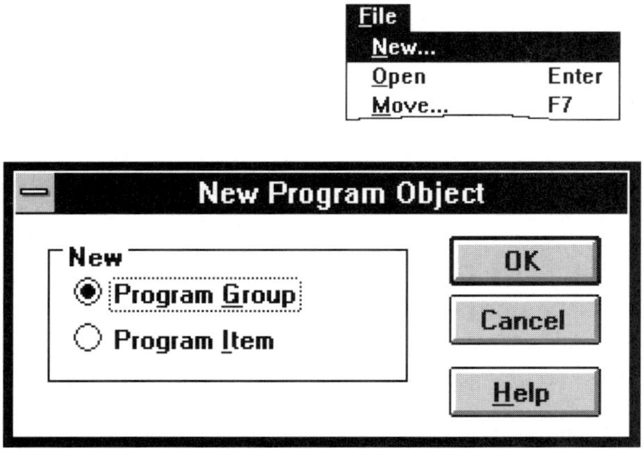


**Figure 2(a).** The *New* command creates either new program groups or new program items in the Program Manager window. When you select this command, a dialog box appears, asking you to select one of these options. Depending on your selection, a second dialog box appears.

### NEW PROGRAM GROUP

**Figure 2(b).** This selection allows you to create a new program group within the Program Manager window.

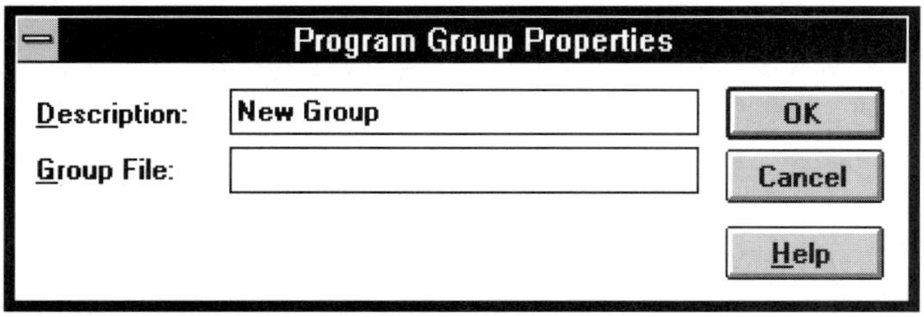


**Figure 3.** Click on the *Description* box to obtain a flashing cursor and enter the caption for this new program group's icon on the screen.

You can leave the *Group File* box empty. A DOS file named after the first eight characters in the description box and having the extension .grp is created automatically. Windows uses this file to store information about the program group but this is all done automatically.

**Figure 4.** When you select *OK*, an empty program group with the name you have given it is created and opened on the screen.

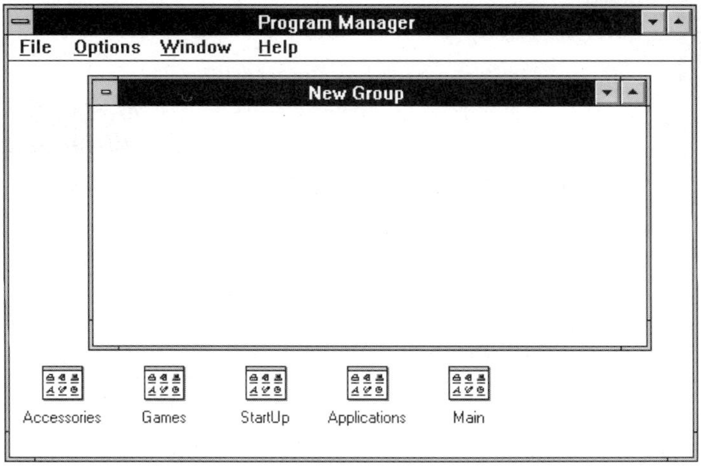


## NEW PROGRAM ITEM

**Figure 5(a).** This selection creates a new program item, which is placed in the currently active program group. Any executable file that you could run from DOS—any file with an .exe, .com, or .bat extension—can be made into a program item.

**Figure 5(b).** If you choose to create a new program item, this *Program Item Properties* dialog box will appear.

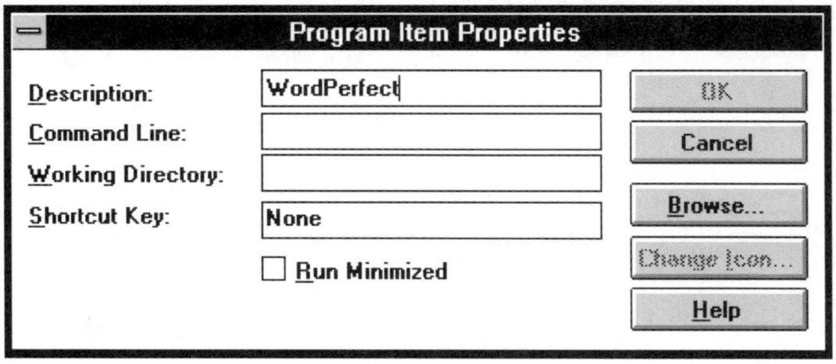


The *Description* you enter (by clicking on the description box and keying in the name) will be the caption under the program item's icon.

In the *Command Line* box, enter the file name—including the full DOS path—of the program you want made into a program item.

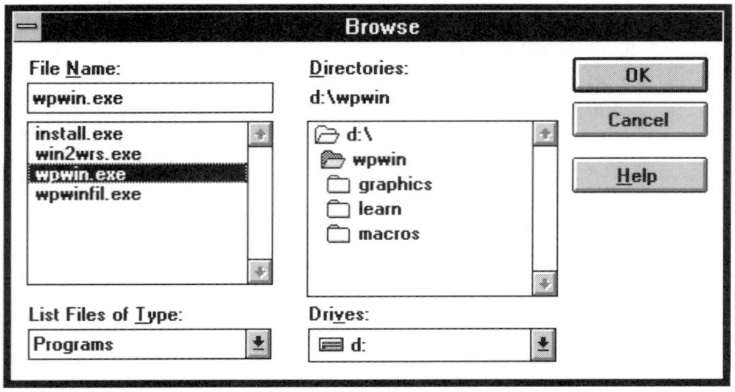


**Figure 6.** If you are unsure of the file's name or location, or if you simply don't want to type it in at the keyboard, click on *Browse* and a file selection dialog box will appear. When you have selected the file through this dialog box, its correct name and path are entered for you in the *Command Line* box of the *Program Item Properties* dialog box, as shown in Figure 8.

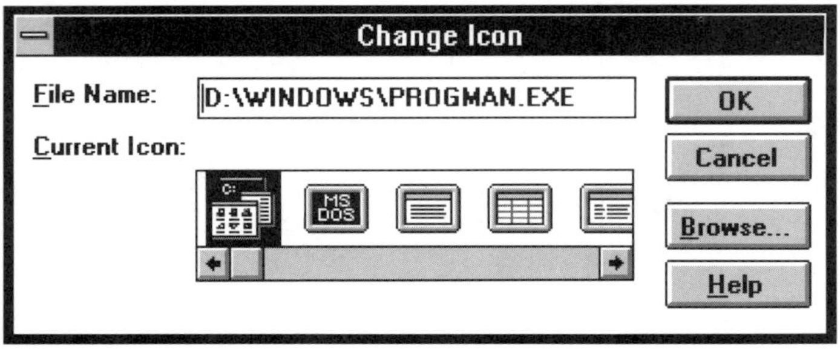


**Figure 7.** If you want to change the icon that is automatically assigned to the program item, select *Change Icon* from the *Program Item Properties* dialog box; the *Change Icon* dialog box will appear.

The available icons are displayed, and the current icon is highlighted. Use the scroll bars to bring the desired icon into view, then select it by clicking on it with the mouse.

Click on *OK* when the desired icon is highlighted.

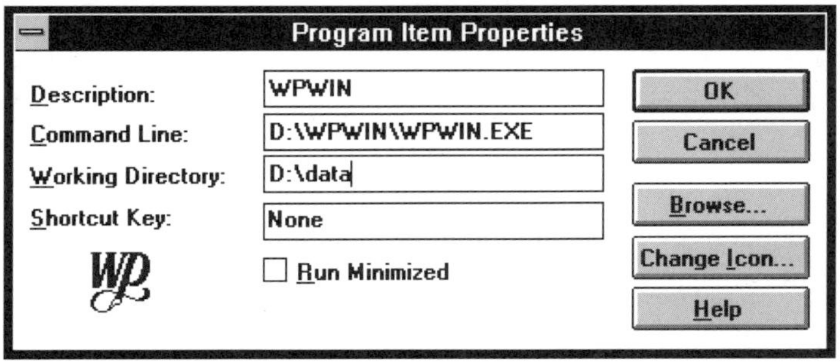


**Figure 8.** The *Working Directory* text box lets you select the default directory to which the program will read and write files. Many programs allow you to select default directories from within the programs themselves. In such cases, these defaults override the settings in this dialog box.

The *Shortcut Key* text box allows you to enter a shortcut key code for this program item. Enter a shortcut code by holding down the Alt key and pressing one of the alphanumeric keys. When the program item being created is running, this key combination will make its window active.

See **Running Multiple Applications** in Chapter 5 for more about switching the active window.

The *Run Minimized* option, if selected, causes the program to run as a minimized icon as soon as it is activated. This feature is handy for programs like the Clock program that you may want to run without occupying too much space on the screen.

It is often convenient to keep frequently used programs minimized on the Desktop. A minimized program can often be activated more conveniently than a program can be run from the Program Manager.

## OPEN COMMAND

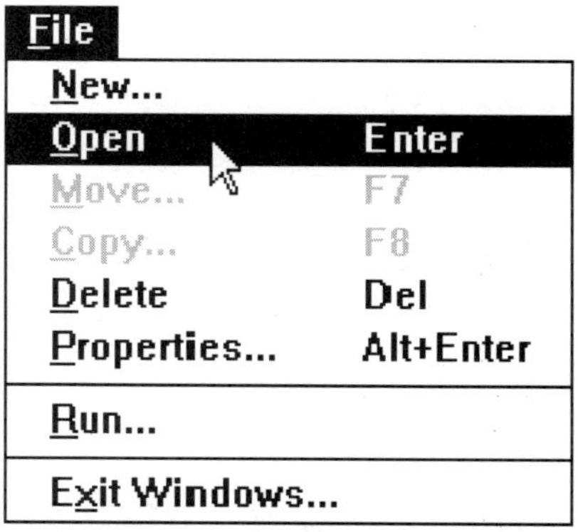


**Figure 9.** The *Open* command works in two ways:

1. If a program group window is open and contains a selected program item, the *Open* command causes the program to be executed.
2. If no open windows are active and a program group icon is selected, the *Open* command opens it into a program group window.

You will usually find it easier simply to double-click on the item directly.

## MOVE COMMAND

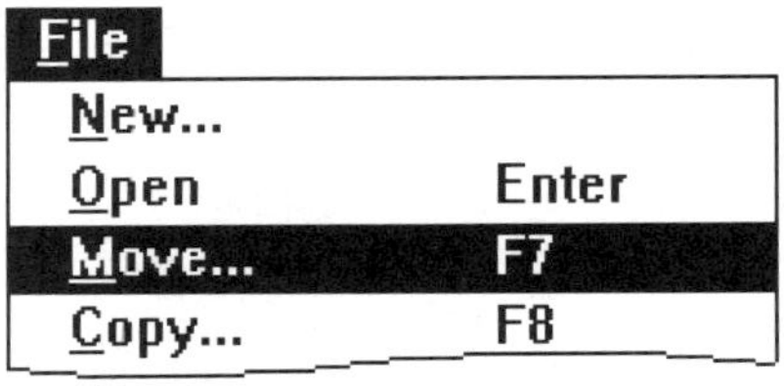


**Figure 10(a).** The *Move* command moves the currently selected program item from one program group to another. It works only when a program group window is open and active; at other times this option is gray and not selectable.

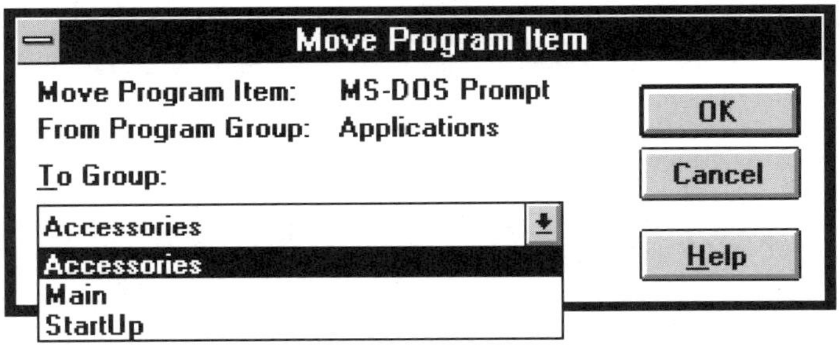


**Figure 10(b).** Selecting the *Move* command invokes the *Move Program Item* dialog box. Select the program group to which the item will be moved from the *To Group* submenu. As a shortcut, you can simply drag the selected item between program groups, as described in Chapter 2, without resorting to the menu.

## COPY COMMAND

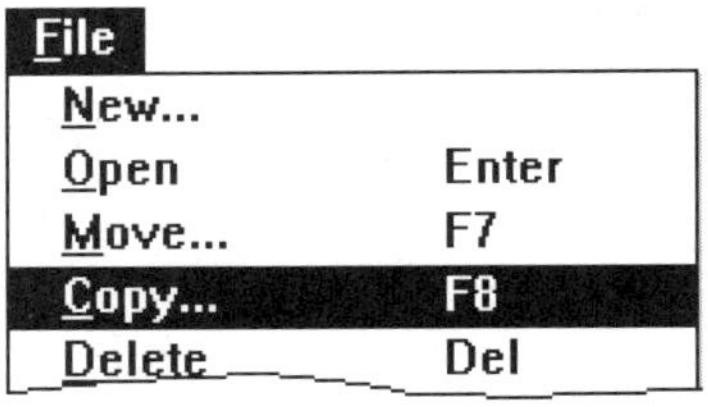


**Figure 11(a).** The *Copy* command copies the selected program item from one program group into another while keeping the item in its original group. A program group window must be open and active for this command to be selectable.

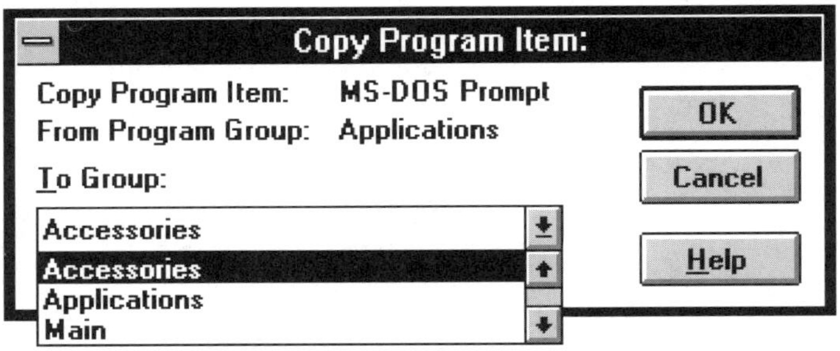


**Figure 11(b).** In the *Copy Program Item* dialog box, select the destination group from the *To Group* submenu. To copy program items without using the menu, hold down the Ctrl key while dragging the desired icon between program groups.

## DELETE COMMAND

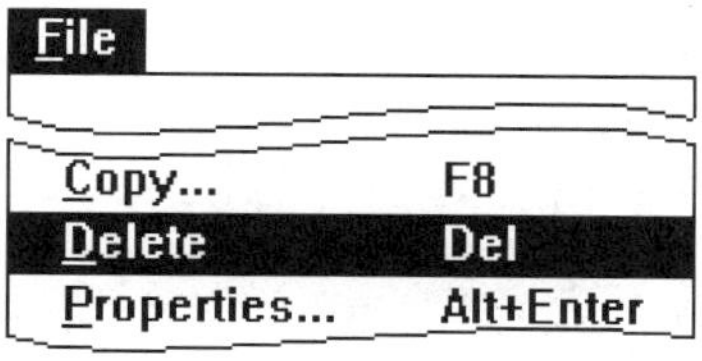


**Figure 12(a).** The *Delete* command deletes the selected icon from the Program Manager window. If the selected icon is a program item, it is removed from its window. If a program group is selected, the entire group, including all of its program items, is removed.

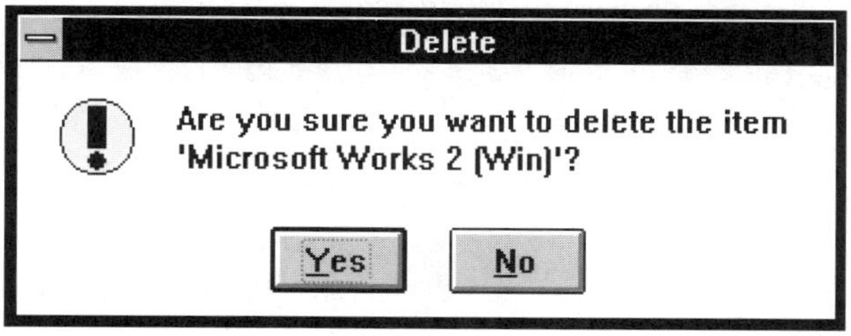


**Figure 12(b).** Because the *Delete* command induces an irreversible change, a warning dialog box will appear before the command is carried out. Select *Yes* to proceed with the deletion.

When icons are removed from the Program Manager window, their associated DOS files remain in your computer system. The Program Manager's *Delete* command only removes icons from the main window. It does **not** delete actual DOS files.

## PROPERTIES COMMAND

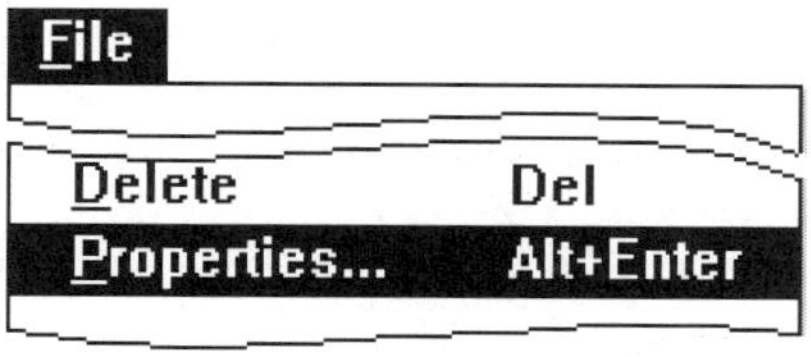


**Figure 13(a).** This command changes the attributes of existing program items or groups.

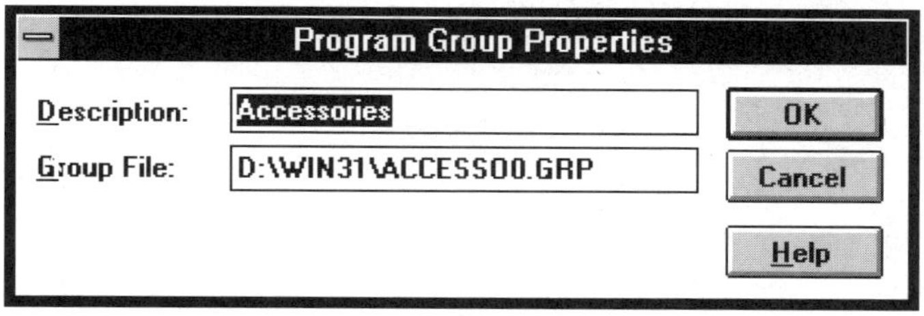


**Figure 13(b).** The *Program Group* (or *Program Item*) *Properties* dialog box appears when you select the *Properties* command (which one depends on whether a group or item is selected). These two dialog boxes have been discussed earlier.

## RUN COMMAND

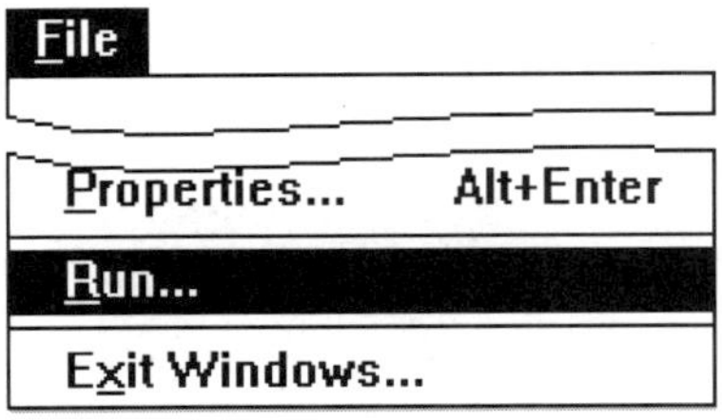


**Figure 14(a).** The *Run* command allows you to run an executable DOS file—one with a .bat, .com or .exe extension—that may not be present in any program group as a program item.

If you select a data file with an extension listed in the extensions section of the win.ini file, the application program that created the data file will be executed and the selected data file will be opened automatically by that application.

Thus, entering chap03.wri, if such a file exists in the subdirectory where Windows files are kept, will execute the Write program and open the file name chap03.wri.

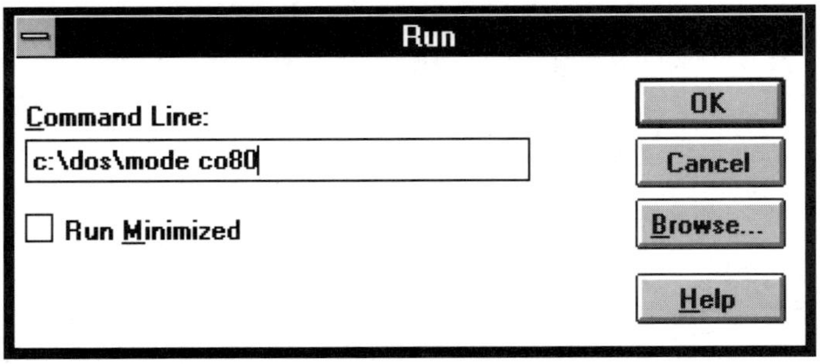


**Figure 14(b).** In the *Run* dialog box, type the program name (including the DOS path) in the *Command Line* box. Type in any parameters, just as you would in DOS.

When you select *OK*, the command is immediately executed.

If you have selected the *Run Minimized* option, the program will run to a minimized icon, which you can restore by double-clicking.

## EXIT WINDOWS COMMAND

**Figure 15(a).** This is the command used to exit the Windows Program. When you exit Windows, any programs that are still running under Windows will terminate. Upon exiting from Windows, you will return to DOS.

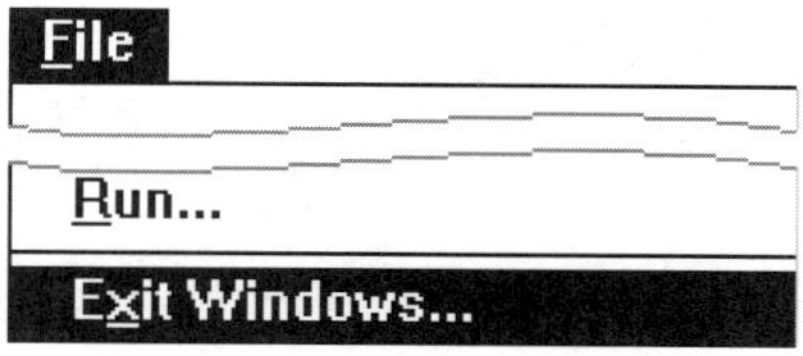


**Figure 15(b).** A warning dialog box will appear to make sure that you really intend to exit the program.

If other applications are running under Windows, you should exit those programs and make sure that any document files are saved before you exit Windows.

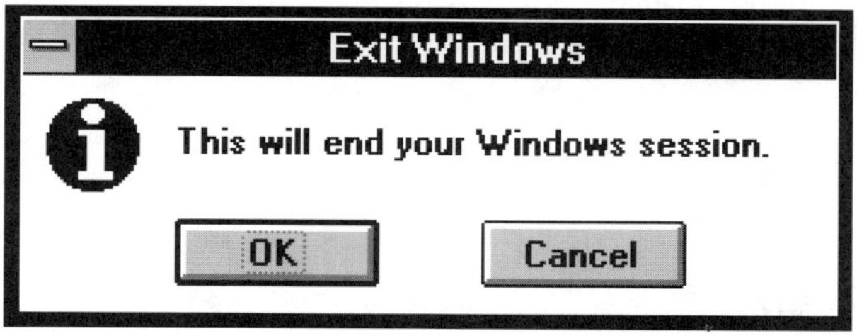


**Figure 16.** A quicker way to exit Windows is to double-click on the main window's Control Menu box.

Control Menu Box

## OPTIONS MENU

**Figure 17.** The choices in the **Options** menu are not commands, as they are in the other menus. The **Options** choices allow you to define in advance how certain situations in Windows are handled.

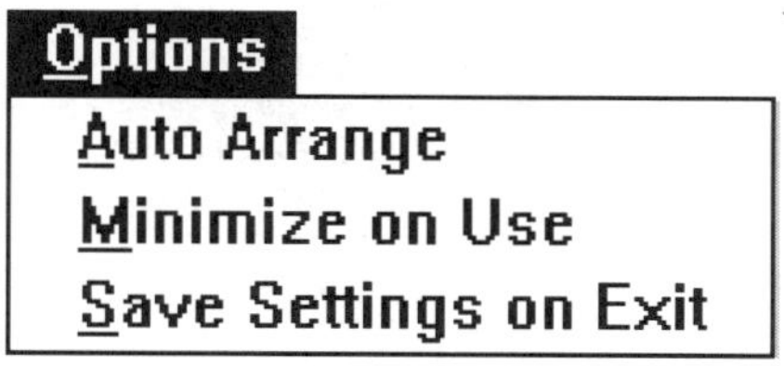


When you make a selection in the **Options** menu, a check mark (✓) appears beside that selection to indicate that it is active. Clicking a selection that already has a check mark deselects the choice by removing the mark.

## AUTO ARRANGE

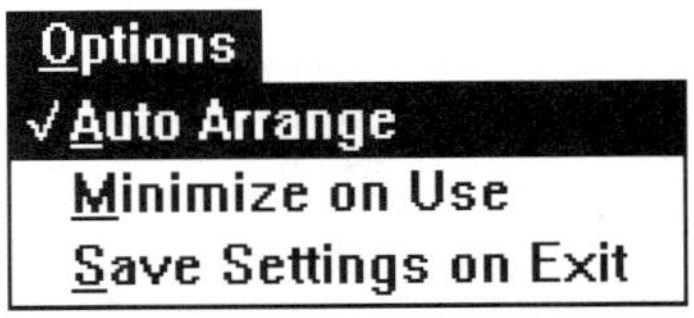


**Figure 18(a).** Program items can be moved within their program group windows (see Chapter 2). As the icons are moved and the sizes of the windows are adjusted, the windows may become cluttered and disorganized and the icons difficult to find.

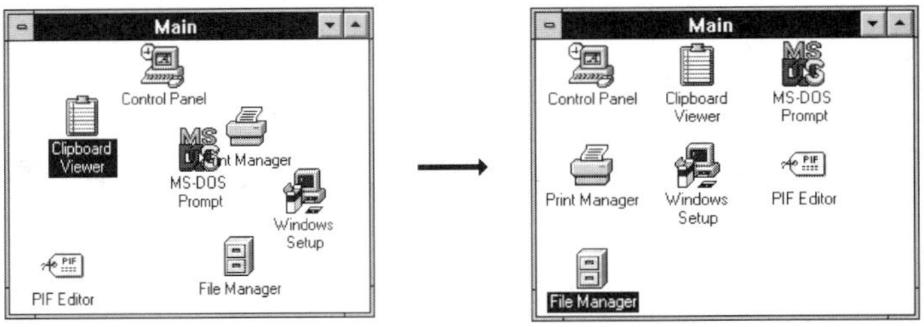


**Figure 18(b).** When the *Auto Arrange* option is selected, the program items in a program group window automatically arrange themselves within the window whenever the window is resized.

## MINIMIZE ON USE

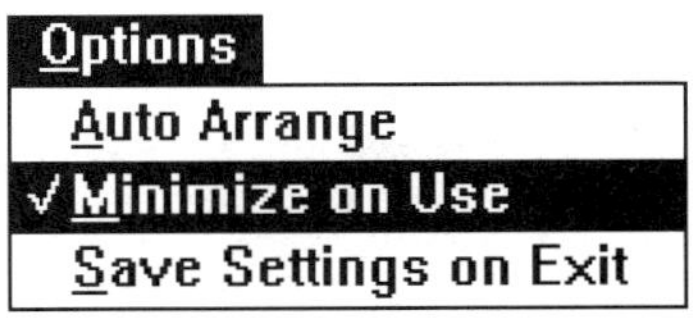


**Figure 19.** The Windows screen can become distracting if a number of windows are open at once and the Program Manager remains open in the background. If you accidentally click on the Program Manager window, it comes to the foreground and your previously selected application is hidden behind it.

**Figure 20.** To keep the screen less cluttered and the background free of distractions, the *Minimize on Use* command causes the Program Manager window to be minimized to an icon when other applications are executed.

To restore the Program Manager, simply double-click on its minimized icon.

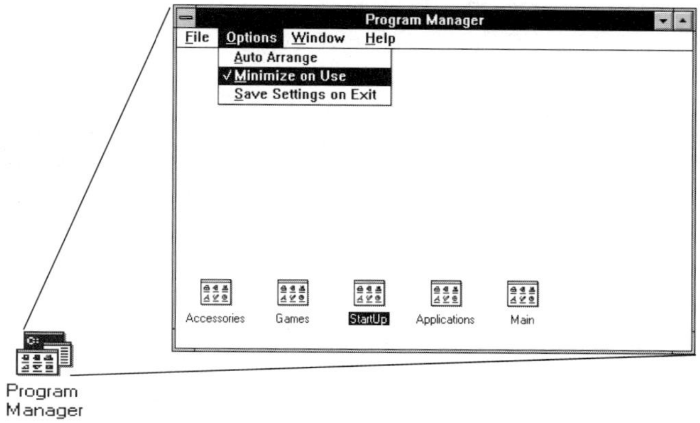


**Figure 21.** If the *Save Settings on Exit* option is selected, changes to the Program Manager's appearance and layout will be recorded when you exit Windows. If this option is not active when you exit Windows, the next time you run Windows it will be set up in the same way as it was when you started the current session.

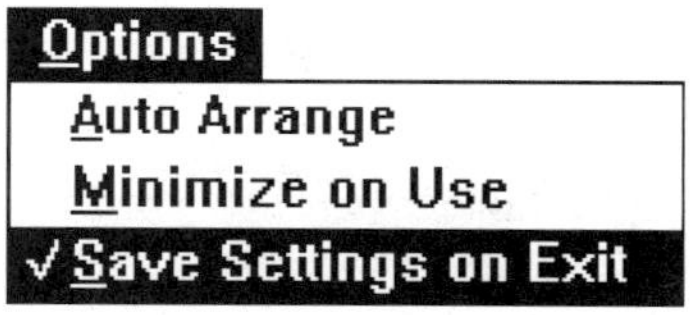


The settings affected by this option include window sizes and positions, icon placement and arrangement, and the settings of the other **Option** commands.

# Window Menu

**Figure 22.** The **Window** menu contains commands for manipulating the appearance of windows and icons on the Program Manager screen. These commands are used to organize the Program Manager window's appearance and to make the screen easier to view.

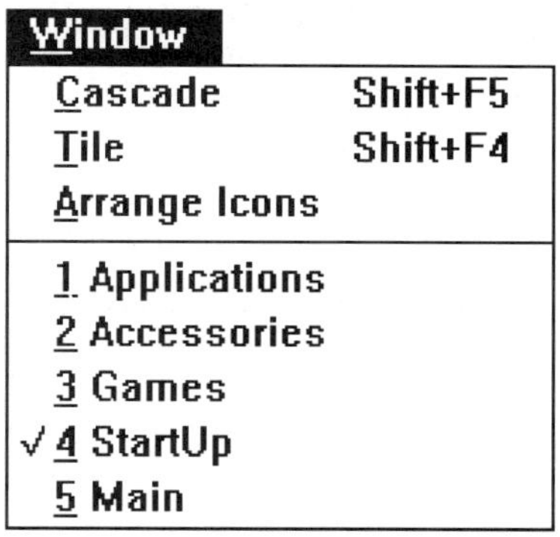

## CASCADE COMMAND

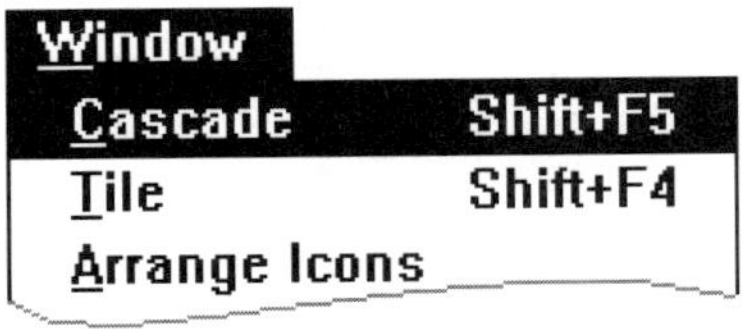


**Figure 23.** While you are using the Program Manager, you can alter the shape and position of program group windows until they overlap and obscure each other on the screen. If a smaller window is fully overlapped by a larger one, it can be hidden from view.

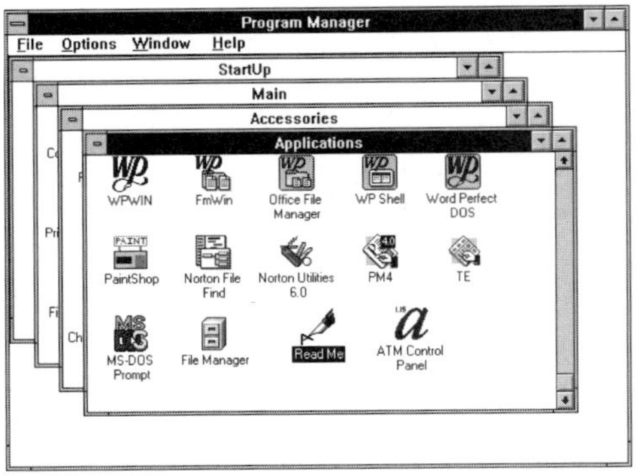


**Figure 24.** The *Cascade* command arranges all the open windows on the screen in an overlapping pattern, so that each window's title bar is visible. You can then select the window of your choice by clicking on its title bar or any other visible part of it.

## TILE COMMAND

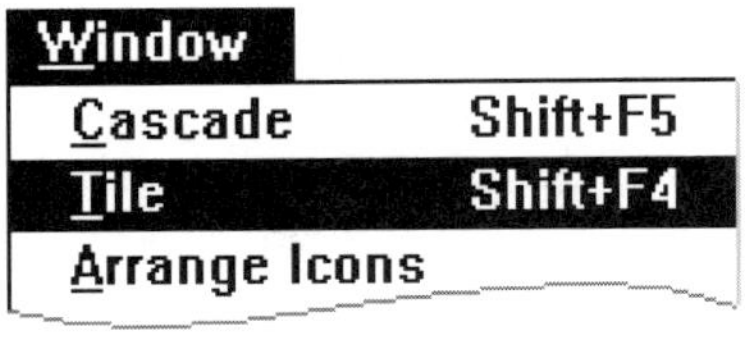


**Figure 25.** You may want the open windows on the screen arranged so that each window is fully visible. This kind of arrangement is useful if you want to switch rapidly between programs or if you want to move icons between windows.

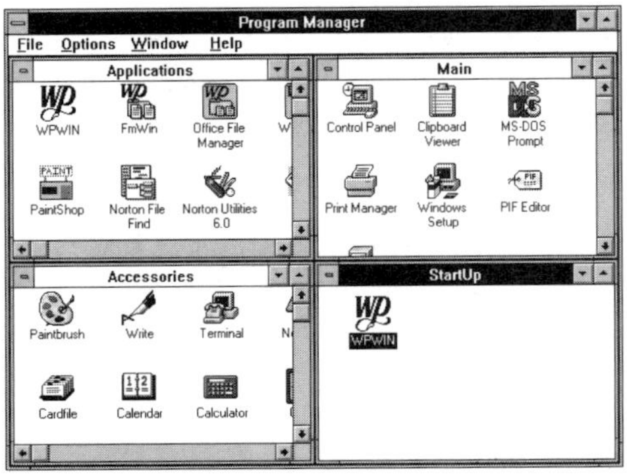


**Figure 26.** The *Tile* command arranges all open windows on the screen in a side-by-side, or *tiled,* pattern. Every window is thus fully visible and not obscured.

Note that scroll bars are automatically placed on windows where necessary.

## ARRANGE ICONS COMMAND

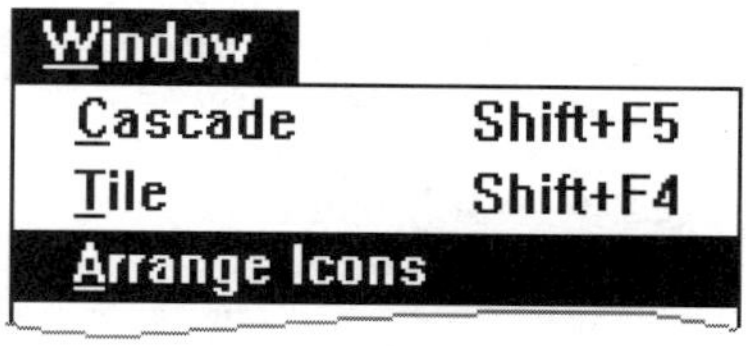


**Figure 27.** If the icons within a particular window become cluttered or disorganized from moving or copying, you will probably want to readjust their positions.

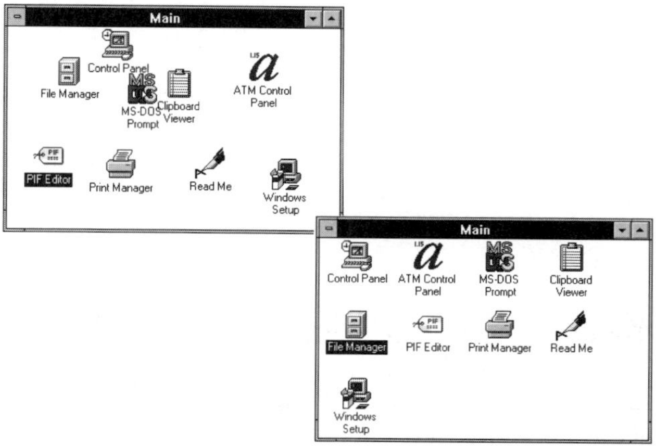


**Figure 28.** The *Arrange Icons* command reorders the icons within the currently selected window. The icons are evenly spaced within the window. This command works only when directly invoked—unlike the *Auto Arrange* command, which remains active once selected.

## OPENING PROGRAM GROUPS

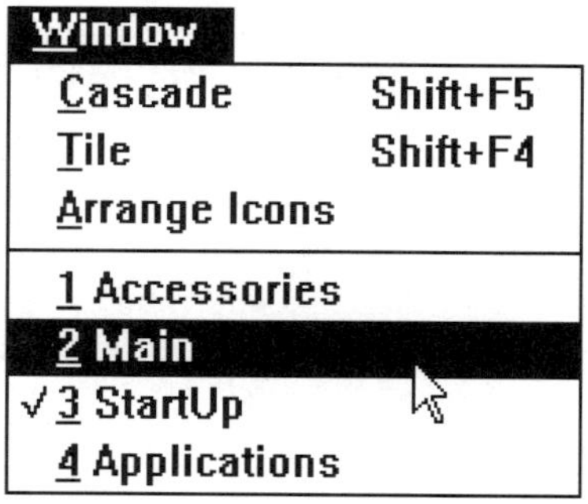


**Figure 29.** Usually, the quickest way to open a program group window is to double-click its icon on the screen. If the window is already open but inactive, it can be made active by clicking anywhere within its borders. However, if a window or its icon is obscured by other windows, accessing the window directly with the mouse may not be possible.

The bottom section of the **Window** menu contains a list of all program groups within the Program Manager. The currently selected group is indicated by a check mark (√). To make a program group current, use the mouse to select that group from this list.

## Help Menu

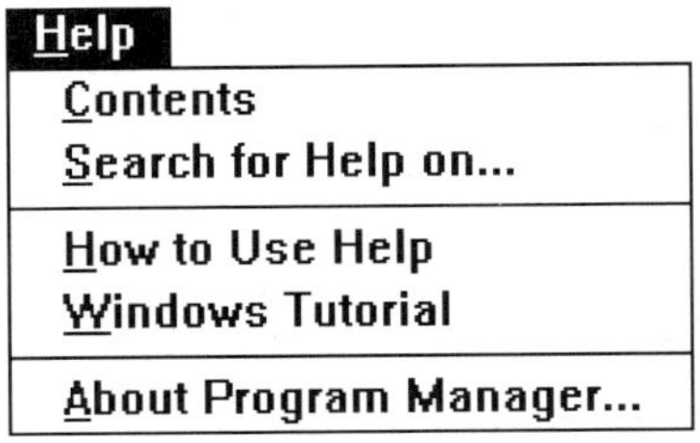


**Figure 30.** Microsoft Windows includes a Help feature in the Program Manager. Help provides you with quick access to information about the Program Manager and its features. This information can jog your memory about specific details of Windows use and allow you to continue working without having to consult the manual.

While it would be difficult to learn Windows using Help, more experienced users may find this feature a useful tool.

### *Help Window*

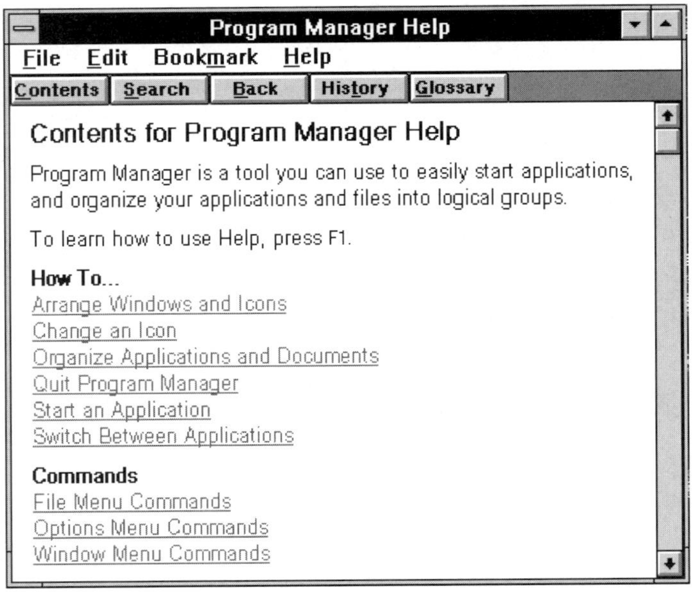


**Figure 31.** When you select a category from the **Help** menu, a special Help window will appear.

The Help window contains information about the topic you have selected. As with any other window, you can use the scroll bars to view the contents of the window. In addition, some special viewing features are available in the Help window.

**Figure 32.** The *History* button lists previously viewed topics in Help. You can select a topic from the History list to return to that topic.

**Figure 33.** The *Back* button returns to the contents of the previous Help window. The Help facility remembers the order in which you have viewed the Help window information. The *Back* key steps you through all the screens you have seen, in reverse order, until you return to the first Help screen of the current Help session.

**Figure 34.** The *Contents* button brings some general Help information into the Help window. This information lists the various topics on which you can obtain more specific help.

As you read this information, you will notice that some words and phrases are underlined; on a color screen this text is in green. These specially marked items represent topics on which more Help information is available.

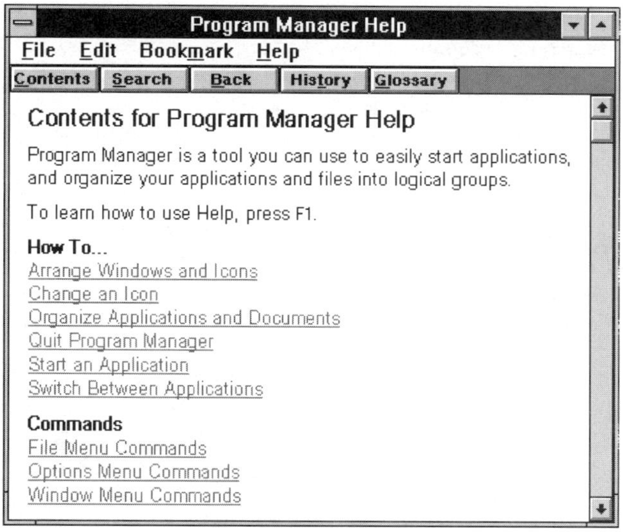


**Figure 35.** As you position the mouse pointer over one of these colored items, it will take the shape of a pointing finger. Clicking the mouse over one of these items brings information about that item into the Help window.

In this figure, the *Arrange Windows and Icons* item is about to be selected. The Help window shown in Figure 36 contains the resulting Help information.

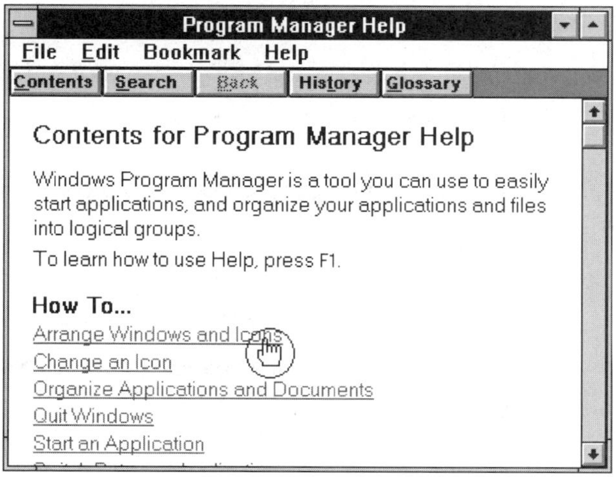

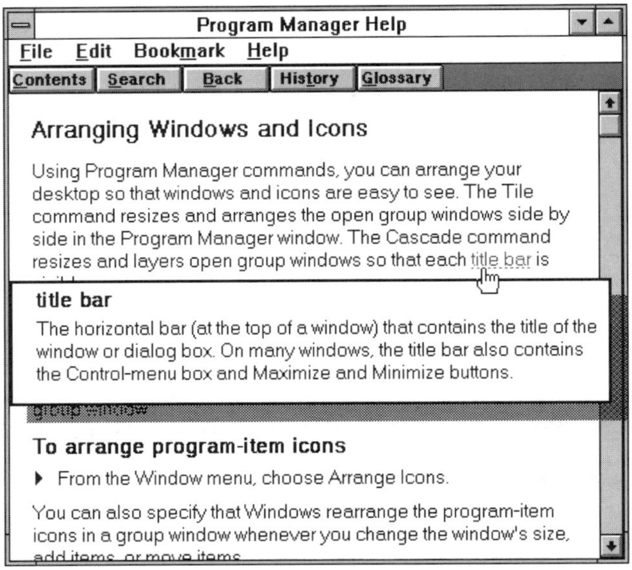


**Figure 36.** If the item is underlined with a broken line, only a small amount of Help information is available for display. In such cases, position the mouse pointer over the item and click the left mouse button.

The information on the item will be displayed in a special information box superimposed over the existing Help information. Clicking anywhere in the Help window will close the information box and return you to the previous Help information.

In this example, the mouse button is held and clicked over the *title bar* item. The resulting information window is shown.

## SEARCH COMMAND

**Figure 37.** If you need help on a specific topic but don't know where to find it in the index, you can use the *Search* button to look up the topic directly.

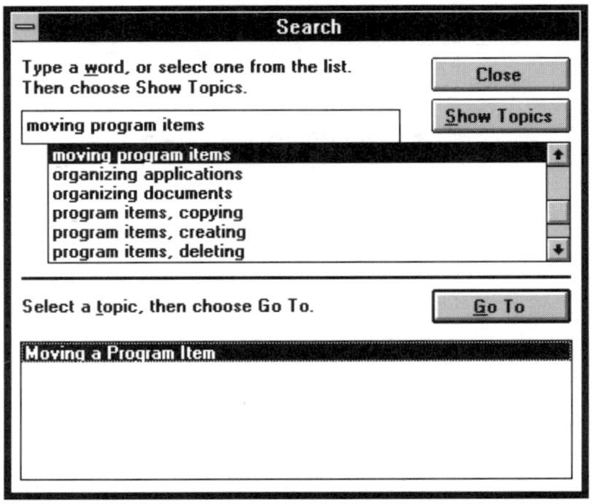


**Figure 38.** When you click on the *Search* button, this special *Search* dialog box will appear. Select the category for which you want help from this list, or type a category name directly in the *text* box above the list. When you have selected a category, click on the *Show Topics* button.

**Figure 39.** If any Help information is available about the category you have selected in the *Search For* dialog box, a list of available topics appears at the bottom of the box. Select the topic for which you want to see Help information and click on the *Go To* button.

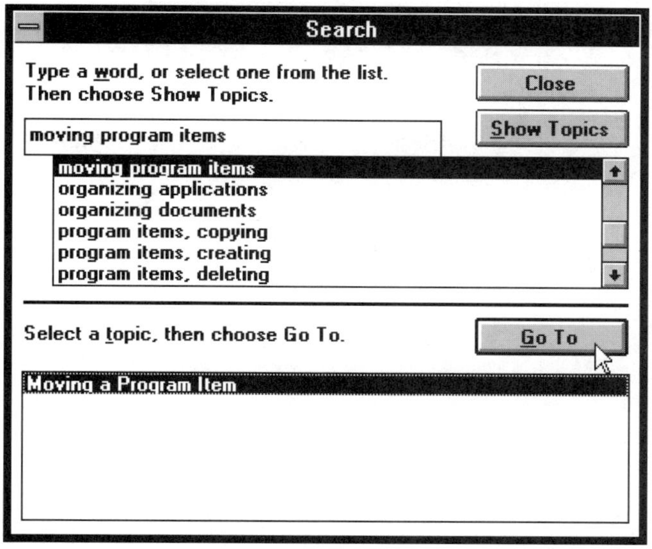


**Figure 40.** The Help window will return to the screen with information on the topic you have selected. You can now view this information just as you would view any other Help information.

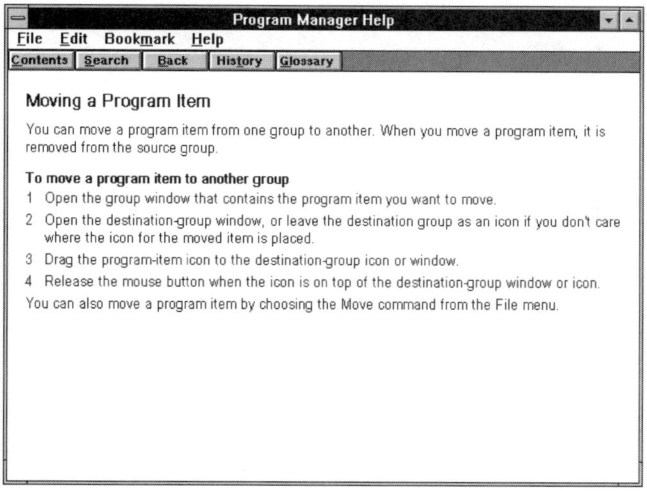


When you want to exit from the Help facility and return to using the Program Manager, simply double-click the Help window's Control Menu box.

# Windows Supplied Programs 4

## Supplied Programs

Version 3.1 of Windows includes an assortment of programs. These programs are distributed among three program groups that are automatically created when you install Windows. You are free to copy or move these programs between their groups or to add new programs to these groups. The initial arrangement is only a suggestion.

## Main Group

**Figure 1.** The Main program group contains a number of programs that replace, and in many cases enhance, commands you would ordinarily use in DOS.

To run one of these programs, double-click on the desired program item icon.

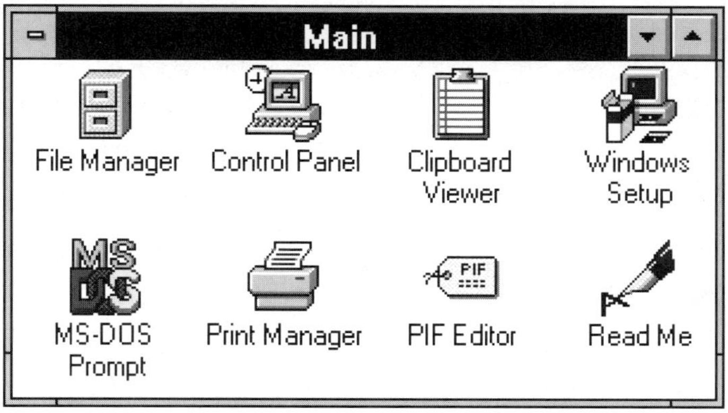


### *FILE MANAGER*

**Figure 2(a).** The File Manager is a utility that enables you to manipulate files and subdirectories on your computer's hard disk and floppy disk drives.

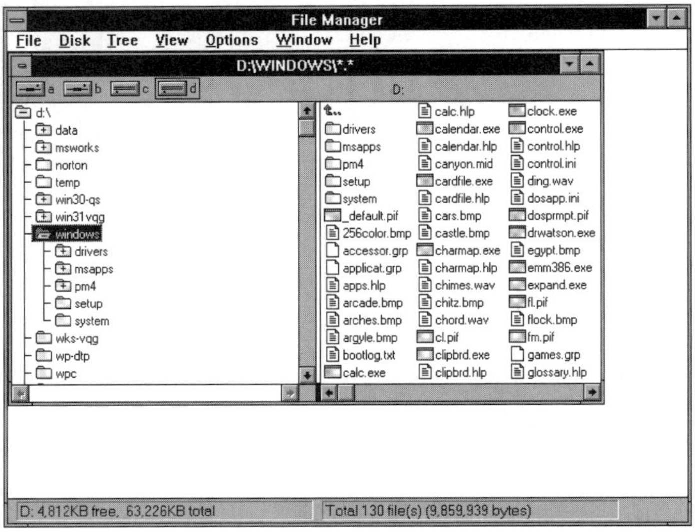


**Figure 2(b).** The File Manager's main window contains a menu bar from which you can select the various file manipulation commands. In the space below the menu bar, the Directory Tree window displays the disk drives available to your system. The area below these icons shows a directory tree of the selected disk.

By using the menu bar and the mouse pointer, you can copy, move, delete, and rename you system's files more easily than you could through DOS. Remember that, unlike the Program Manager, changes made with the File Manager do permanently affect the DOS files on your system.

Chapter 7 deals in detail with the File Manager.

## CONTROL PANEL

**Figure 3(a).** The Control Panel is a special program group window that is activated when you run the Control Panel program item.

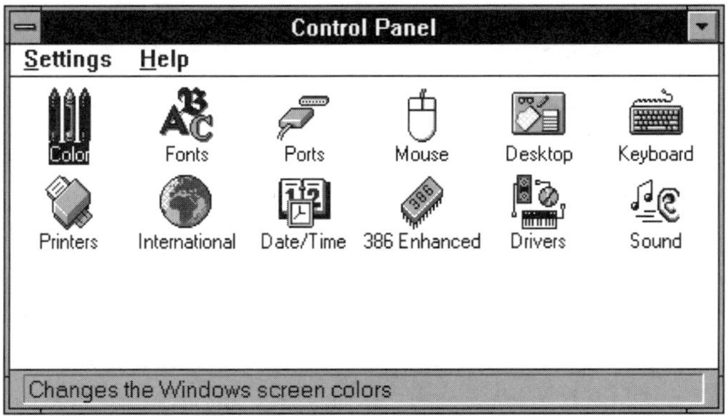


**Figure 3(b).** The Control Panel window contains a set of utility programs for customizing the Windows interface to your specific needs. Included are utilities for changing the screen colors, mouse and keyboard options, and printer details.

In contrast to other program group windows, you can neither add to nor delete from the programs in the Control Panel.

Chapter 6 explains each program in the Control Panel window.

## CLIPBOARD VIEWER

**Figure 4(a).** The Clipboard is a special utility program that enables Windows to perform one of its most valuable features: the easy transfer of data between Windows applications.

All Windows applications that deal with data of any sort have a *Cut*, a *Copy*, and a *Paste* command. These commands, usually located in the **Edit** menu, are not only used to arrange data within the application itself but also help facilitate its transfer to other Windows applications.

Whenever you use the *Cut* or *Copy* commands, the selected data is copied into a special part of your system's memory called the Clipboard. When you use the *Paste* command, the contents of the Clipboard are placed back onto the active screen.

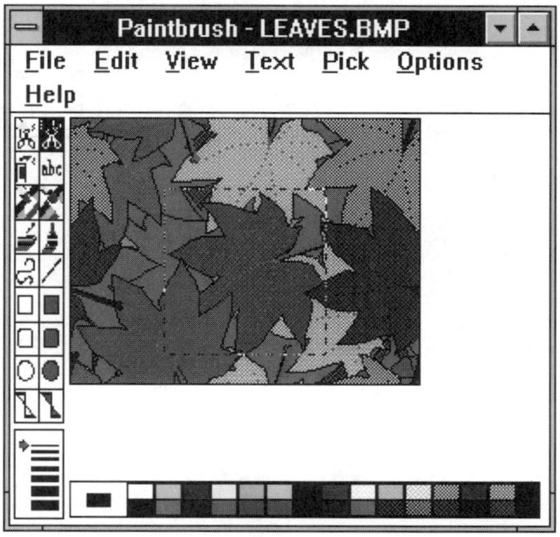


**Figure 4(b).** Using this feature, you can *Copy* or *Cut* data in one Windows application, switch to another program, and then use the *Paste* command to introduce the data into the second application.

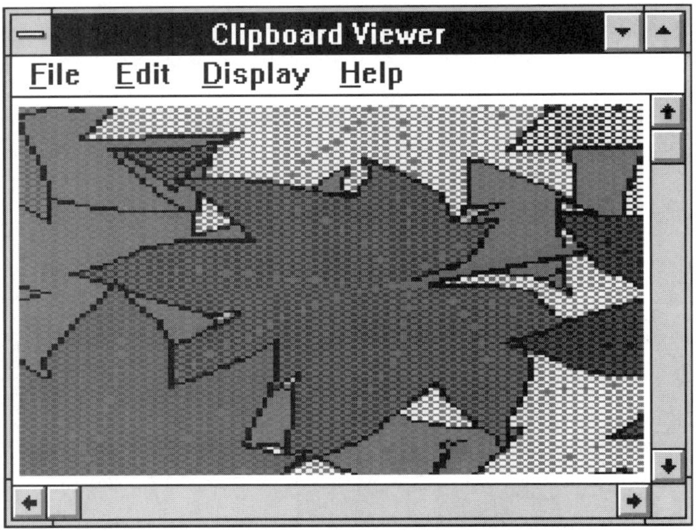


**Figure 5.** The Clipboard program allows you to see the current contents of the Clipboard and to save the Clipboard's contents for later retrieval.

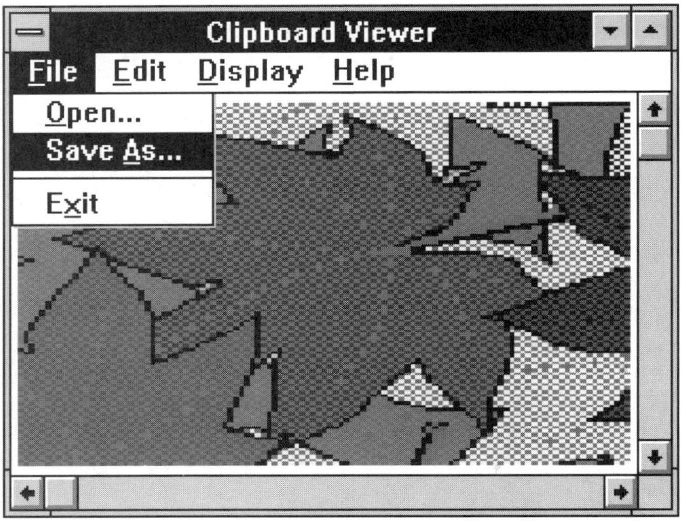


**Figure 6.** To save the Clipboard's contents, use the *Save As* command from the **File** menu in the Clipboard's menu bar. The data will be saved in a file with a .clp extension. Using the *Open* command, you can load a previously saved .clp file into the Clipboard.

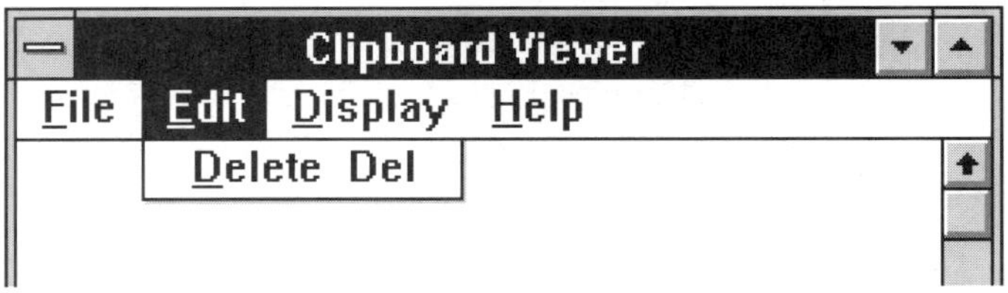


**Figure 7.** The **Edit** menu in the Clipboard program's menu bar has only one command: *Delete.* This command is used to clear the Clipboard. Be sure to save the contents before *Deleting* because the data is not retrievable once it has been deleted.

A final function of the Clipboard is to "capture" the appearance of the Windows screen. If you press the Print Screen key (often labeled as Prt Sc) while running Windows, a graphical image of the entire screen will be placed into the Clipboard. If you hold the Alt key while pressing the Print Screen key, only the active window will be captured.

Using this feature you can easily demonstrate the appearance of the Windows screen in special situations without having to recreate those special conditions each time. Some of the screen images used in this guide were made with the help of the Windows Clipboard.

## WINDOWS SETUP

**Figure 8(a).** The Windows Setup program allows you to identify to the Windows interface what components make up your computer system and whether you are operating under a local area network.

**Figure 8(b).** When you run the Windows Setup program, the Windows Setup window appears. This window, which lists the current system settings, also has a menu bar along the top.

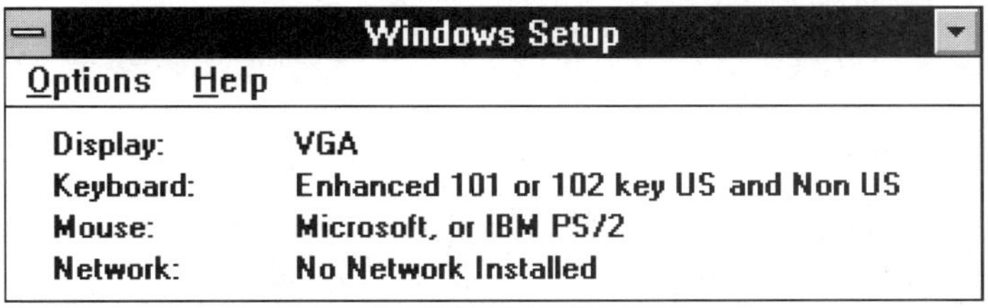


**Figure 9.** The settings listed in this window will have been specified during the initial installation of the Windows program, but it is not necessary to reinstall Windows if you alter your system's setup.

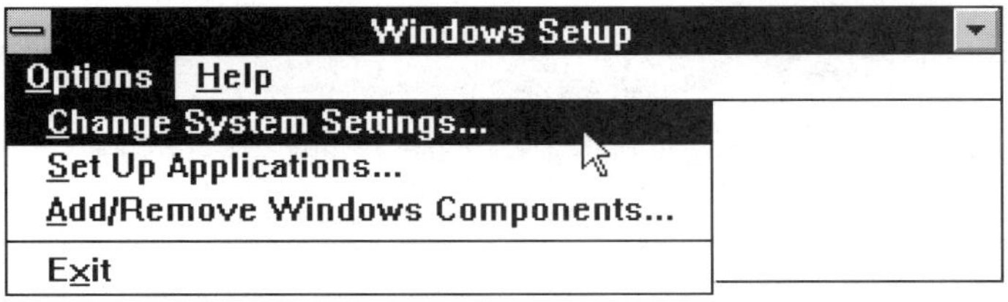


To change these settings, select *Change System Settings* from the **Options** menu.

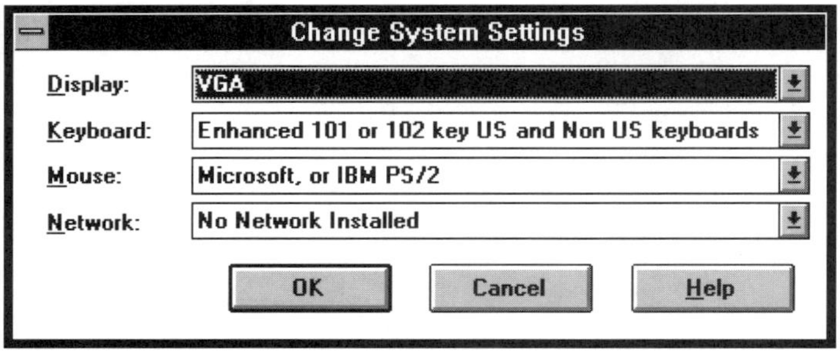


**Figure 10.** A set of submenus will appear in the *Change System Settings* dialog box, from which you can select the items that most accurately describe your system's makeup.

You may want to consult the documentation included with your system's components to ensure that you are identifying them correctly. Some items, like the computer's monitor, may be capable of operating in several modes. You will need to decide which mode is best for your application, then select it from the submenu.

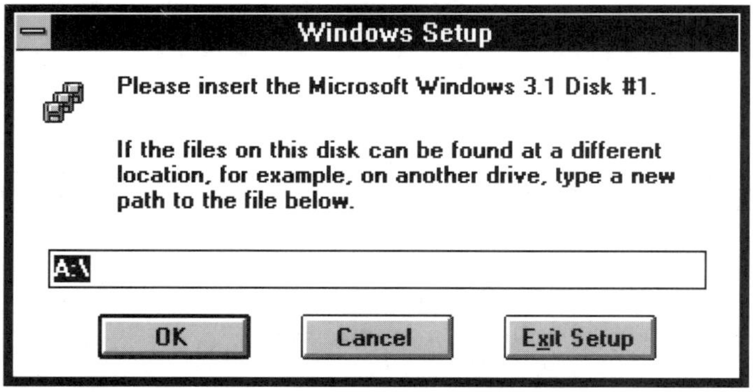


**Figure 11.** If you change the selected equipment, Windows may need to read information about your selection from one of the original setup disks. A dialog box will appear to tell you which disk is required. Insert the requested disk in the suggested drive, or key in the correct path.

**Figure 12.** Restart Windows to make the new changes take effect. A dialog box gives you the option of restarting the program immediately or continuing.

A second function of the Windows Setup program is to allow you to install application programs as program items in the Program Manager. This feature of the Setup program is outlined in more detail in Chapter 5.

**Figure 13.** Use the *Set Up Applications* selection from the Windows Setup **Options** menu to install application programs whose files are already located on your hard disk.

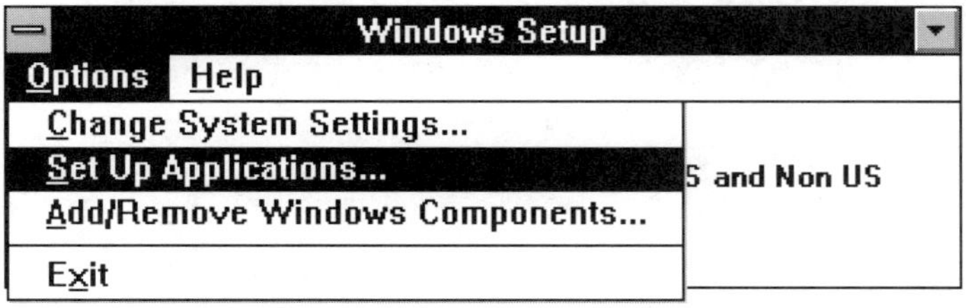


## *MS-DOS PROMPT*

**Figure 14(a).** If, while running Windows, you want to return to DOS for a short time, you can do so without having to exit and restart the Windows program.

**Figure 14(b).** When you double-click on the MS-DOS icon from the Main group, the Windows display will vanish and be replaced by the usual DOS prompt display. Though Windows is still present in your computer's memory, the DOS operating system will respond to typed DOS commands in the usual way.

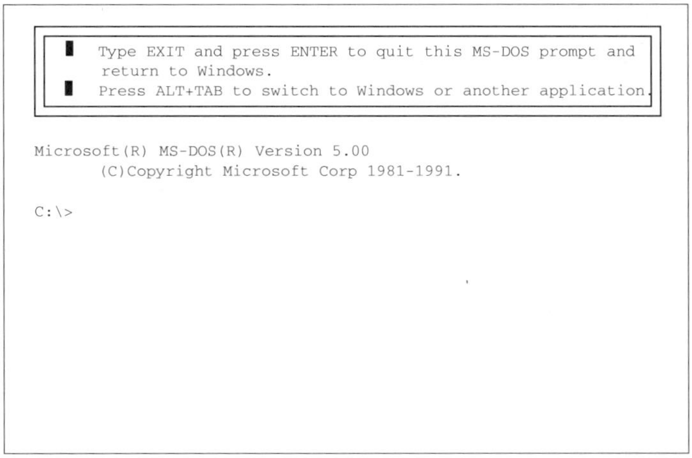


When you are ready to return to Windows, type EXIT at the DOS prompt and you will be returned to the Windows interface.

When you use the DOS icon in Windows, remember that Windows is still in memory! Because there is no indication in the DOS display that Windows is still active, it is easy to forget that you are not just in DOS.

If you try to start up Windows, forgetting that it is already active, a message appears to tell you that you are already running Windows. The message that appeared when you first switched to the MS-DOS prompt (shown in the previous figure) is also repeated.

## PRINT MANAGER

**Figure 15(a).** Because an application program can send data to a printer faster than the printer can assimilate and translate the data, applications must spend extra time sending the data more slowly, all the while suspending any other use of your computer system. The Print Manager utility limits the amount of time that is lost when applications transfer data to the printer.

With the Print Manager, applications do not send their data directly to the printer but to a part of your system's memory reserved for the Print Manager. This transfer can be completed much more quickly than the slow transfer of data to the printer. You are then free to return to your application, while the Print Manager program, running in the background, sends the data to the printer at the required rate.

If the *Use Print Manager* option is selected from the Printers program in the Control Panel, the Print Manager is activated automatically every time you print from an application running in Windows.

**Figure 15(b).** When you run the Print Manager program, a window showing the data sent to the Print Manager appears. This window shows the order in which the items will be printed, the size of the items, and the times at which they were sent to the Print Manager. For the item currently being printed, indicated by a printer icon, the percentage of the data already sent to the printer is also shown.

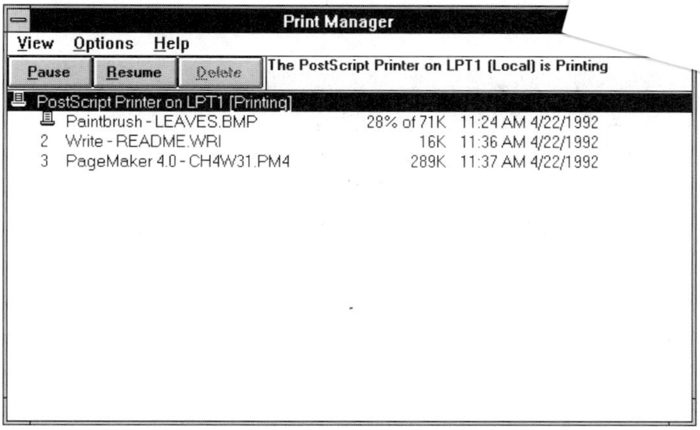


## *PIF EDITOR*

**Figure 16(a).** The PIF Editor creates and modifies Program Information Files (PIFs). These files contain information about non-Windows applications that helps the Windows interface to run these programs.

**Figure 16(b).** The PIF Editor contains different options, depending on whether the non-Windows application being defined is intended to run in Standard or in 386 Enhanced mode.

Select the mode from the **Mode** menu of the PIF Editor window. You can create PIFs for both Enhanced and Standard modes, regardless of the mode in which Windows is running at the time. Be sure, however, that Windows is running in the correct mode when you actually run the application.

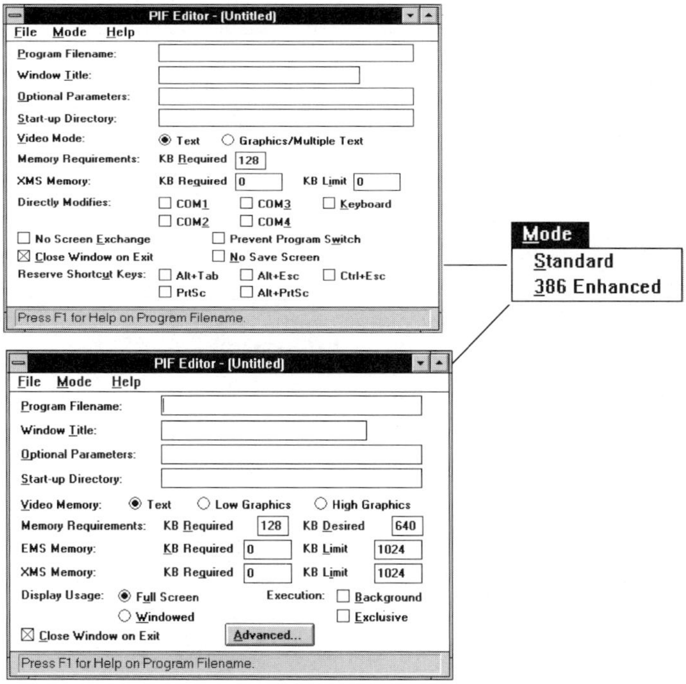

## STANDARD MODE

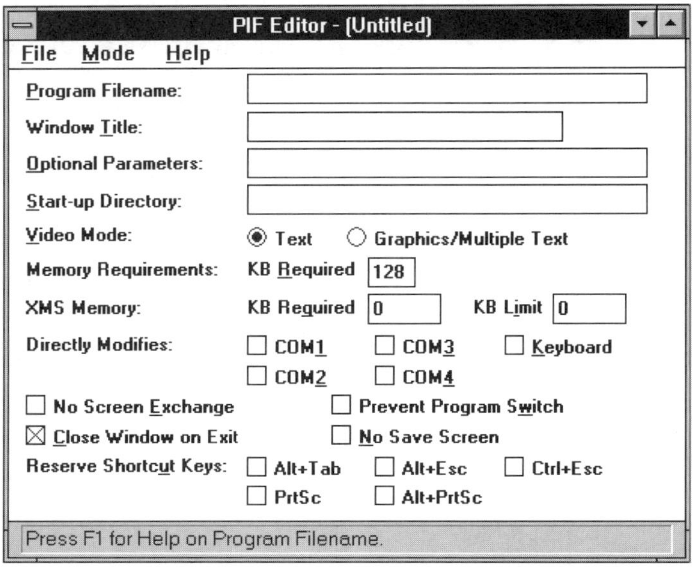


**Figure 17.** The upper part of the standard mode PIF Editor window allows you to enter such basic items as the program's name, location, and any parameters that should be included when the program is executed.

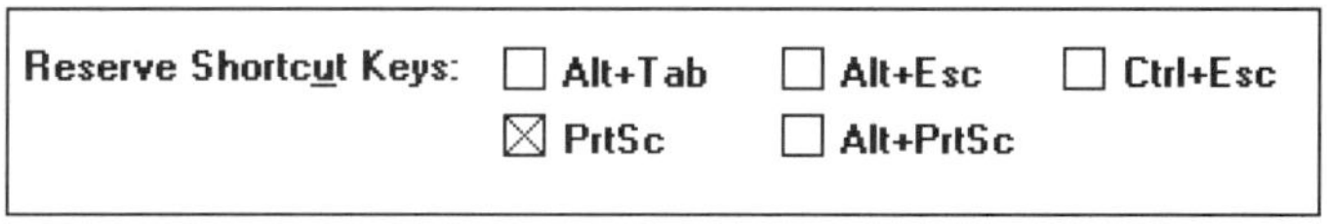


**Figure 18.** Many programs written to run under DOS will use key combinations that have special meanings under Windows.

If the program you are installing uses such keystrokes, select them from the list shown here, which occurs at the bottom of the dialog box shown in Figure 17. This will ensure that Windows' interpretation of these keys is suspended while the application is running.

## ENHANCED MODE

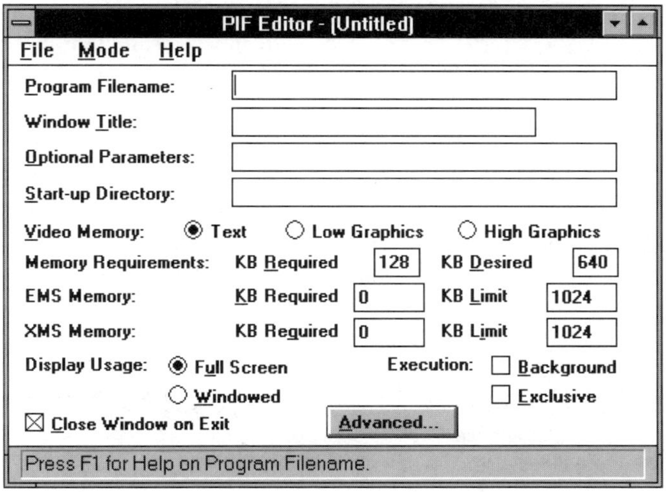


**Figure 19.** The basic 386 Enhanced PIF Editor window requests much of the same file name and parameter information as the Standard mode window.

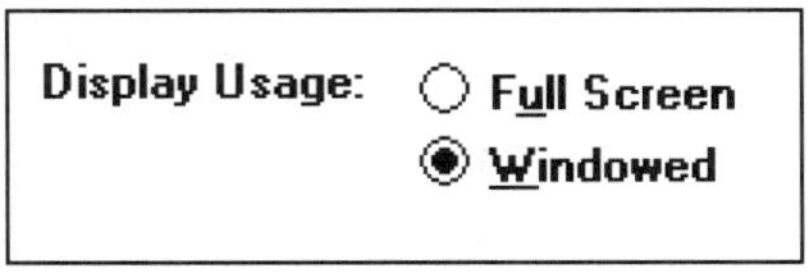


**Figure 20.** In 386 Enhanced mode, non-Windows applications can also run within a window, while in Standard mode they must occupy the entire screen. Use the *Display Usage* radio buttons to select *Full Screen* or *Windowed* execution for the application you are defining.

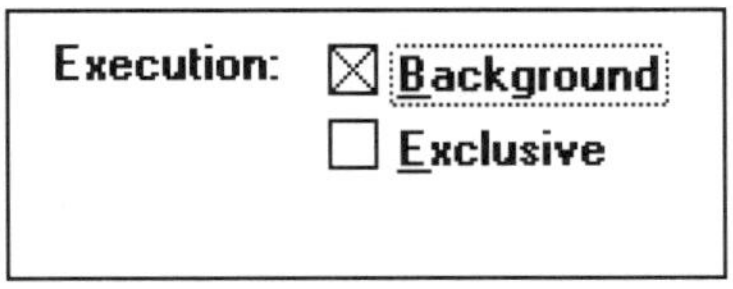


**Figure 21.** In 386 Enhanced mode, Windows has the ability to execute several programs at once, running one in the active window (foreground) while the others run in inactive or minimized windows (background). The *Execution* check boxes provide options that relate to the handling of multitasked applications.

If the non-Windows application can run in the background—for example, like a spreadsheet that may take time to recalculate without user involvement—select the *Background* check box.

If you want your system's full resources devoted to the application when it is in the active window, select the *Exclusive* check box. Processing of all inactive windows will be suspended while the application is active, but will resume when the application is closed or moved to an inactive window.

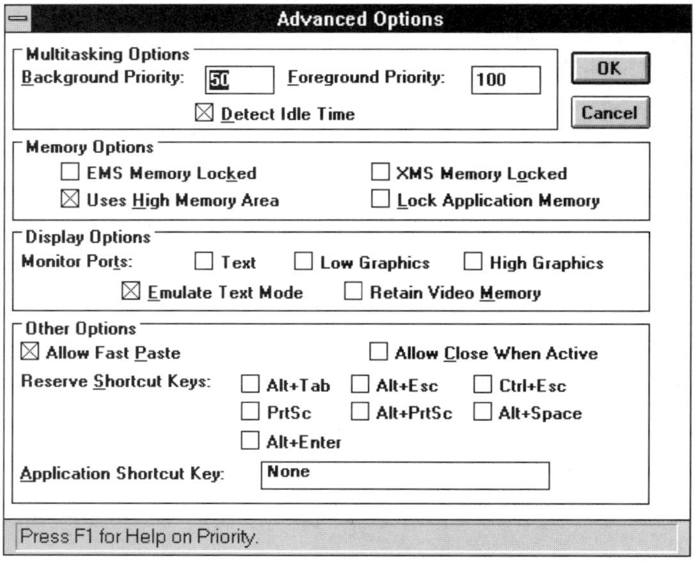


**Figure 22.** In addition to the window pictured in Figure 19, the 386 Enhanced PIF Editor has an advanced set of options. When you select the *Advanced* button in the Figure 19 dialog box, this *Advanced Options* window appears.

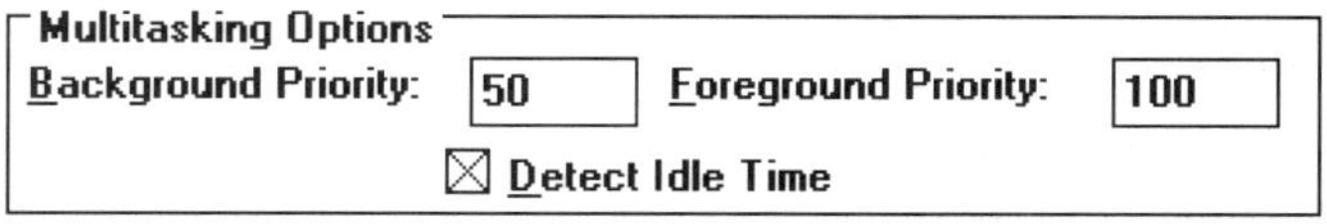


**Figure 23.** When Windows is multitasking, it switches its attention rapidly between each of the different programs that are currently running. The amount of time given to each application is based on the priority you have assigned to it.

Every application has a priority number between 1 and 1000. The percentage of the processor's time that is devoted to an application is the ratio of the application's priority number to the sum of the priority numbers of all the applications currently running. You can assign a higher priority to an application when it is in the foreground than when it is in an inactive window.

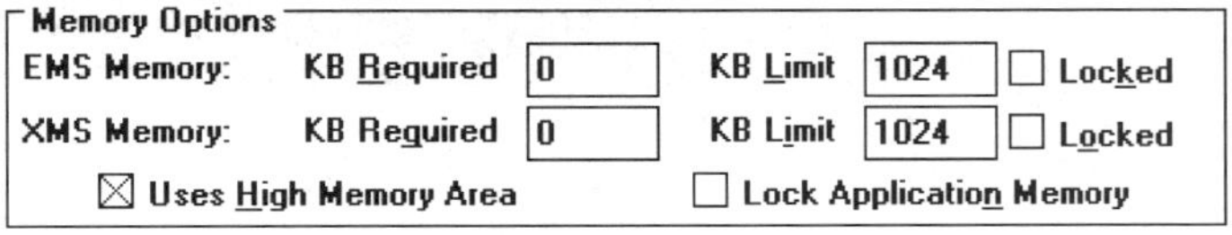


**Figure 24.** If your system has extended (XMS) or expanded (EMS) memory and the application you are defining makes special use of one of these kinds of memory, you can specify the application's memory requirements. The documentation included with the non-Windows application will explain its memory requirements.

# Accessories Group

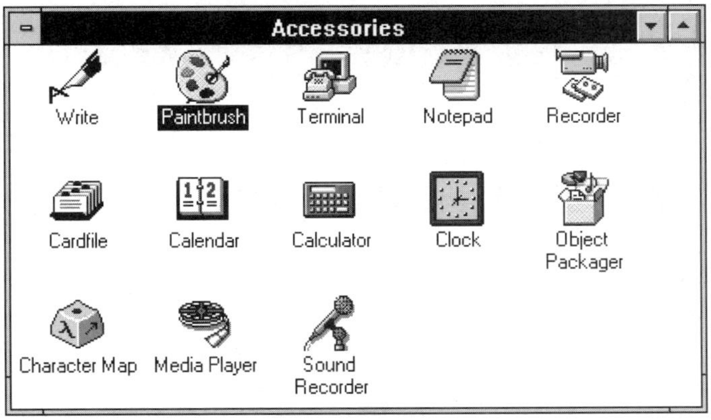


**Figure 25.** The Accessories program group contains a collection of utility programs that are not essential to the use of Windows. Though not vital, these programs are very useful to have in the Windows environment. To run one of these programs, double-click on the appropriate icon.

## CALCULATOR PROGRAM

**Figure 26(a).** The Calculator program causes a window shaped like a pocket calculator to appear.

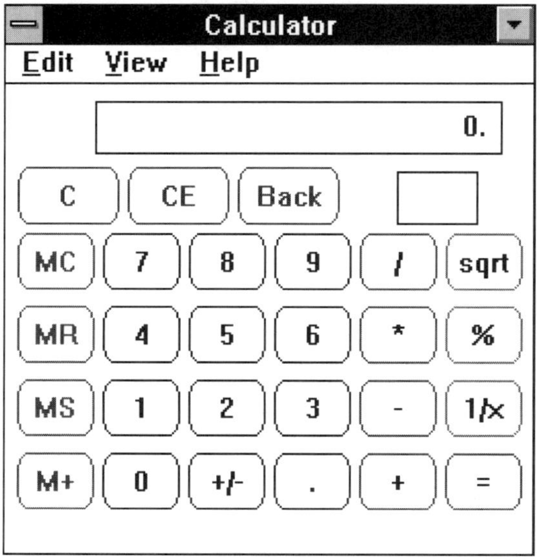


**Figure 26(b).** To operate the calculator, click the mouse pointer on the calculator's keys or use the number pad on your keyboard.

The **Edit** menu in the Calculator's menu bar allows you to either *Copy* the displayed number to the Clipboard or to *Paste* the Clipboard's contents (if applicable) into the Calculator's readout.

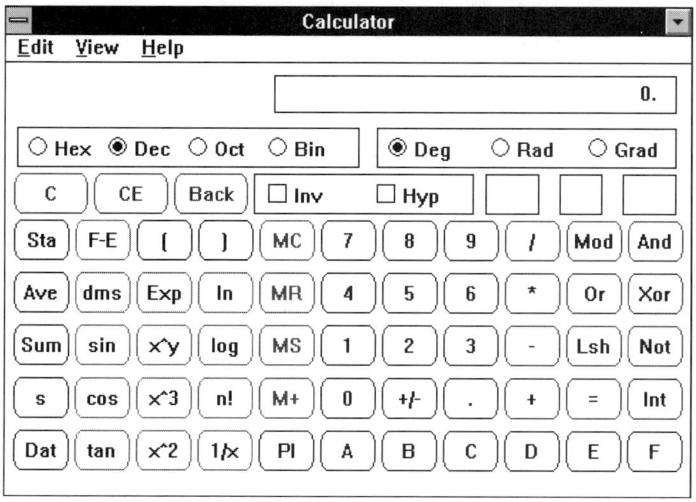


**Figure 27.** The **View** menu lets you choose between the standard calculator layout (pictured in Figure 26(b)) and the full-function scientific calculator layout shown here.

# CALENDAR PROGRAM

**Figure 28(a).** The Calendar program displays a window that resembles a desk calendar and operates like a personal appointment diary.

**Figure 28(b).** The **File** menu commands of the Calendar let you save, retrieve, and print Calendar information.

The **Edit** menu's *Cut, Copy,* and *Paste* commands link the Calendar to the Clipboard.

The **View** menu lets you select a daily or monthly display format.

The **Options** menu allows you to mark appointments and special events on the Calendar.

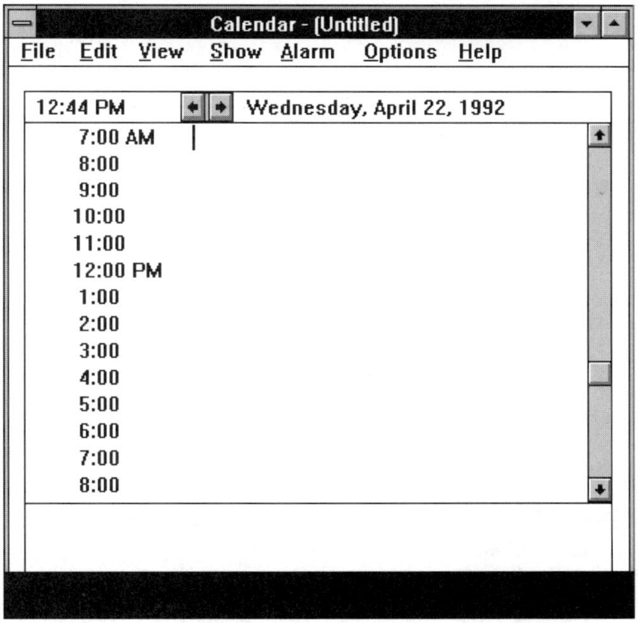


# CARDFILE

**Figure 29(a).** The Cardfile, as its name suggests, is a computerized index card filing system. The "cards" are sorted alphabetically using the data entered on the top line of each card as an index.

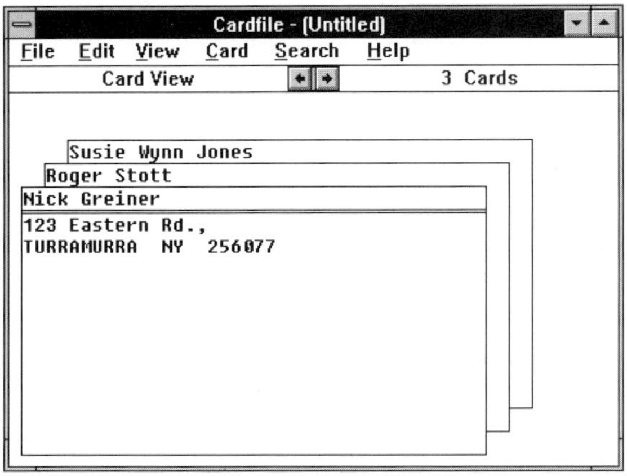


**Figure 29(b).** The desired card can be brought to the front of the stack by clicking the mouse pointer on its index heading.

The **File** menu lets you save, retrieve, and print Cardfile data.

The **Edit** menu links the Cardfile to the Windows Clipboard. Using the Clipboard, graphical images as well as text data can be included on the file cards.

## CHARACTER MAP

**Figure 30(a).** The Character map program is a utility that allows you to view the various fonts available in Windows and to copy specific characters to the Clipboard.

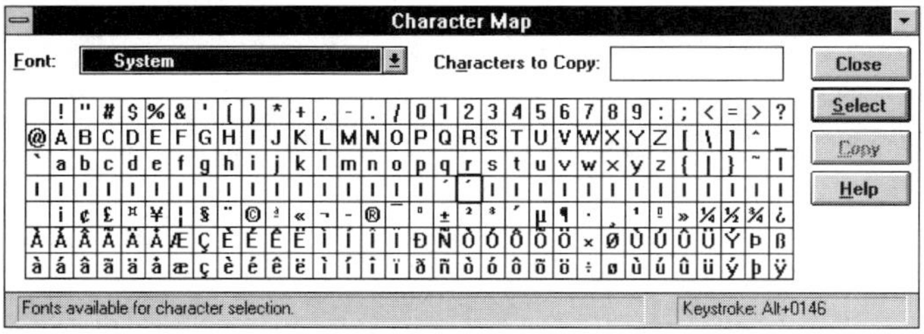


**Figure 30(b).** The *Character Map* dialog box contains a chart that lists all the characters in the currently selected typeface. The *Font* submenu lets you select the typeface to be viewed in this dialog box.

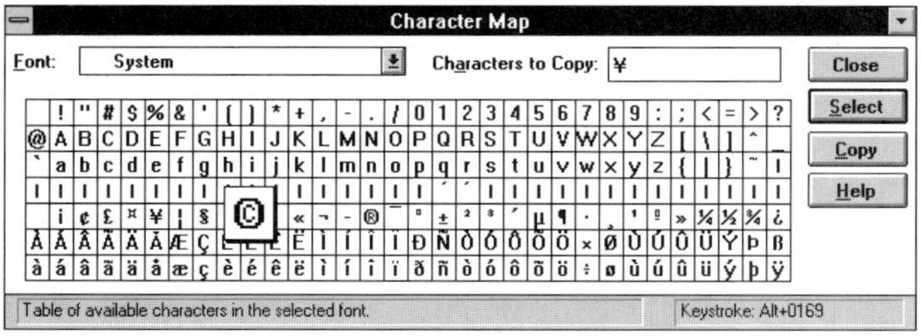


**Figure 31.** Click on any of the characters in the chart and hold down the mouse button to display an enlarged view of that particular character.

Double-click on a character to add it to the *Characters to Copy* text box, from which it can be copied to the clipboard using the *Copy* button.

## CLOCK PROGRAM

**Figure 32(a).** The Clock program produces a window containing either an analog or digital clock-face, displaying the current time.

**Figure 32(b).** This program is useful because it continues to display the correct time, even when it has been minimized to an icon.

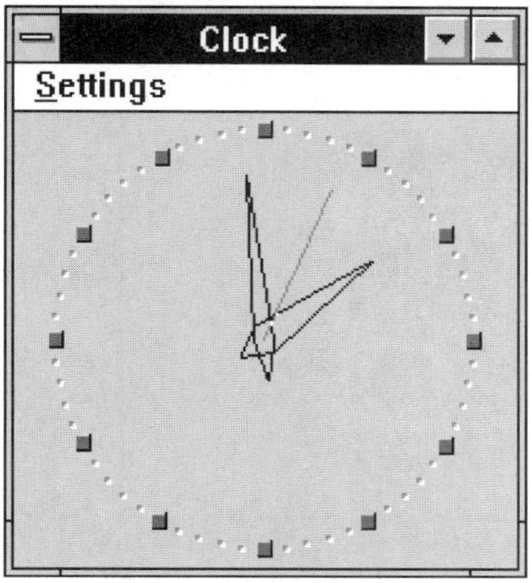


## NOTEPAD

**Figure 33(a).** The Notepad is a simple text-editor program that allows you to write and modify text files in your computer system.

**Figure 33(b).** The Notepad is ideal for creating or modifying DOS files like autoexec.bat, or config.sys. Programmers may find the Notepad to be convenient for writing code without having to exit Windows or the application they are using.

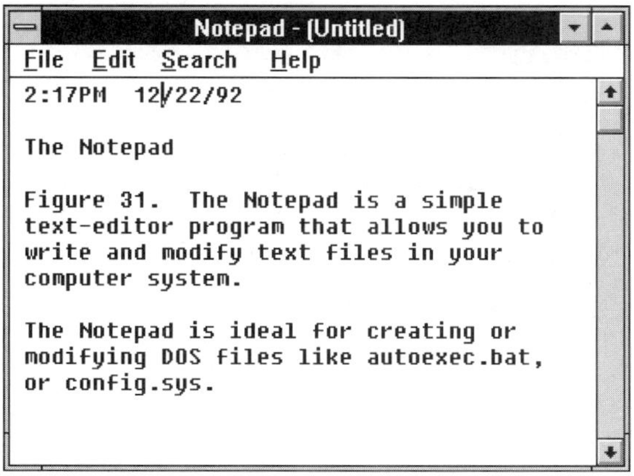

## PAINTBRUSH PROGRAM

**Figure 34(a).** Paintbrush is a graphical drawing program that lets you create and modify graphic images.

**Figure 34(b).** Paintbrush includes a variety of tools that allow you to create colored or black-and-white pictures. You can also load images created elsewhere and modify them in Paintbrush.

Some of the screen images in this guide were captured with the Clipboard and customized in Paintbrush.

## MACRO RECORDER

**Figure 35(a).** If there is a series of keystrokes and mouse movements that you use often, you can use the Macro Recorder program to "memorize" these actions and play them back at will. A recorded sequence of actions is called a macro.

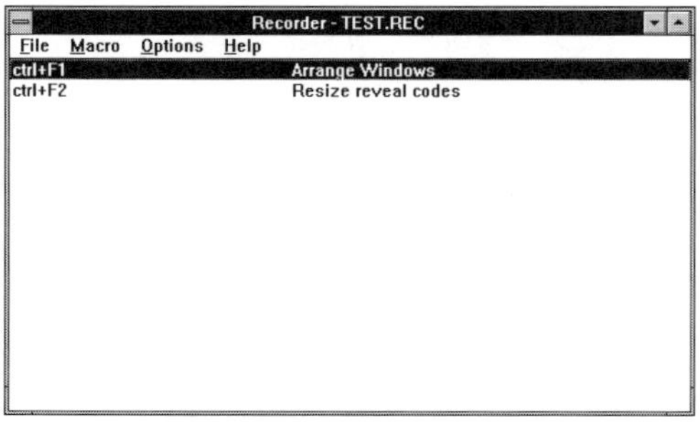


**Figure 35(b).** The Recorder program window contains a menu bar and a list of macros.

The **File** menu lets you load, save, merge, or delete lists of macros.

**Figure 36.** When you select the *Record* command from the **Macro** menu in the Recorder dialog box pictured in Figure 35(b), the *Record Macro* window appears. In this window you can name and describe the sequence you want to record, as well as set a number of options.

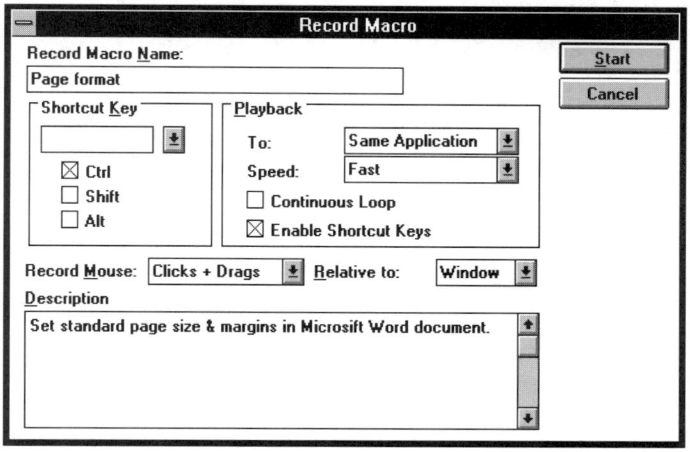


When you select *Start*, the Recorder program appears as a flashing icon on the lower left of the desktop. Perform all the actions, using the mouse and keyboard, that you want to record, then click on the flashing icon to stop the recording.

If the Recorder icon is obscured by another window, you can stop recording by holding down the Control key (Ctrl) and pressing the Break key.

## WRITE PROGRAM

**Figure 37(a).** The Write program is a word processing package that is included with Windows.

**Figure 37(b).** This program does not possess some of the advanced layout and formatting features found in more sophisticated word processing packages, but it is not intended to replace these programs.

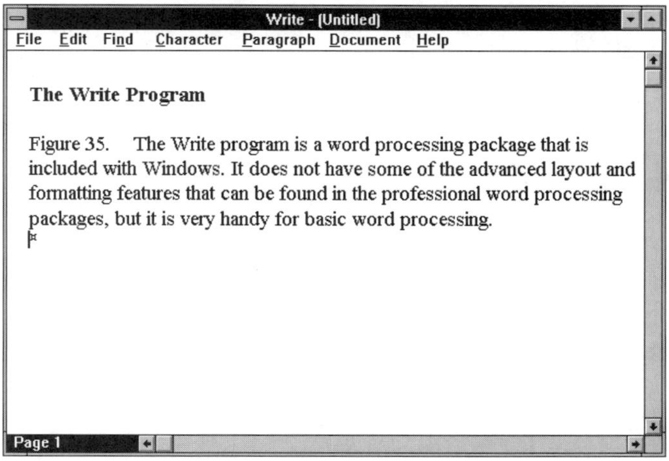


The Write program is ideal for putting together short letters or memoranda. If you use a desktop publishing package that has an awkward text-editing facility, you can use Write to create the text portions of your documents.

Documents written in Write can also be saved in ASCII text format or in the format used by Microsoft Word.

## OBJECT PACKAGER

**Figure 38(a).** As described in Chapter 5, Windows 3.1 allows you to embed or link various files into a single document. The Object Packager is used to assign specialized icons to linked or embedded objects. Using this feature, the object itself need not be visible in the document in which it is linked or embedded; only the assigned icon, with its caption, will be visible on the screen.

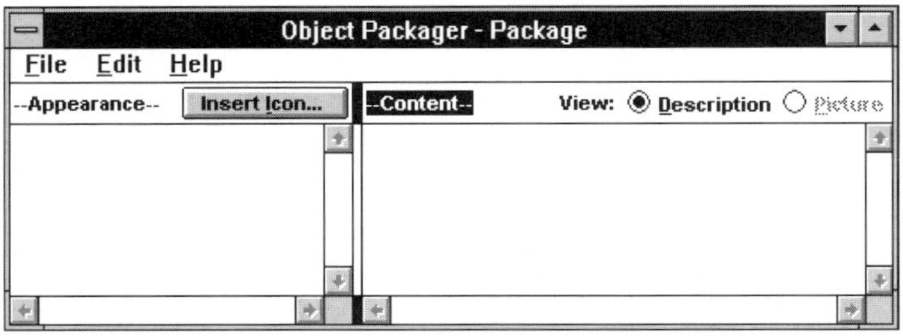


**Figure 38(b).** The Object Packager window is divided into two sides: *Appearance* and *Content.* As you use the Object Packager, the *Content* section of the window lists what is included in the selected object, while the *Appearance* side shows the icon that will take the object's place in a document.

The menu commands in the Object Packager window affect the half of the window that is selected. To select a specific side of this window, click anywhere on that side using the left mouse button.

**Figure 39.** To assign a document to be packaged, select the *Import* command from the **File** menu. Use the file selection dialog box that appears to select the file that is to be packaged.

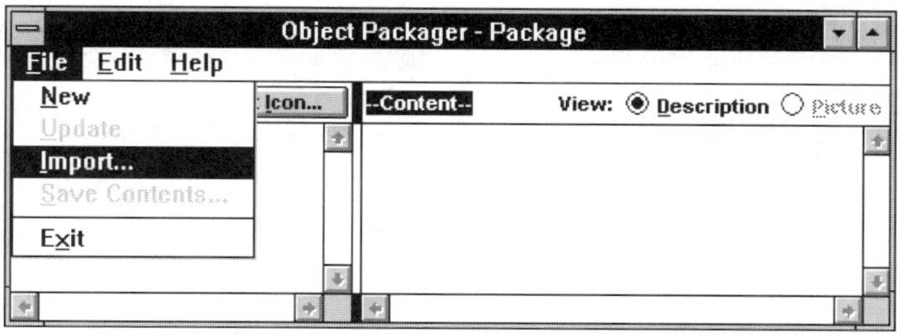


**Figure 40.** The name of the selected file will appear in the *Content* section of the window, while an icon representing the program in which the selected file was created—in this case Paintbrush—will appear on the *Appearance* side.

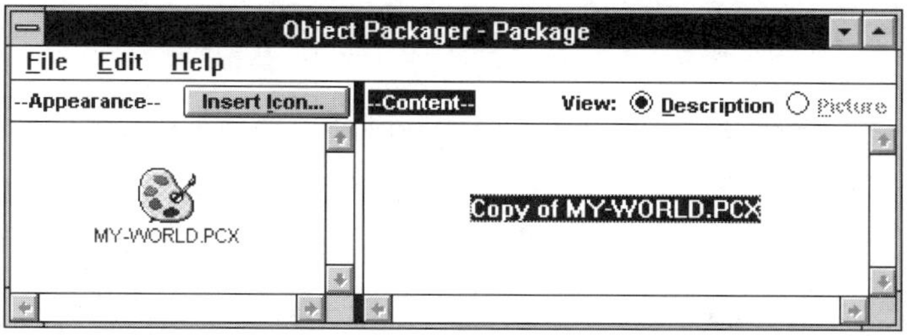


**Figure 41.** Using the *Label* command in the **Edit** menu, the icon's caption can be modified to better describe the selected file's contents. Because this icon will appear in a document in lieu of the file it represents, an accurate caption is useful in identifying the file's contents.

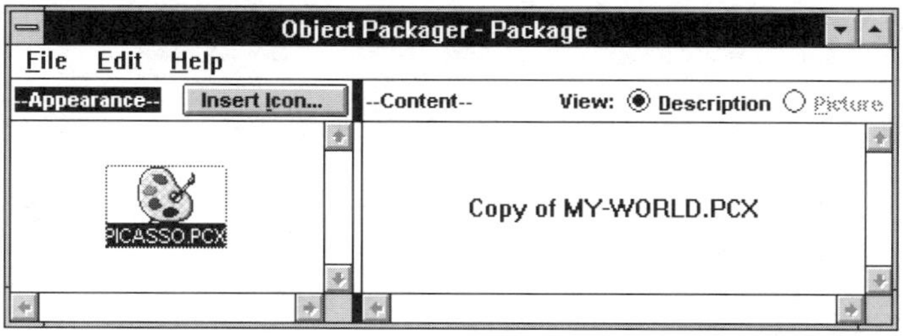


**Figure 42.** To insert the packaged file into a document, select the *Copy Package* command from the Object Packager's **Edit** menu.

Then open the program into which the package is to be inserted and select either *Paste* or *Paste Link* from the newly opened application's **Edit** menu.

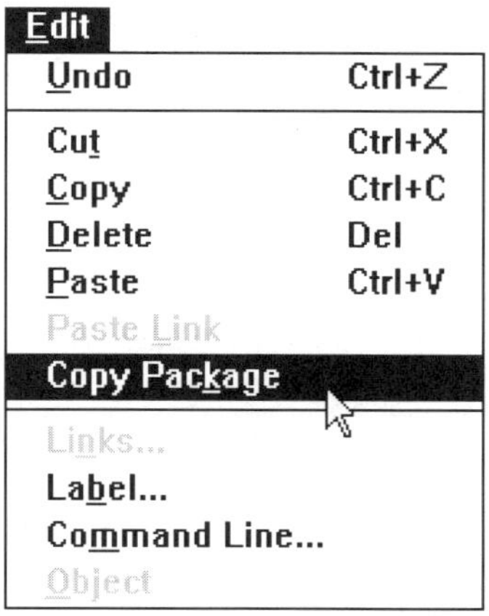

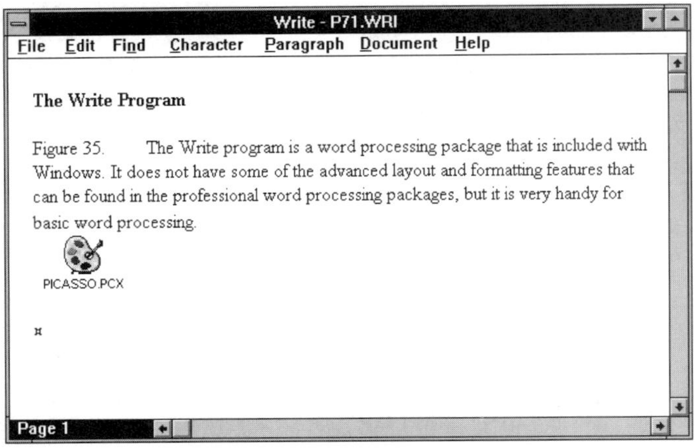


**Figure 43.** The packaged object will appear on the screen in the form of the icon and caption from the Object Packager's *Appearance* section. When the document is printed, the full contents of the packaged object will be included in the output.

## TERMINAL PROGRAM

**Figure 44(a).** Terminal requires specific hardware in order to perform. If you want to connect to a computer in the same room, you need to attach a special serial cable called a *null modem cable.* To communicate with computers in different locations, you need the null modem cable and a modem.

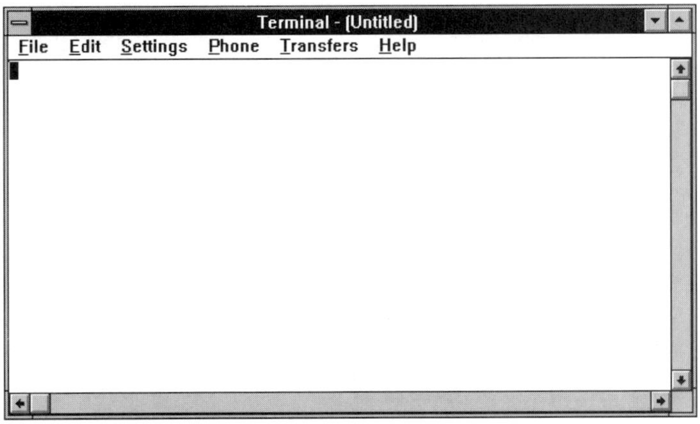


**Figure 44(b).** Terminal enables you to communicate to other computers that have been connected to your system. When computers are connected, you can exchange data via a communications device. For example, you can hook up on-line to such information services as the Dow Jones News/ Retrieval®.

**Figure 45.** When the correct equipment is in place, you are ready to connect. When you choose *Dial* from the **Phone** menu, Terminal automatically dials the number specified in the *Dial* text box.

Once the computers are connected and communicating properly, you can send and receive text or binary files.

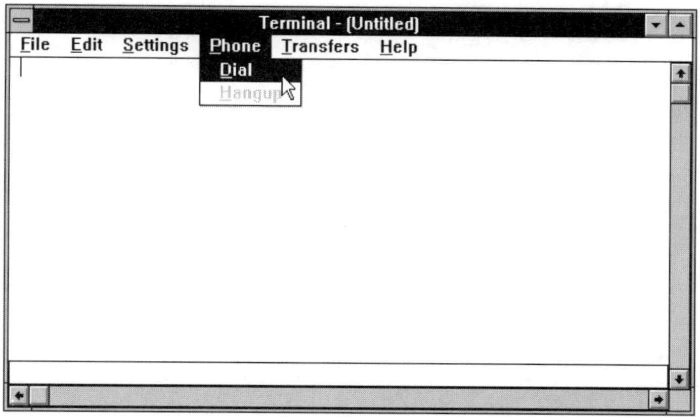


## MEDIA PLAYER

**Figure 46(a).** The main purpose of the Media Player is to play animation, sound, and MIDI sequencer files. The Media Player can also control various types of hardware—such as CD-ROM drives and video disk players.

To use the Media Player, a Media Control Interface (such as a sound card) must be installed in your system. Once in place, the appropriate Media Control Interface driver needs to be installed through *Drivers* in the Control Panel. In addition, a speaker or headphones must be used as an output device for the sound.

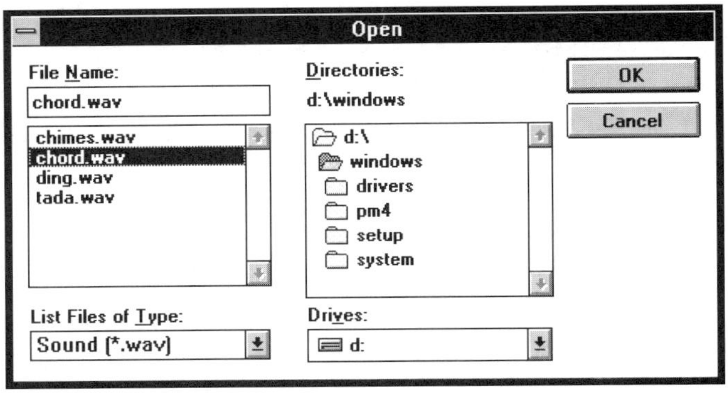


**Figure 46(b).** One type of sound file in Windows is a WAVE file. It has an extension of .wav. When Windows 3.1 is installed, sample .wav files are copied into the Windows 3.1 directory. These can be heard using the Media Player—provided your computer has supporting hardware.

To play one of these files, start the Media Player and select *Open* from the **File** menu. From the *Open* dialog box, select the file you want to hear and click on *OK*.

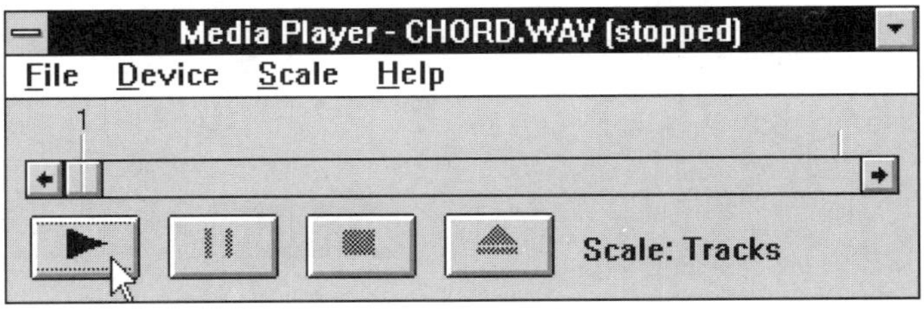


**Figure 47.** The file is loaded into the Media Player, displaying the file name in the title bar. To play the sound, click on the *Play* button. The sound is played through the speakers. Various options within the Media Player are specified using the other two menu commands.

**Figure 48.** **Device** enables you to select the type of Media Control Interface you wish to use. The contents of the **Device** menu depends on which devices are installed. In this case there are only two Media Control Interfaces installed—*Sound* and *MIDI*.

**Figure 49.** The two options in the **Scale** menu let you view the sound file in *Tracks* or *Time.* When *Time* is selected (as shown), the length of the sound is shown in minutes, seconds, and/or milliseconds. When *Track* is selected, the scale in Media Player is measured by the number of tracks in the sound.

## SOUND RECORDER

**Figure 50(a).** You can create sounds of your own and save those files in a WAVE format using the Sound Recorder. You will need an input device, such as a microphone, and a Media Control Interface of some kind installed.

**Figure 50(b).** To record a new sound, all you need do is click on the *Record* button. To record a voice, speak into the microphone for up to one minute. To turn the recorder off, click on the *Stop* button.

**Figure 51.** After you have created a sound, you may want to edit it using the options in the **Edit** menu. Once complete, however, you will want to play your masterpiece back. This is done by clicking on the *Play* button.

This sound can then be saved as a file and can be used in other parts of Windows, such as the Media Player, or in Sound in the Control Panel, (covered in Chapter 6).

## GAMES GROUP

**Figure 52(a).** Two game programs are included with Microsoft Windows and are placed in the Games program group.

### *SOLITAIRE*

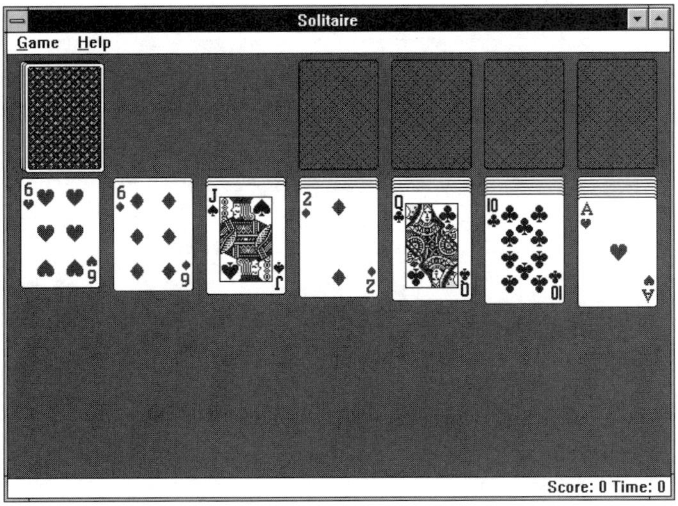


**Figure 52(b).** Solitaire lets you play a number of different versions of that game. The *Options* selection in the **Game** menu lets you set your preferences among a number of rules. The *Deck* selection lets you change the image on the backs of the cards.

## MINESWEEPER

**Figure 53.** In the game of Minesweeper, you try to guess the positions of "mines" hidden on an imaginary mine field.

You "step" on squares by clicking on them with the left mouse button. If no mine is hidden under the square, a number indicating the number of mines adjacent to that square, will appear.

Mark the sites of mines by clicking with the right mouse button.

## STARTUP GROUP

**Figure 54(a).** The Startup Group is used by Windows to determine which applications to load when Windows is initially started.

You can put any application items into the Startup window. An application in the Startup window will be automatically loaded when Windows itself is loaded into memory.

**Figure 54(b).** By default, the Dr. Watson program is inserted into Startup and therefore will start each time you start Windows.

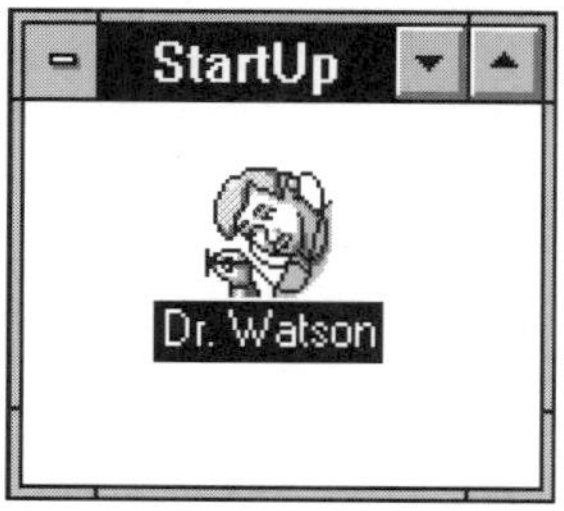

# Application Programs 5

## Applications

Windows is designed to act as an intermediary between you—the user—and any programs you want to run on your computer system. In addition to the programs that are part of the Windows package, almost any application program that runs on your computer can run through Windows. In some cases, the programs run in Windows just as they would in DOS, but the advantages of Windows can often improve the performance of these application programs.

## Setting up Applications

You can run a program from Windows at any time by using the *Run* command in the **File** menu. However, if you want to use an application regularly, you should first set the program up as a program item icon.

Before a program can be represented by a program item icon, all of its files must be installed on your hard disk. Most applications include a special installation program that copies the required files onto your hard disk. The details of these programs are specific to each application; you can consult the program's documentation to determine how best to install it on your hard disk.

You can use the *New* command in the **File** menu (described in Chapter 3) to make a single application into a program item. This method will set up only one program at a time. If you have many programs, however, this can be very slow and time consuming. A more efficient method of adding applications is to use the Windows Setup program, described below.

**Figure 1.** The Setup program item in the Main program group allows you to set up a number of applications at once.

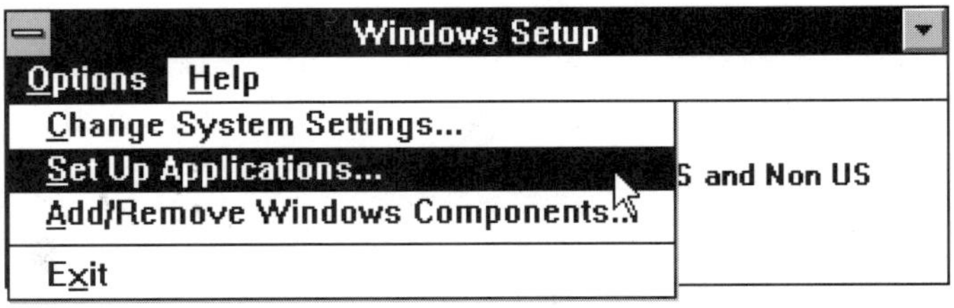


**Figure 2.** Select the *Set Up Applications* command from the **Options** menu of the Setup program. Your computer system's disk drives will be searched for application programs that you can set up as program items.

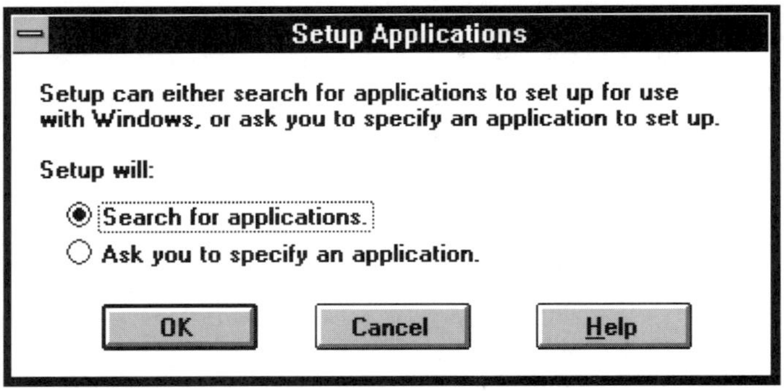


**Figure 3.** Windows gives you the option of searching for all applications or allowing you to specify a particular application.

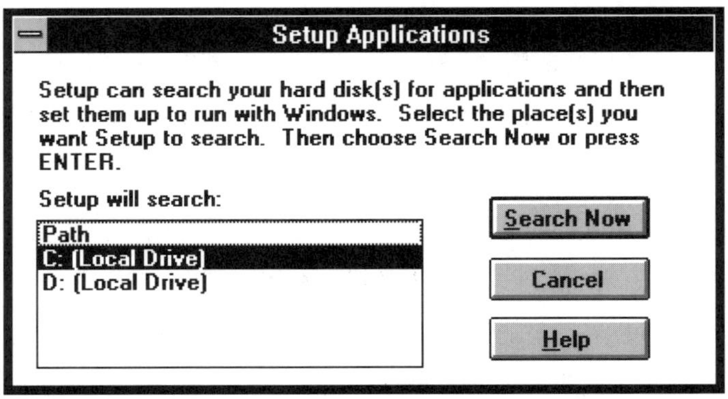


**Figure 4.** This dialog box allows you to select parts of your computer system to be searched for application programs. All of the hard disks on your system—in this case there are two—are available for selection. In addition, the default path usually set in your autoexec.bat file will also be available as an option.

One or more options can be selected simultaneously.

**Figure 5.** As the Setup program searches your disks for applications, an information window will let you follow its progress through your files. A gauge indicates what percentage of disk space has been searched. Above the gauge, the names of application programs are shown as they are found on disk.

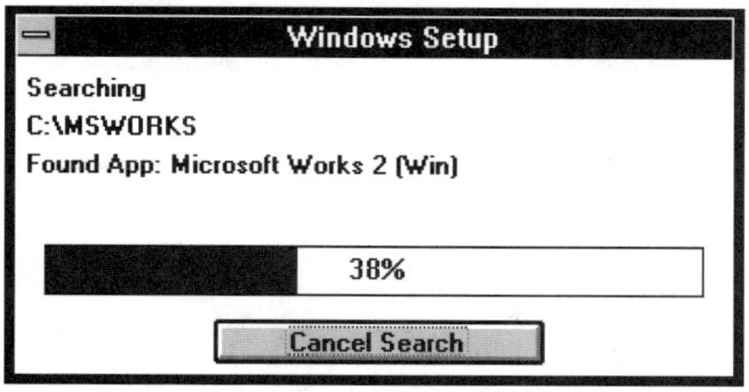


**Figure 6.** Windows will alert you if it finds any programs about which it is unsure.

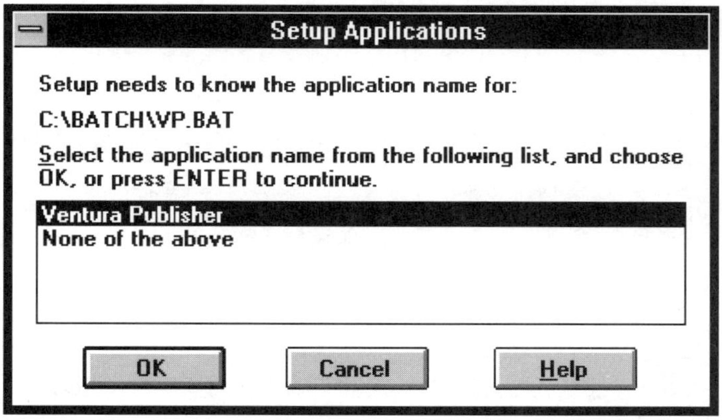


**Figure 7.** Once the specified disk space has been searched, the *Setup Applications* dialog box appears. On the left of the dialog box, all application programs that were found on your computer's disks are listed.

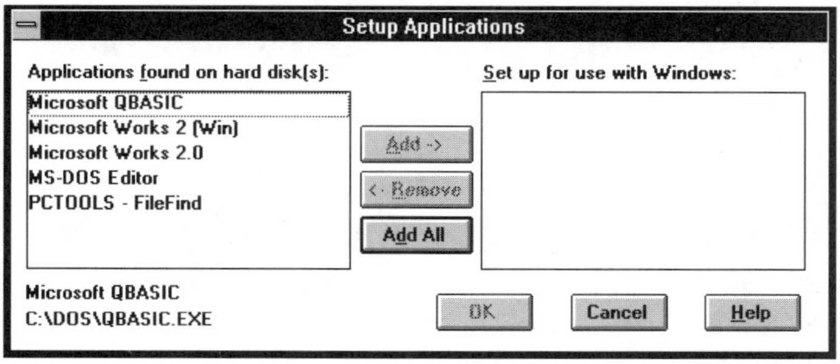

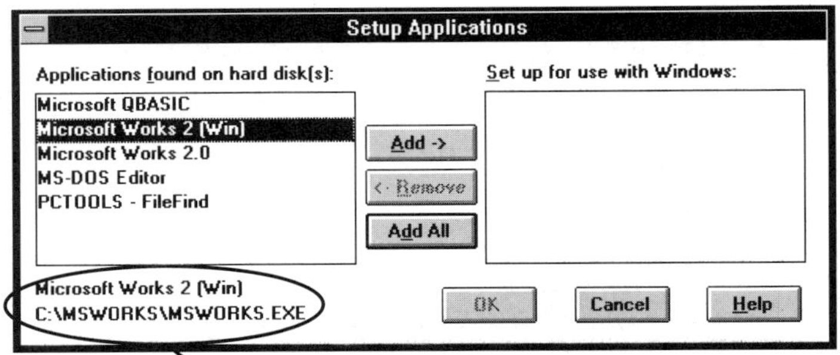


**Figure 8.** Select the programs that you want to set up by clicking on their names in the left-hand box. Use the scroll bar to view names further down the list. As you click on a program name, it will be highlighted. Clicking again will deselect the name.

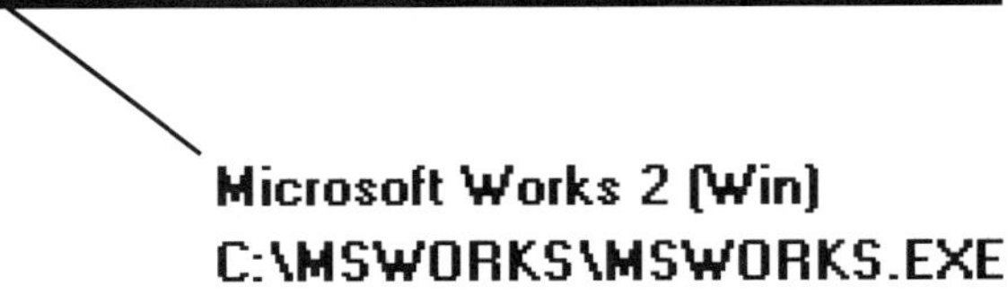


**Figure 9.** When you select a program name from the list, its name and DOS path are displayed in the lower left-hand corner of the dialog box.

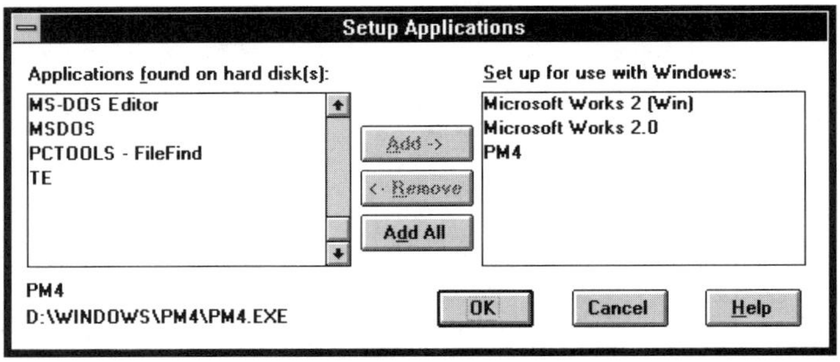


**Figure 10.** Once the names of those programs that you want set up as program items have been highlighted, click on the *Add* button to transfer the names into the list box on the right side of the dialog box.

If you want to set up all applications listed, simply click on the *Add All* button.

When all programs that you want to set up are listed in the right list box, click on *OK.*

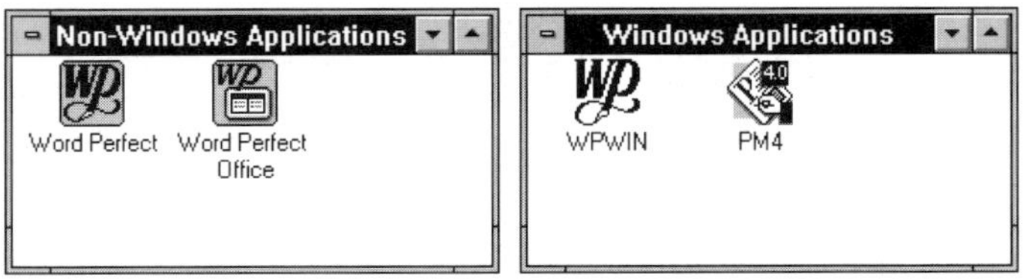


**Figure 11.** The Setup program will, if necessary, create two program group windows in which to place the applications as program items.

Programs specially written for Windows will be placed in a program group labeled *Windows Applications* (discussed below).

Regular DOS programs will be put in a program group called *Non-Windows Applications* (also discussed below).

## WINDOWS APPLICATIONS

Many application programs have been specially designed to run in the Windows environment. The Setup program will put these program items in a program group labeled *Windows Applications*, as shown in Figure 11. You are, however, free to move them to other program groups.

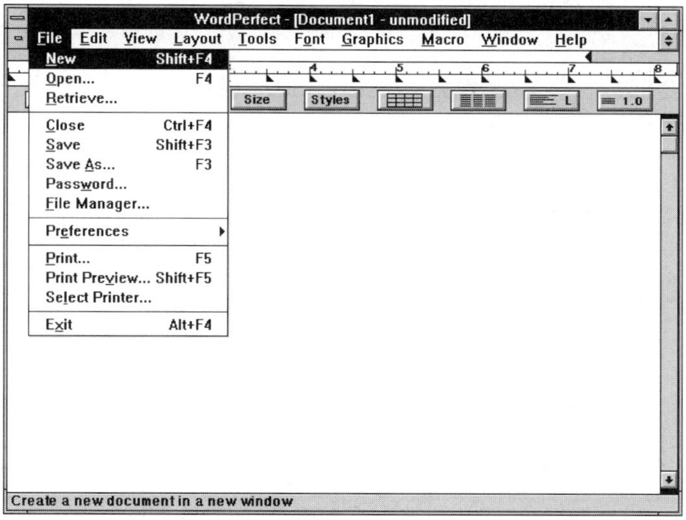


**Figure 12.** Windows applications are designed to take advantage of the special features of the Windows program. They use a system of windows and menus that match those of the Program Manager.

The "look and feel" of Windows applications—the way the program appears on screen and the way its menus and commands are organized—is consistent with that of Windows itself. Once you are familiar with Windows programs, it is relatively easy to learn new Windows applications.

As use of Windows becomes widespread, more application programs are being offered with a Windows version.

## Non-Windows Applications

Many application programs that were not written especially to run under Windows can still be used in Windows. You may want to continue using such programs after you have installed Windows onto your computer system.

**Figure 13.** These programs can be set up as program items using the Setup program; they will be placed in the program group marked *Non-Windows Applications.*

Non-Windows applications that have been installed with the Setup program are handled slightly differently from programs installed with the *New* command.

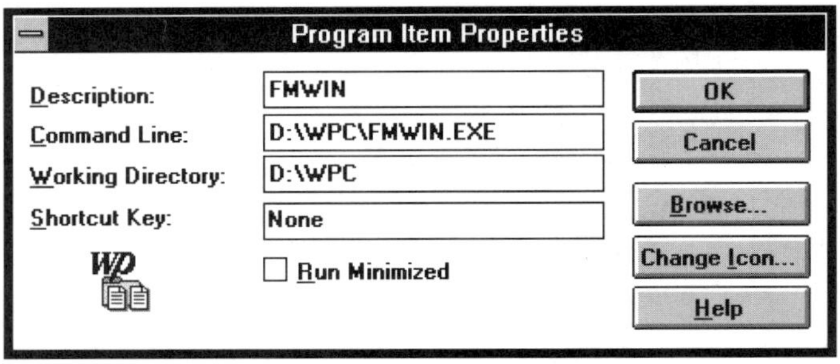


**Figure 14.** If you highlight a program item installed through the *New* command and select the *Properties* command from the **File** menu, you will see the name of the program's executable DOS file in the *Command Line* box.

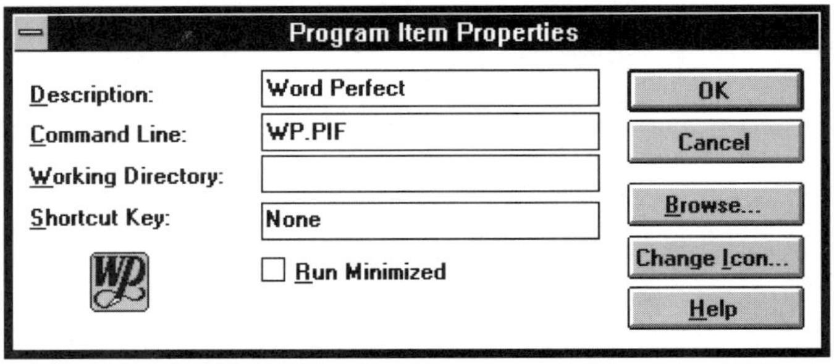


**Figure 15.** If you examine the *Properties* of a non-Windows application installed through the Setup program, you will see that the *Command Line* lists a program with a .PIF extension.

PIFs—Program Information Files—are files that record specific information, such as memory and graphics requirements, about non-Windows applications.

Windows uses this information to help run the programs more efficiently, even though they have not been designed to run under Windows.

Using a Windows Accessory called the PIF Editor, you can create or modify these special files for all your non-Windows applications. The use of the PIF Editor is discussed in Chapter 4.

# RUNNING MULTIPLE APPLICATIONS

One of the principal advantages of Windows over DOS is the ease with which it allows you to use several applications at once. You can switch between programs without the cumbersome and time consuming task of exiting from one application and loading up another.

## *SWITCHING BETWEEN ACTIVE PROGRAMS*

### USING THE MOUSE

**Figure 16.** If several applications, running within Windows are all visible on the screen at once, you can switch between these programs by clicking on the window that you want to make active.

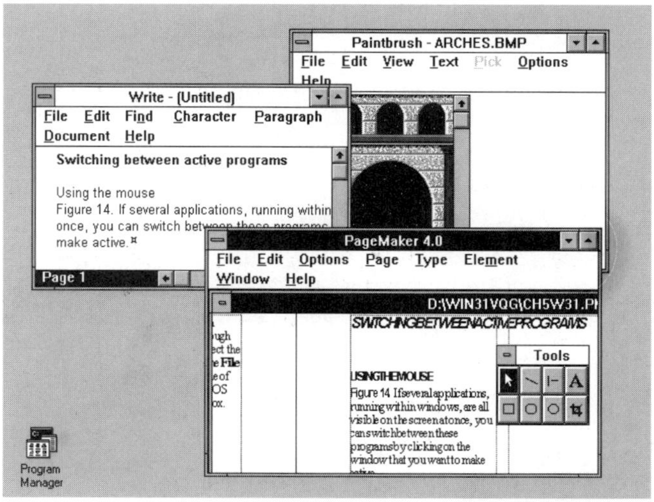


### USING THE KEYBOARD

If the windows are not all visible on the screen simultaneously, the keyboard can be used to cycle through the open windows. To do this, hold down the Alt key and press the Escape (Esc) key.

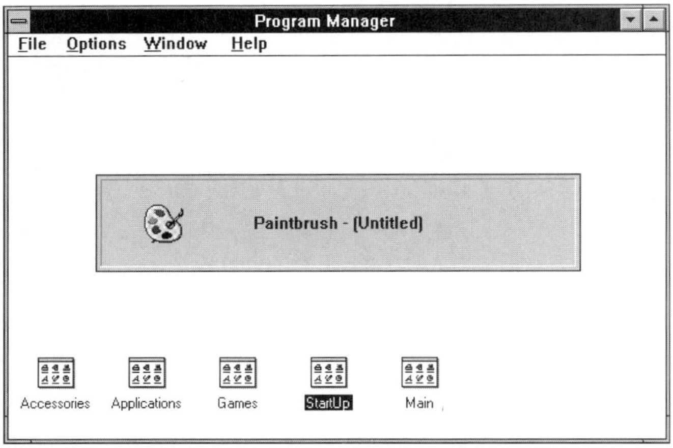


**Figure 17.** Alternatively, each time you press Tab while the Alt key is depressed, the name of the next application in the task list is displayed in a dialog box. Repeat this until the desired window is shown.

When the name of the required window appears, release both keys to display the application window you need to use.

## TASK LIST

Windows has a special utility, called the Task List, for helping you manage many applications at once. It takes the form of the Task List dialog box and can be called up at any time while Windows is running.

### DISPLAYING THE TASK LIST

**Figure 18.** One way to display the Task List is from the Control Menu of any window. Click on the Control Menu box in the upper left-hand corner of any window and select the *Switch To* menu choice.

You can also call up the Task List by double-clicking on the desktop background, the screen surface usually found behind the Program Manager window.

Finally, the Task List can be activated from the keyboard by holding down the Control (Ctrl) key while pressing Escape. This method is often the only way to activate the Task List if you are using a non-Windows application that fills the entire screen.

## USING THE TASK LIST

**Figure 19.** A list box in the *Task List* dialog box contains the names of all programs that are currently open under Windows.

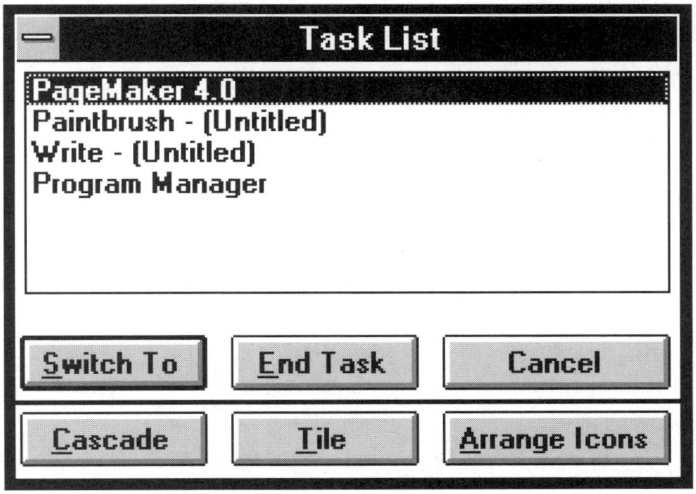


**Figure 20.** To switch to a given application, highlight the program's name in the list by clicking on it, then click on the *Switch To* button below the list box. You may find it easier to simply double-click on the application's name in the list.

**Figure 21.** Clicking on the *End Task* button in the *Task List* dialog box will close the window containing the highlighted application and will stop running that program.

It is usually a good idea, especially with non-Windows applications, to exit programs through their own exit facility rather than with the Task List.

**Figure 22.** If you try to close a Windows application using the Task List *End Task* button, a warning dialog box will appear if this closure will result in the loss of files or data.

**Figure 23.** The *Cascade* and *Tile* buttons in the *Task List* dialog box let you arrange open program windows on the screen in either the overlapping *Cascade* pattern or the side-by-side *Tile* pattern.

**Figure 24.** The *Arrange Icons* button causes the icons on the desktop, representing minimized windows and applications, to be arranged in an orderly fashion on the bottom left of the screen.

**Figure 25.** The *Cancel* button allows you to quit the Task List without altering your work environment.

## Embedding and Linking

A new feature of Windows, introduced with version 3.1, is the ability to embed or link files within other documents.

Because this is a new feature, it may not yet be available with all Windows applications. As these applications are updated for Windows 3.1, linking and embedding facilities will be added.

The Windows Accessories programs Write and Cardfile can accept embedded or linked files. The Paintbrush program can create files that can be embedded or linked.

## EMBEDDING FILES

A file is said to be embedded when a copy of that file is added to another document.

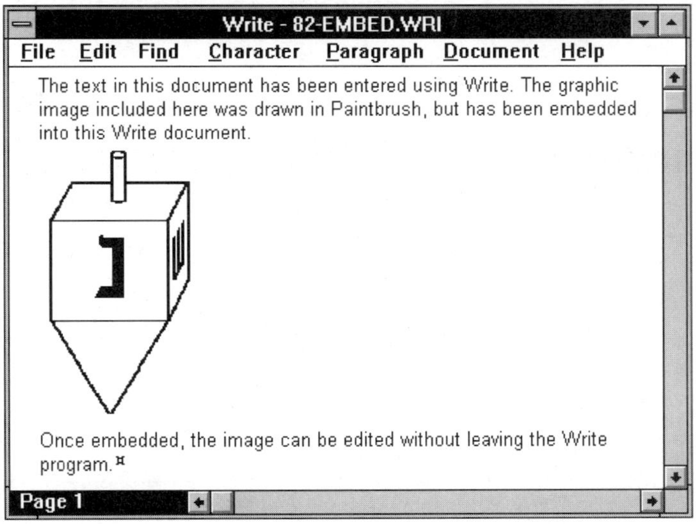


**Figure 26.** Typically, a graphic file, such as an image created in Paintbrush, can be embedded in a document file, such as a letter written in Write.

An advantage of embedding a file, rather than simply pasting it into the document, is that an embedded file can be modified without leaving the program into which it was embedded.

To modify an image that was pasted into a Write document, you would have to exit from Write, open a graphics program, redraw or modify the graphic, and paste it into the Write document.

If the original graphics file was no longer on your computer system, or if the document had been moved to a different computer, there would be no way of modifying the image other than recreating it from scratch.

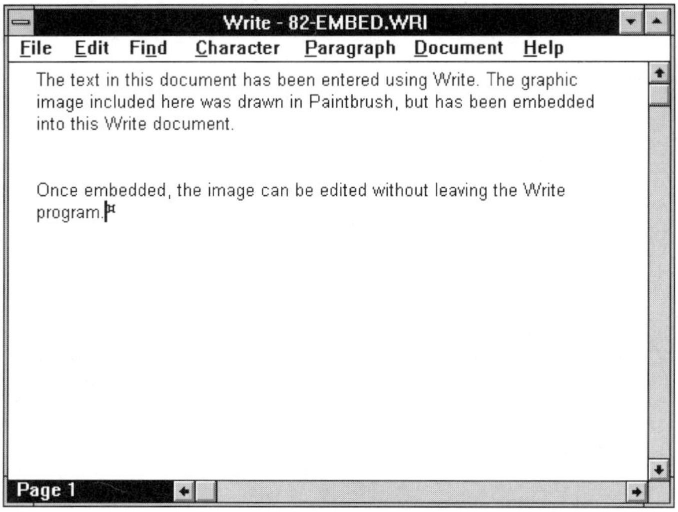


**Figure 27.** To embed an object into a document, open the program into which the file will be embedded. In this case an image created in Paintbrush will be embedded into the Write document that has been started in this figure.

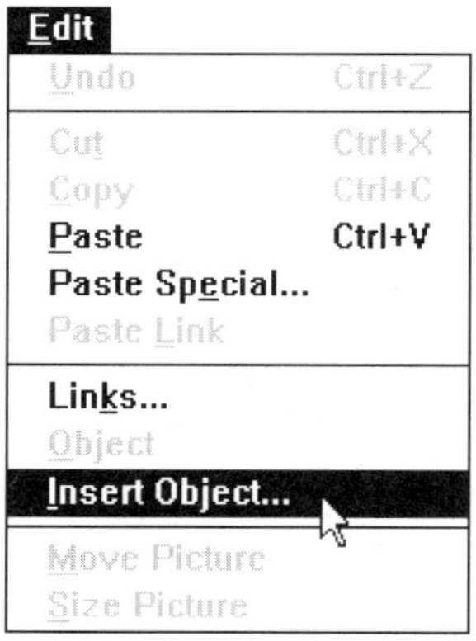


**Figure 28.** To embed the image into the document, place the text cursor in the position where the image is to appear and select the *Insert Object* command from the **Edit** menu.

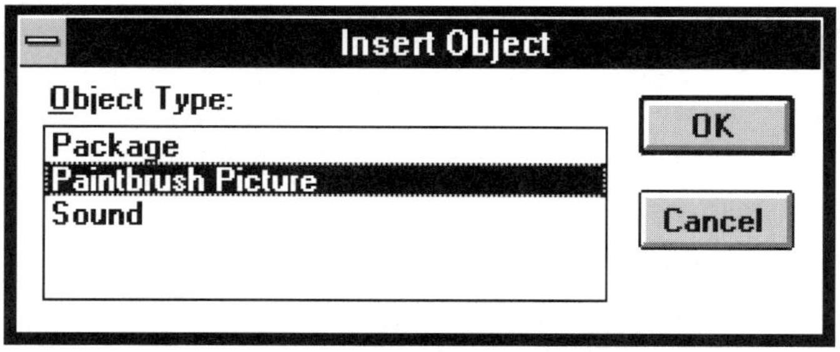


**Figure 29.** In the *Insert Object* dialog box that appears, select the kind of image that will be embedded. In this figure, the *Paintbrush Picture* option has been selected.

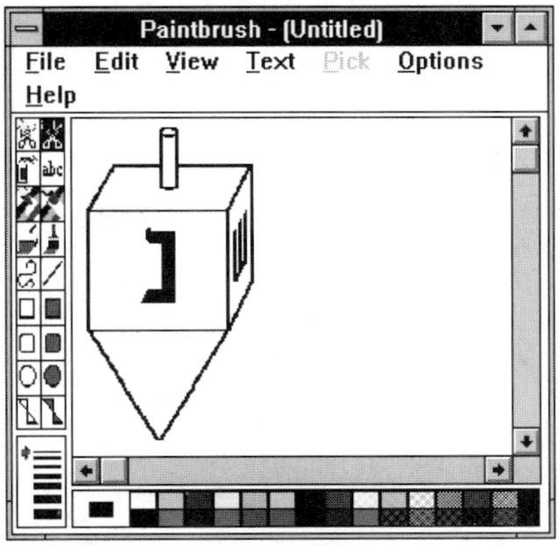


**Figure 30.** The appropriate application program, in this case Paintbrush, will be activated. Use this program to create the desired image. If the image already exists on a file, you can use the *Paste From* command in the **Edit** menu to load it onto the screen.

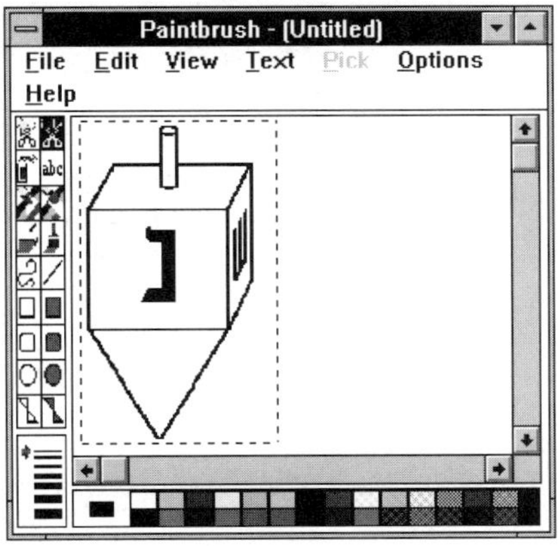


**Figure 31.** You must use the *Exit & Return to (file name)* command in the **File** menu to close down the Paintbrush program and return to Write. The image will be imported into the document using its original dimensions. In the warning dialog box that appears, click on *Yes* to complete the embedding process.

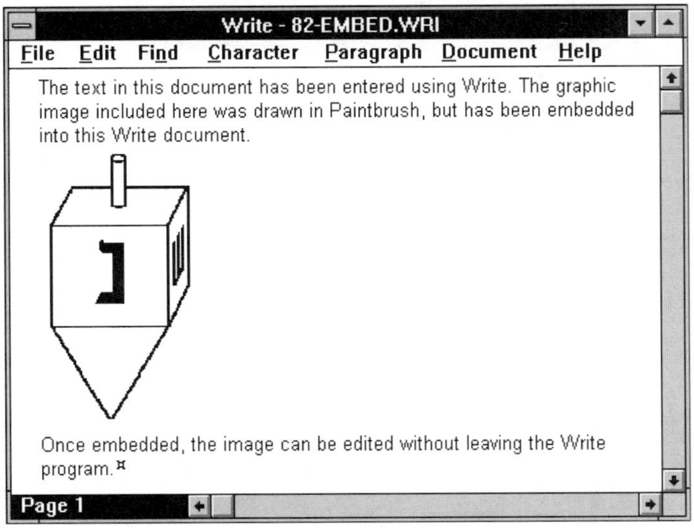


**Figure 32.** Back in the Write program, the selected graphic now appears as part of the document.

To edit this image at any time, simply double-click on it with the mouse pointer and Paintbrush will automatically be activated from within the Write program.

When you choose *Exit and Return to (file name)* from the **File** menu within Paintbrush, the changes made to the graphic will be reflected in the Write program.

Changes made in this way affect only the graphic that appears in the Write document. Any file from which the graphic originated will not be affected.

## LINKING FILES

Linking, like embedding, is a way in which the data in files created using one application can be made part of a document created in a second application.

When an object is *embedded* into a document, an entire copy of the item becomes part of the new document. When a file is *linked* to a document, only a reference, or link, to that file occurs in the new document.

Linking uses less memory and disk space than embedding. If a large graphic file is embedded in a document, that document must contain a complete copy of the embedded file. Every time a file is embedded, a new copy has to be made. Linking always uses the same amount of space because only a reference to the file, regardless of its size, is added to the document.

Linking can also save you a lot of time and effort in situations where the contents of the linked file are subject to change. When a file is added to a document using the linking process, any changes to the original file are automatically reflected in that document.

If the linked graphic represents a chart or graph, the document will not have to be updated every time the data in the image changes.

**Figure 33.** To link a file with another document, open the program, in this case Paintbrush, in which the linked file will be created. Create and then save the file using this program. If the file already exists, load it onto the screen using the *Open* command in the **File** menu.

It is important that a file already exists on disk *before* the linking process is carried out. If a file has not been previously saved, Windows will not be able to link the files.

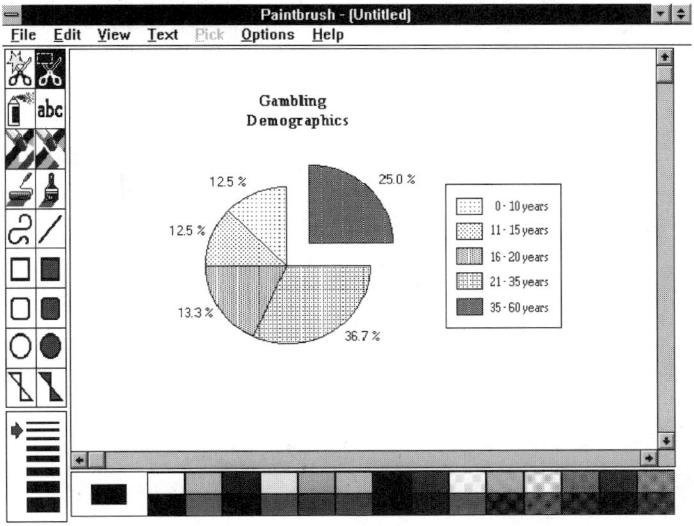


**Figure 34.** In Paintbrush, select the entire image and *click* on the *Copy* command in the **Edit** menu to place a copy of the image into the Clipboard.

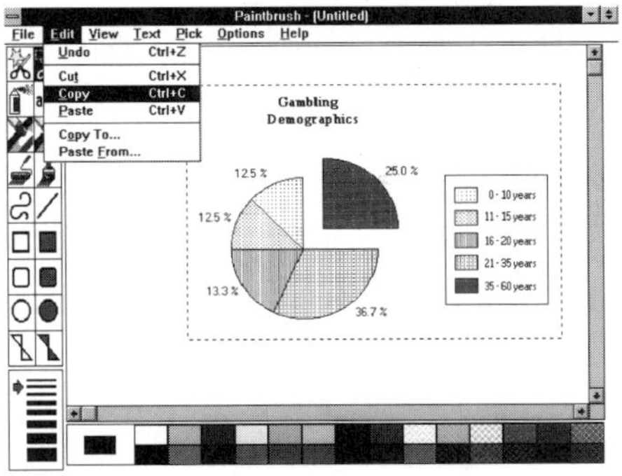


**Figure 35.** Open the program, in this case Write, to which the file will be linked. In this figure, Write is shown with a document already started and the text cursor positioned in the location at which the linked file will appear.

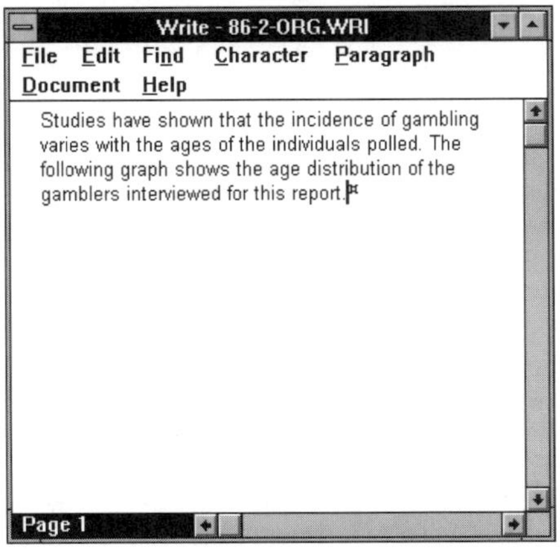

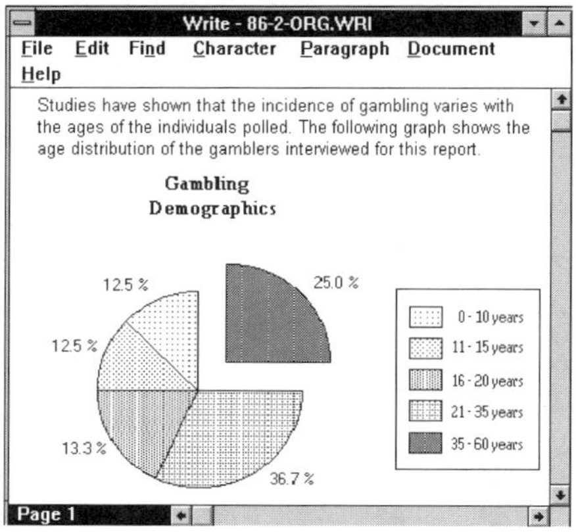


**Figure 36.** To actually link the graphic file to this document—remember that the graphic is still in the Clipboard—select the *Paste Link* command from the **Edit** menu.

If *Paste Link* is not available, check that the Paintbrush file has been saved. The linked graphic will appear in the document.

As with embedded objects, a linked file can be edited by double-clicking with the mouse pointer to open the program in which it was created.

Unlike an embedded object, when a linked item is edited, the original file is updated to reflect the changes, and all documents linked to this item are also affected.

# The Control Panel

6

## Using the Control Panel

The Control Panel window contains a variety of utility programs. Each of these programs allows you to set or define some aspect of the Windows environment.

## Control Panel Window

**Figure 1(a).** The Control Panel icon is found in the Main program group. You can open the Control Panel window by double-clicking on this icon.

**Figure 1(b).** The Control Panel window differs from other windows that contain program items. It contains a fixed set of utility programs, and you cannot add to, or delete from, this group.

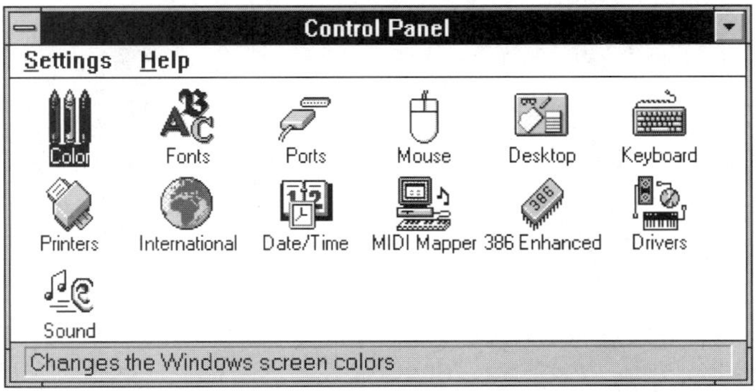


A status bar at the bottom of the Control Panel window gives a brief description of the program item that is highlighted.

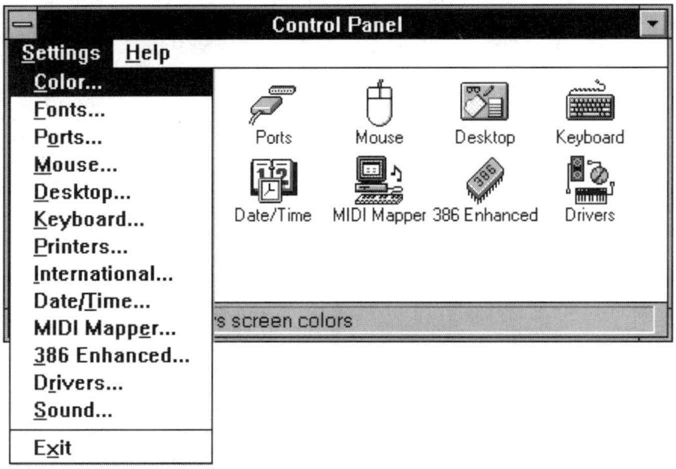


**Figure 2.** The Control Panel contains a small menu bar. The **Settings** menu lists all the utility programs in this window. A program can be run either by double-clicking the appropriate icon or selecting the program's name from the **Settings** menu.

The **Help** menu allows you to obtain Help information about each of the Control Panel's programs.

## CUSTOMIZING THE WINDOWS INTERFACE

### *COLOR*

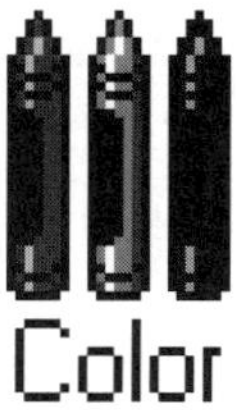


**Figure 3(a).** The colors used in the Windows display—or the shadings used on monochrome monitors—can be set to suit your preferences. Select the Color program from the Control Panel to change the displayed colors.

## SELECTING COLOR SCHEMES

**Figure 3(b).** The Color dialog box contains a *Color Schemes* submenu in which you can select from a list of predefined color combinations.

Because this is a dialog box, the screen colors will not actually change until you have clicked on *OK*. However, sample windows, which appear below the *Color Schemes* submenu, do change color immediately so that you can see what effect your changes will have on the appearance of the screen.

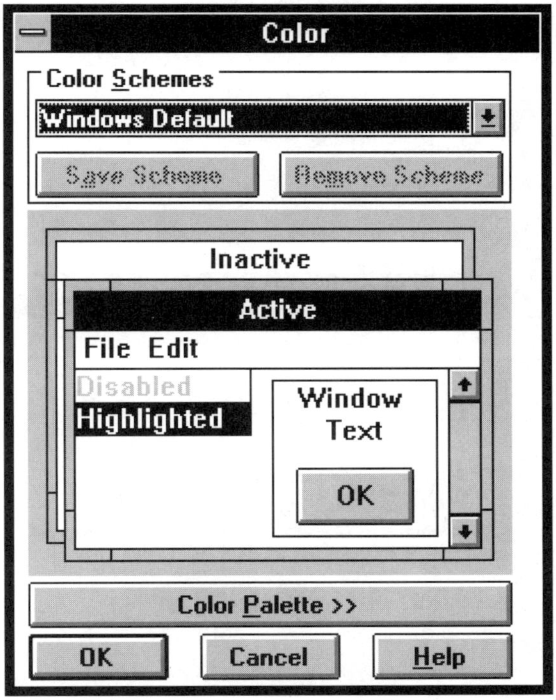


## COLOR PALETTE

**Figure 3(c).** If the color arrangement you want is not already available in the *Color Schemes* submenu, you can create a customized color scheme by selecting *Color Palette.*

**Figure 4.** When you select *Color Palette,* a new section appears on the right side of the *Color* dialog box.

The *Screen Element* submenu lets you pick what part of the Windows display you want to modify.

An array, or palette, of colored rectangles lets you select the color for the *Screen Element* you have selected.

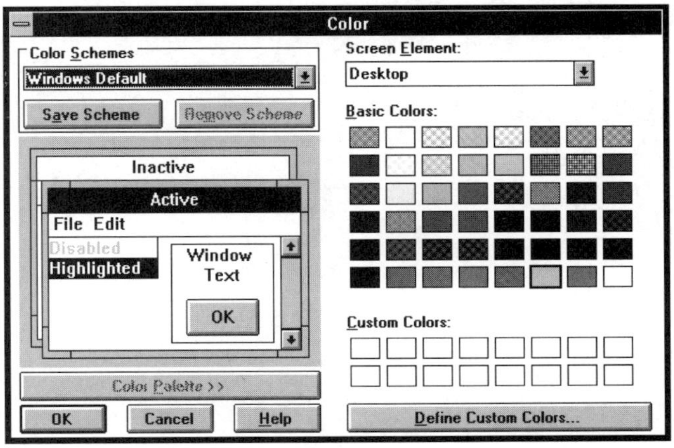

You can also select a screen element by clicking directly on its sample below the *Color Schemes* submenu. This method is often easier than selecting from the *Screen Element* submenu.

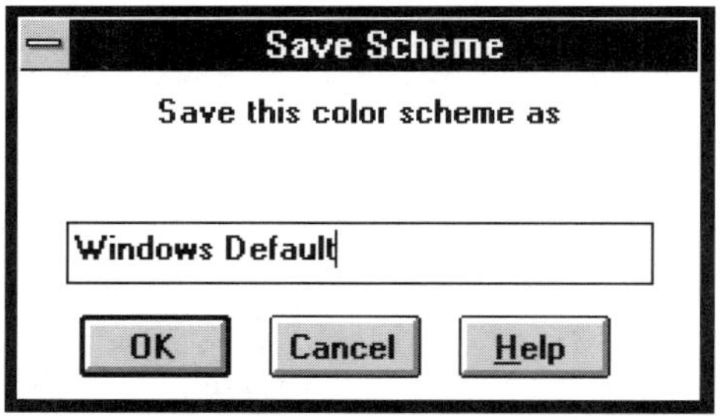


**Figure 5.** You can add your personalized color choices to the *Color Schemes* submenu by clicking on *Save Scheme* and entering a new name for your color choices in the dialog box that appears.

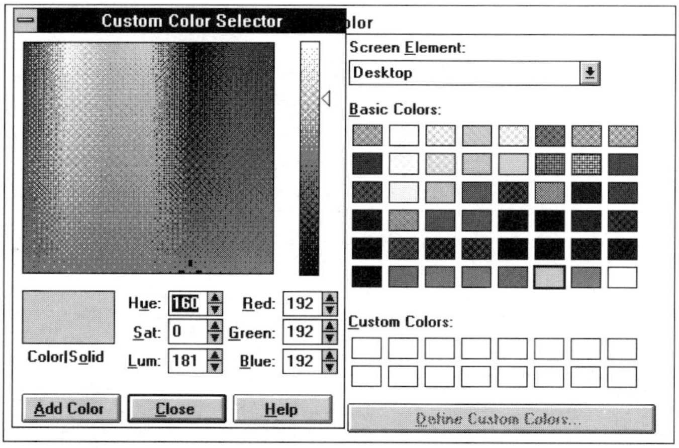


## CUSTOM COLORS

**Figure 6.** The Color program also lets you define up to sixteen *Custom Colors* by clicking on the *Define Custom Colors* button. The *Custom Color Selector* dialog box lets you define colors by selecting the desired shade and hue from the multicolored Color box using the mouse.

Alternatively, you can define the color numerically by setting either the Hue, Saturation, and Luminosity values or the Red, Green, and Blue values for the color you want.

Click on *Close* to return to the *Color* dialog box and *Cancel* to return to the screen.

## DESKTOP SETTINGS

**Figure 7(a).** The Desktop is the background surface of the Windows display. If all open windows, including the Program Manager, are moved aside, the Desktop will be exposed. If no maximized windows are open, part of the desktop will probably be visible.

**Figure 7(b).** The Desktop program allows you to change the appearance of the Desktop part of your display, as well as letting you set several other characteristics of Windows.

The various aspects of this dialog box are described in Figures 8 through 19.

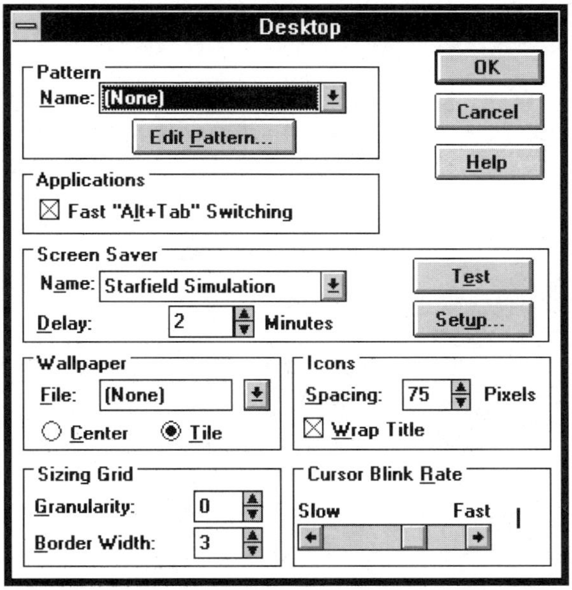


### PATTERN

The Desktop's colors are set with the Color program, but the Desktop program can also be set to display a pattern.

**Figure 8.** Select a background pattern from the *Name* submenu in the *Pattern* section of the Desktop dialog box. If you select [*None*], the background will remain plain.

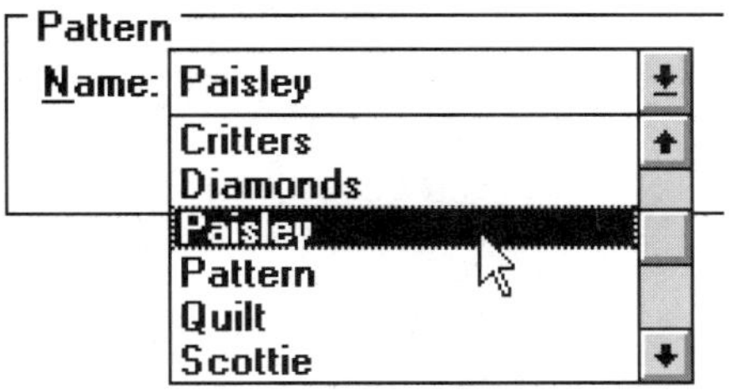


You can also design your own pattern by clicking on the *Edit Pattern* button shown in Figure 7.

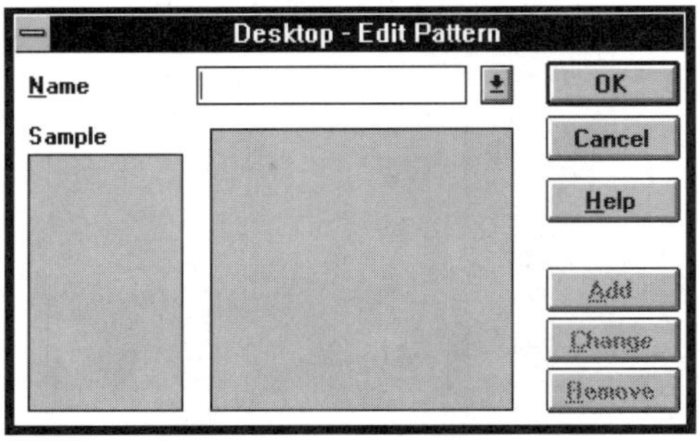


**Figure 9.** From the *Edit Pattern* dialog box, you can select a pattern to be modified from the *Name* submenu or create your own pattern from scratch.

When you select a pattern, its graphical composition will appear in the Design box, the large square in the center of the dialog box. A sample of the pattern's overall appearance will be shown in the *Sample* box to the left.

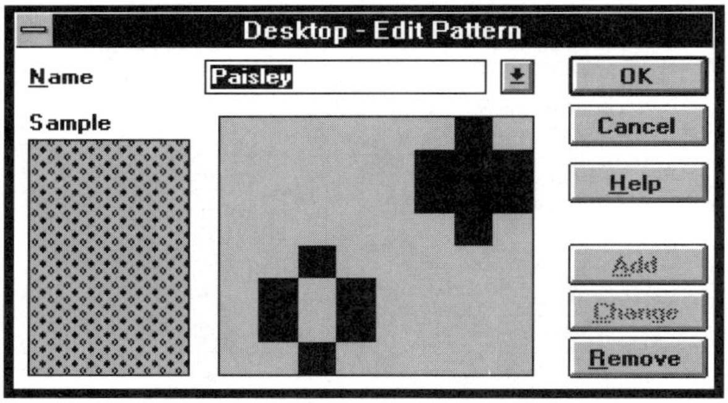


**Figure 10.** The Design box is divided into an eight-by-eight grid. Click on each grid square to switch its color between the colors defined for "Desktop" and "Windows Text" in the Colors program.

The pattern you define in the Design box will be repeated continuously to make up the Desktop's background pattern.

If you want to save a newly designed pattern, click in the *Name* box, key in a name for the pattern, then click on *Add.* To remove an undesired pattern, select it from the *Name* submenu and click on *Remove.* Click on *Cancel* to remove the *Edit Pattern* dialog box.

## APPLICATIONS

The *Applications* section of Figure 7 enables you to specify how to change between programs that are running in Windows 3.1. To change between programs, press Alt and Tab simultaneously.

**Figure 11.** When *Fast "Alt+Tab" Switching* is selected, Windows displays the name of the program on the screen before switching to it. This feature enables you to scroll through all open programs before actually changing the one you want to use. When this option is deselected, Windows simply switches to the next program in the task list.

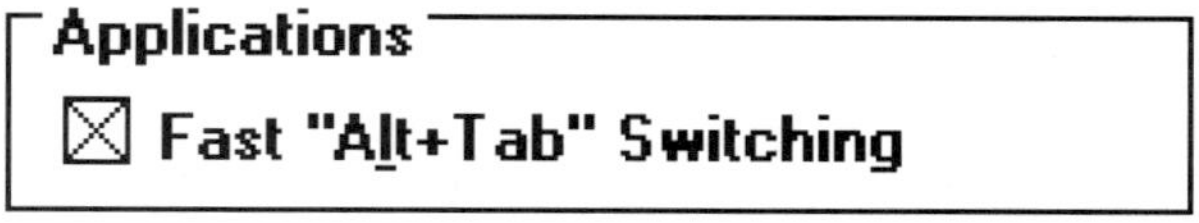


## SCREEN SAVER

**Figure 12.** The *Screen Saver* option is a feature of Windows designed to protect the monitor when Windows is running but the computer is not being used. If the same screen displays for too long, it may "burn" its pattern onto the surface of the monitor.

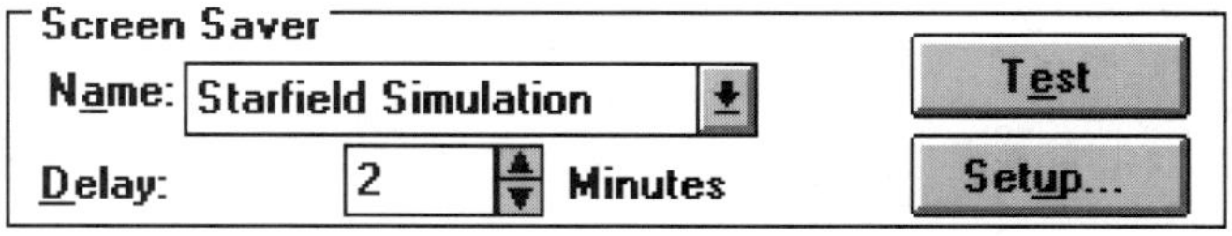


If neither the keyboard nor the mouse are used for the amount of time specified in the delay text box, the screen saver will display one of several changing patterns that can be selected from the *Name* submenu.

These ever changing displays do not endanger the monitor in the way that a static display can. If you press any key or move the mouse, the original screen display will be restored.

**Figure 13.** The color, text, and speed of some of the individual screens can be altered using the *Setup* dialog box. This is opened when the *Setup* button shown in Figure 12 is pressed. To protect the screen setup from change, you can give it a password in the *Setup* dialog box.

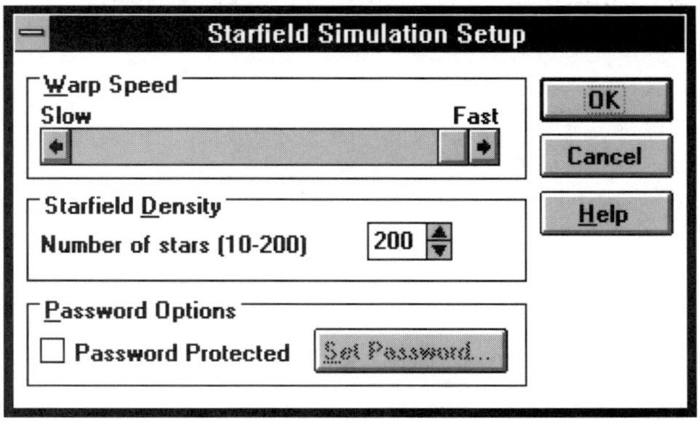

## WALLPAPER

Instead of displaying a simple pattern from the *Pattern* submenu, you may want the desktop to display a graphic image. Windows 3.1 comes with a selection of graphic images that can be displayed on the desktop. You can, however, use any graphic image files with .BMP extensions in your \WINDOWS subdirectory.

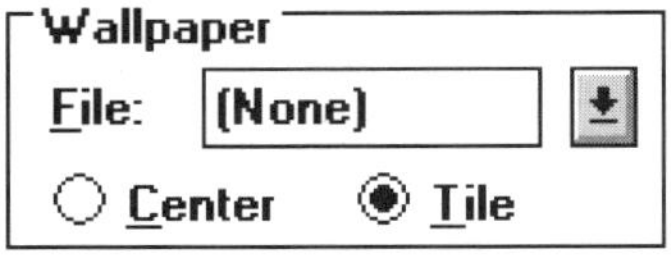


**Figure 14.** Select the desired image file from the *File* submenu in the *Wallpaper* section of the *Desktop* dialog box—shown in Figure 7. Use the radio buttons to indicate whether the image should be displayed in the *Center* of the screen or repeated in a *Tiled* pattern.

Some graphics, when centered, are big enough to fill the entire screen. Smaller graphics will cover only a portion of the desktop and may be covered by open windows. It is best to tile these images.

## ICONS

When icons are arranged in a window or on the desktop, they are spaced at even distances from each other. These distances are measured in pixels, where one pixel represents one dot on the screen.

**Figure 15.** By changing the value in the *Icons Spacing* box, you can determine the size, in pixels, of the spaces between the icons.

Icon spacing can be set between zero and 512 pixels.

**Figure 16.** The Wrap Title option allows long icon captions to be displayed on several lines if they are too long to fit within the set *Spacing* width.

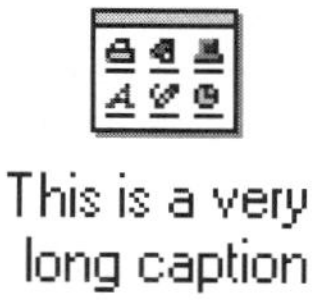


## SIZING GRID

In Windows, the screen's surface is organized in an invisible grid of vertical and horizontal lines. This grid is used internally by Windows to keep track of the positions of windows and icons on the screen.

**Figure 17.** The value in the *Granularity* box in the *Desktop* dialog box represents the distance, in units of eight pixels, between these grid lines. If this value is set at zero, objects on the screen such as icons and window borders can be placed in any position.

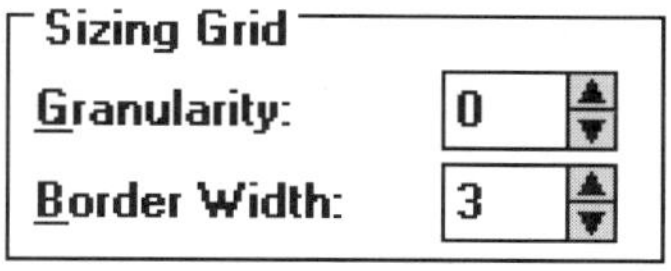


If the granularity is greater than zero, objects can be placed only on the intersection of grid lines. An object placed on the screen will automatically move, or snap, to the nearest grid intersection.

Just as playing pieces placed on the grid of a checker board are more ordered than counters scattered at random on a table, increasing the granularity will increase the orderliness of the Windows screen display.

Values for granularity may range from zero to forty-nine eight-pixel units, representing distances of between zero and 392 pixels.

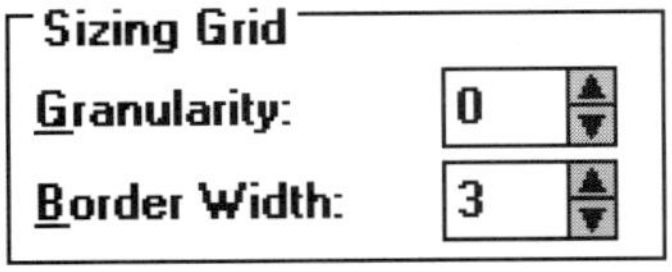


**Figure 18.** The value in the *Border Width* box represents the thickness, in pixels, of the borders surrounding on-screen windows. Windows with wider borders are easier to resize but may add to screen clutter.

Borders may be between one and forty-nine pixels in width.

## CURSOR BLINK RATE

When you enter text from the keyboard, the position on the screen where the text characters will appear as they are typed is indicated by a vertical line called a cursor. To make the cursor more visible, and to distinguish it from the text itself, the vertical line flashes, or blinks, at a regular rate.

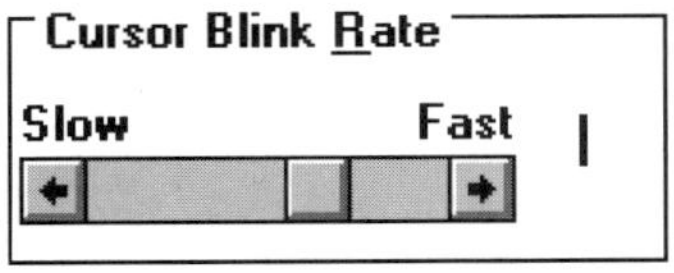


**Figure 19.** You can adjust the blink rate using the *Cursor Blink Rate* scroll bar in the *Desktop* dialog box. Position the scroll box by clicking the scroll arrows or dragging the scroll box. A sample cursor below this scroll bar will blink at the newly selected rate. Cancel the *Desktop* dialog box and return to the screen.

## MOUSE SETTINGS

**Figure 20(a).** The Mouse program lets you customize the workings of your mouse under Windows.

### TRACKING SPEED

The speed with which the mouse pointer moves across the screen in response to the mouse's movement on your desktop is called the tracking speed. A higher tracking speed requires less desk space but makes the pointer more difficult to aim precisely.

**Figure 20(b).** The speed is adjusted using the *Mouse Tracking Speed* scroll bar in the *Mouse* dialog box. As you adjust the scroll bar, the tracking speed changes immediately. You can move the mouse pointer around the screen to test the new setting.

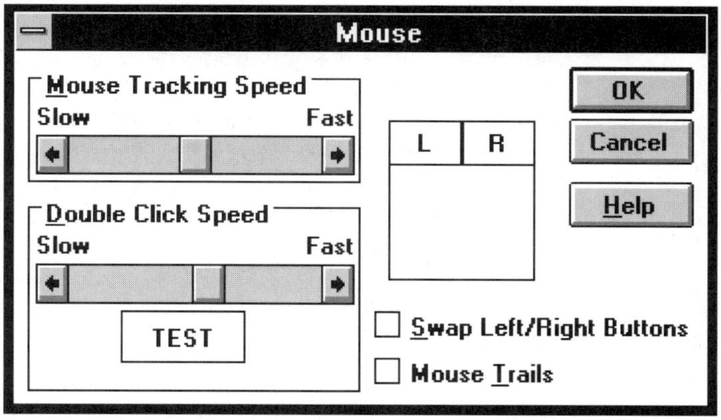


Even though the change in speed is effective before *OK* has been selected, clicking on *Cancel* in the *Mouse* dialog box will return this and other settings to their previous values.

### DOUBLE CLICK SPEED

**Figure 21.** The speed at which you must click the mouse for the action to be recognized as a double-click is also adjustable in the *Mouse* dialog box. After setting the scroll bar to the desired position, double-click in the box labeled "TEST." A successful double-click will reverse the text from dark-on-light to light-on-dark.

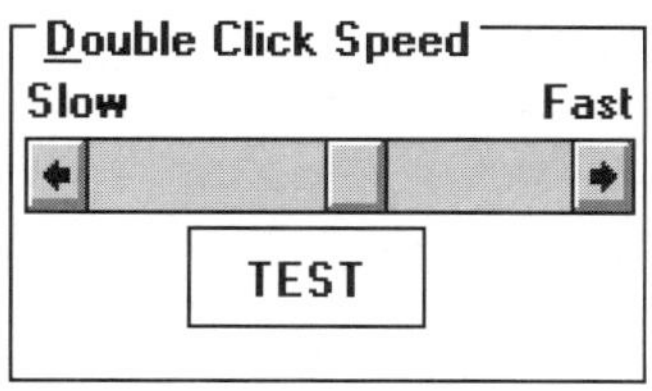

## SWAP LEFT/RIGHT BUTTONS

**Figure 22.** Windows uses the left mouse button because this button is easier to press when the mouse is being used by right-handed people. If you are using the mouse with your left hand, or simply prefer clicking with the right mouse button, select the check box labeled *Swap Left/Right Buttons.*

## THE MOUSE BUTTON INDICATOR

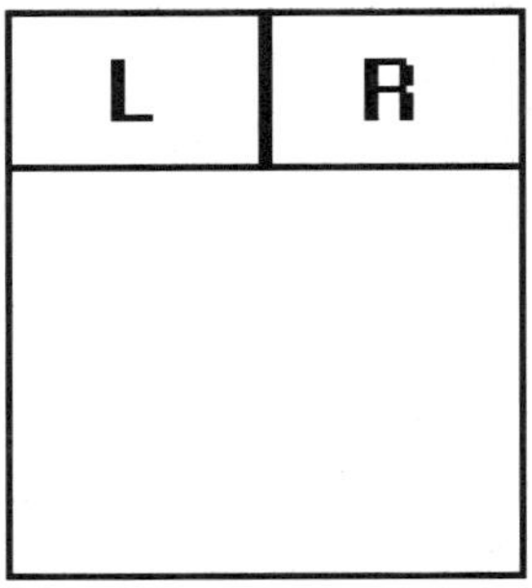


**Figure 23.** Whenever you click one of the mouse buttons while the mouse pointer is within the *Mouse* dialog box of Figure 20, the corresponding button on the Mouse Button Indicator will be highlighted. If you reverse the buttons with the *Swap* option, the indicator's buttons will reverse as well.

## MOUSE TRAILS

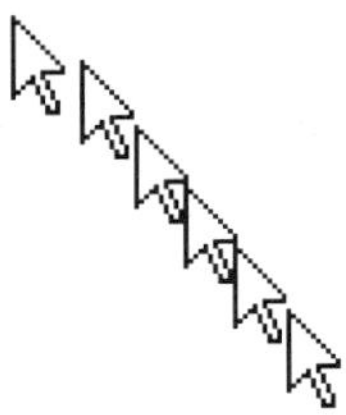

**Figure 24.** When *Mouse Trails* is selected in the *Mouse* dialog box, the mouse leaves a temporary trail across the screen when the mouse is moved. This is useful for laptop screens, as the cursor is often hard to locate. Click on *Cancel* in the *Mouse* dialog box to return to the screen.

## KEYBOARD SETTINGS

**Figure 25(a).** When a key is held down on the keyboard, it will begin to repeat. This feature allows you to type a long string of the same character without having to strike the keyboard repeatedly. Windows also allows you to set the amount of time before the character is repeated.

**Figure 25(b).** To modify the setting, adjust the scroll bar to the desired speed. To test the new speeds, click in the *Test* box to obtain a cursor and then try holding down a key to observe the new rate.

Click on *Cancel* to return to the screen.

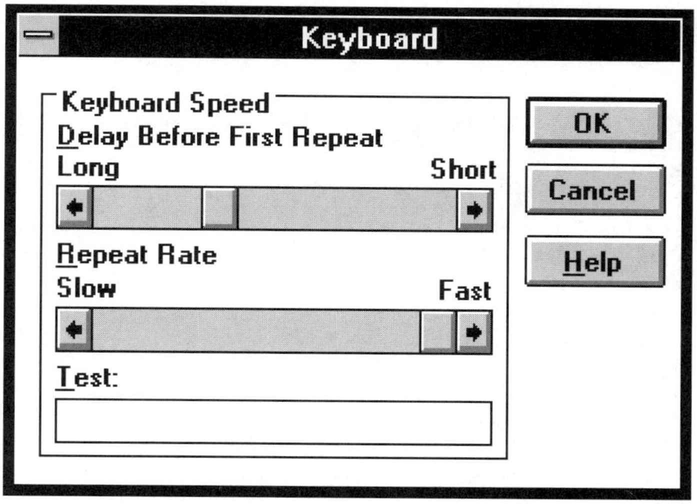


## CONFIGURING PRINTERS AND PORTS

In Windows, you can set up and define your printers and output characteristics once and these settings will be valid for all Windows applications. This is one of the key advantages of Windows.

## PRINTERS PROGRAM

**Figure 26(a).** Because different printer models interpret output in different ways, there are special programs, called *drivers*, that translate your output into a code that specific printers will understand. The Windows set up disks include drivers for over 150 different printers. The Printers program allows you to install and customize the drivers to suit your equipment.

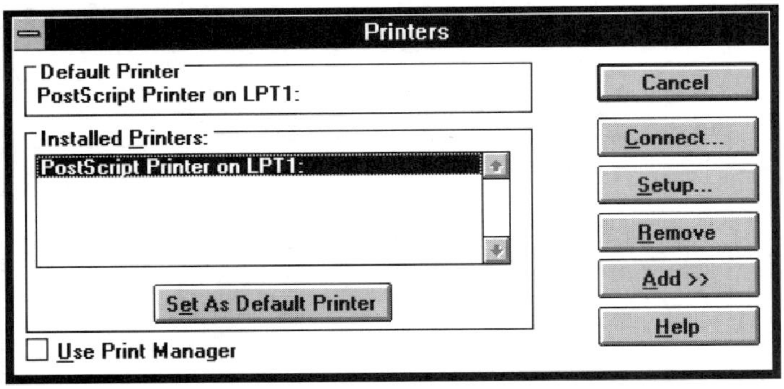


**Figure 26(b).** The *Printers* dialog box—which appears when you run the Printers program—contains an *Installed Printers* list-box that lists those printers for which drivers have been selected. If you have not yet installed any printer drivers, this box will be empty.

### ADDING PRINTERS

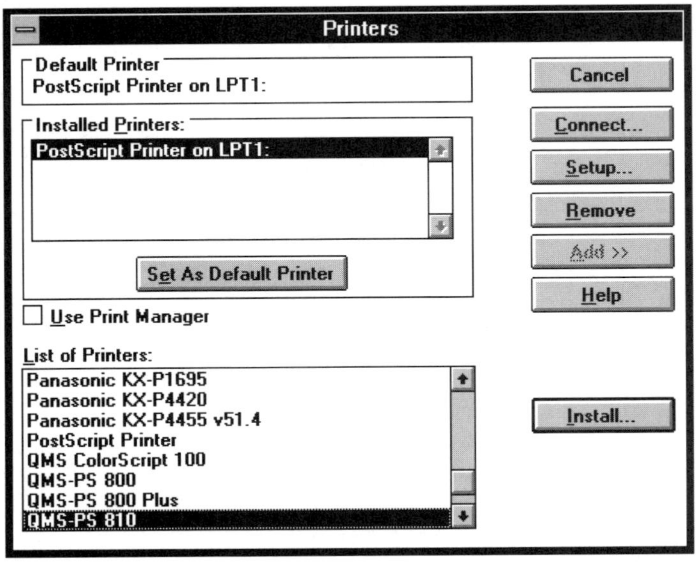


**Figure 27.** To add a new printer to this list, click on the *Add* button. An additional section, containing a *List of Printers*, will appear at the bottom of the dialog box.

To add one of these printers to the list of *Installed Printers*, click on its name to highlight it in the list and click on *Install*.

The printer drivers are kept on the Windows Setup disks because it would be inefficient to keep so many programs on the hard disk when most systems use only one or two printers.

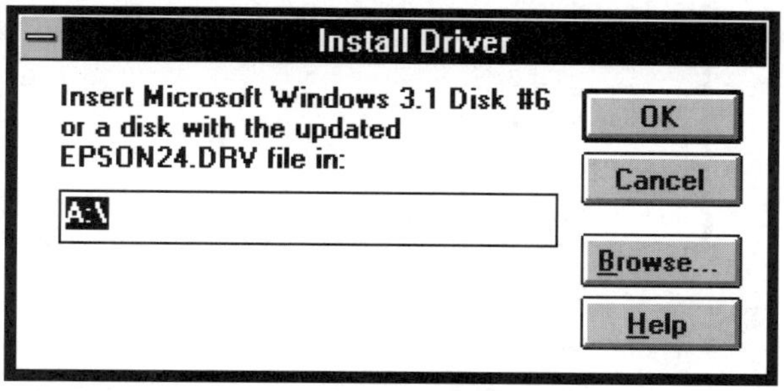


**Figure 28.** If you want to install a new printer, a dialog box may appear, instructing you to insert the appropriate Setup disk. Place the diskette in the indicated disk drive, or type in the new drive name, and click on *OK*.

The required driver will be loaded and the printer will be added to the *Installed Printers* list.

## DEFAULT PRINTER

If more than one printer is installed, Windows must be told which one is the default printer—the printer that is automatically used when a print instruction is given. To select the default printer, double-click on that printer's name in the *Installed Printers* list and its name will appear in the *Default Printer* box in Figure 26(b).

## PRINTER CONFIGURATION

Once a printer has been installed, you will want to specify how it is used. The port to which the printer is connected, the size and orientation of the paper it is using, the fonts available for that printer, and similar information, are all part of what is called the printer's *configuration*.

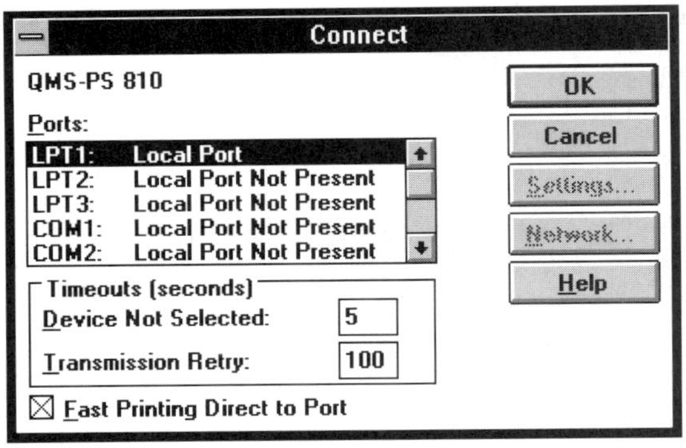


**Figure 29.** To set the configuration for a printer, highlight its name in the *Installed Printers* list and click on *Connect.* The *Connect* dialog box will appear. In the center of this dialog box is a list of output ports available on your system. To select the port to which the nominated printer is connected, highlight it in this list.

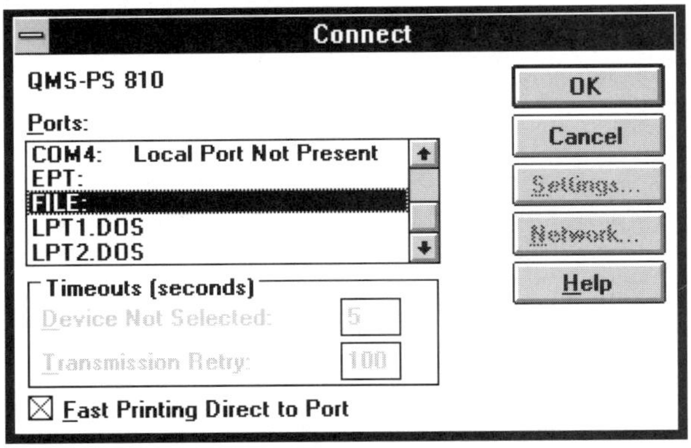


**Figure 30.** Selecting the *FILE* option instructs Windows to generate a disk file in the format understood by the selected printer.

This feature allows you to "print" a document at a work-station not connected to the selected printer. You can later print the file at a different computer where the appropriate printer is connected without using the application that created the file.

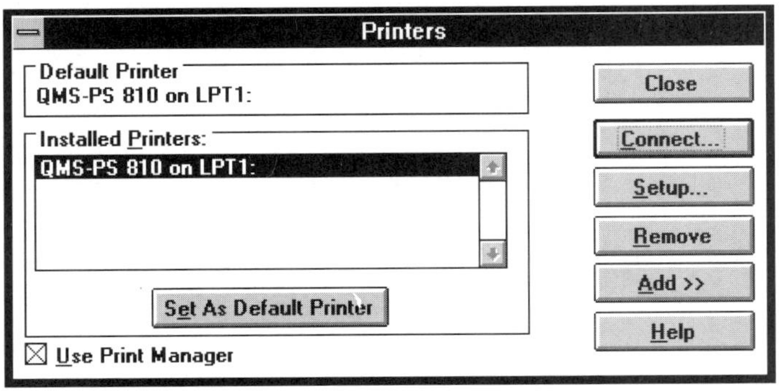


**Figure 31.** To delete the selected printer from the list of *Installed Printers*, click on the *Remove* button back in the original *Printers* dialog box. A warning dialog box will determine if you truly intended to remove the selected printer from the list. If you do inadvertently Remove a printer from the list, you can always Install it again if necessary.

The *Setup* button allows you to set printer-specific characteristics such as paper size, available fonts, and graphic resolution.

**Figure 32.** This is the *Setup* dialog box that appears when a PostScript-type printer is selected. Because different printers have different characteristics that need setting, this dialog box will differ between printer types. Choose *Cancel* to return to Figure 31.

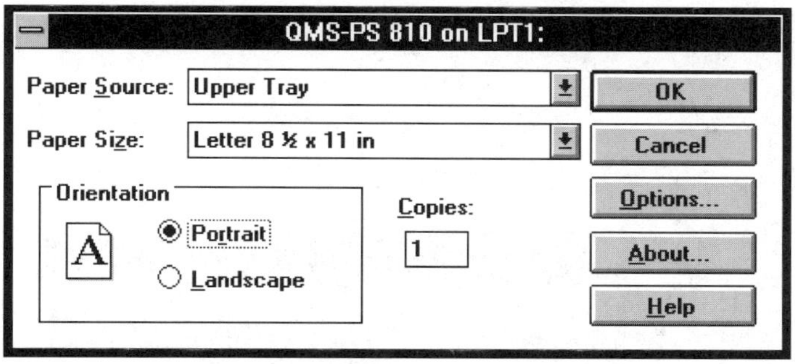


## USE PRINT MANAGER

The Print Manager, described more fully in Chapter 4, is a program that helps manage the printer output from Windows applications.

**Figure 33.** The *Use Print Manager* check box allows you to enable or disable the use of Print Manger. When this option is selected, the Print Manager will operate automatically when printing.

Close the *Printers* dialog box and return to the Control Panel screen.

## PORTS PROGRAM

**Figure 34(a).** The way in which the computer communicates with various peripherals through the communications, or COM, ports can be configured using the Ports program. Up to four communications ports can be configured.

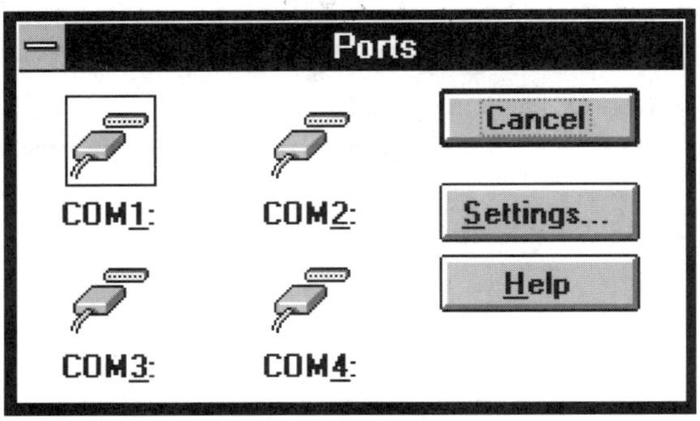


**Figure 34(b).** The *Ports* dialog box allows you to select which of the four COM ports you want to configure.

Click on the desired port's icon and select *Settings* or simply double-click on the port icon.

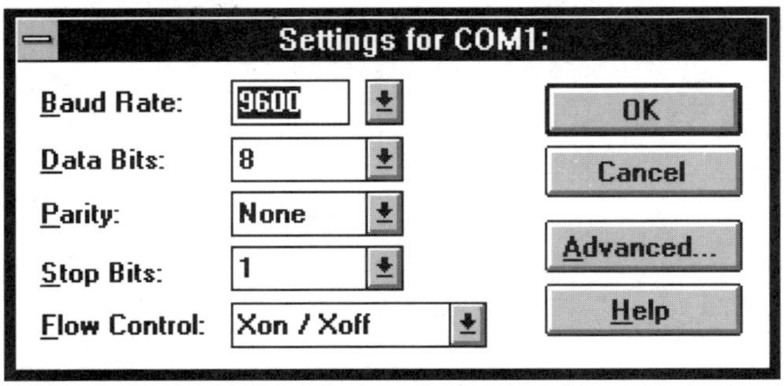


**Figure 35.** In the *Settings* dialog box, the *Baud Rate* submenu lets you set the rate at which data is transmitted through the selected port. The other submenus let you specify various communications conventions.

Devices that use the communications ports, like modems, some printers, and some mice, may require specific settings for these values. Consult the documentation included with those peripherals. Cancel the *Ports* dialog box to return to the Control Panel screen.

# Miscellaneous Control Panel Settings

## THE INTERNATIONAL PROGRAM

**Figure 36(a).** Because Windows is used all over the world, and certain standards and conventions differ from country to country, the International program lets you select the settings appropriate to your environment.

**Figure 36(b).** The *International* dialog box contains four submenus in which you can specify a number of features that vary internationally.

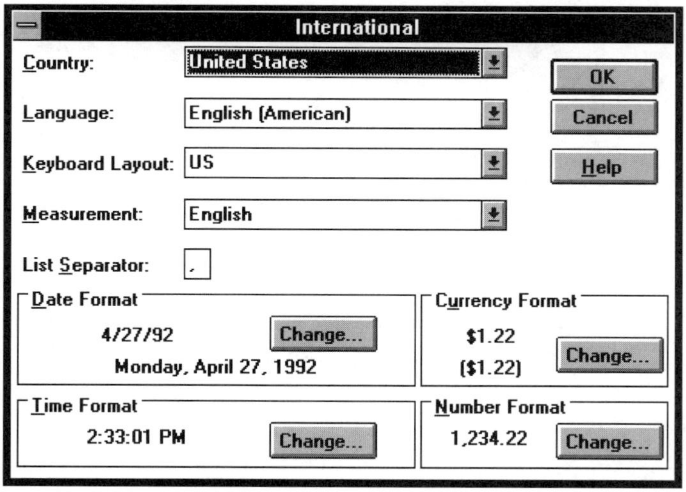


### COUNTRY SETTING

**Figure 37.** From the *Country* submenu, you can select the country whose conventions for date, time, currency, and numeric format you follow.

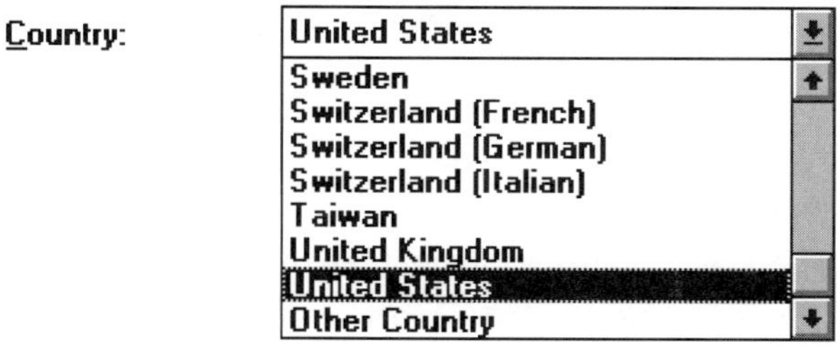

As you select a country from this list, the samples of these four formats listed at the bottom of the *International* dialog box will change automatically. These formats can also be changed directly by clicking on their individual *Change* buttons.

## LANGUAGE SETTING

**Figure 38.** The *Language* submenu lets you identify the language in which you are working. Some Windows applications have language-specific functions, like spelling programs, and use this setting to determine which language to use.

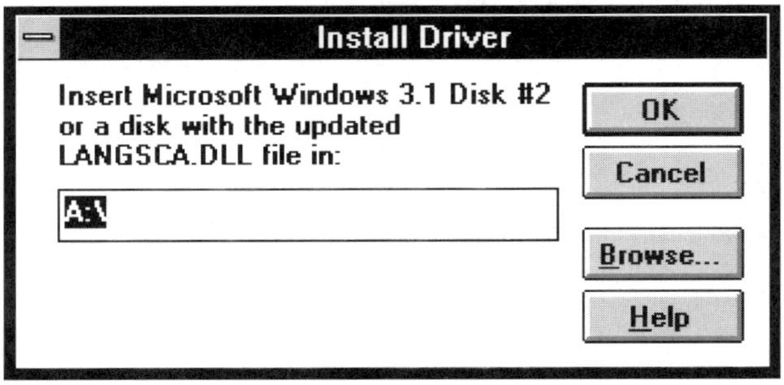


**Figure 39.** Windows does not keep information for every language on your hard disk. If you change the *Language* selection, you will be prompted, after clicking on *OK*, to insert one of the Setup disks so that the required language information can be added to your system.

## KEYBOARD LAYOUT

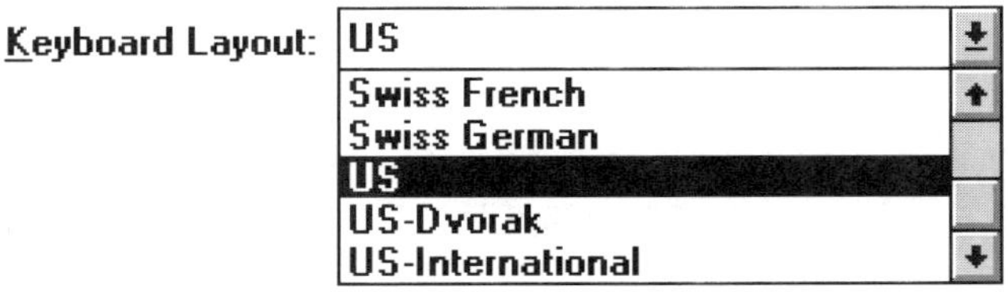


**Figure 40.** The keyboards of different countries contain specific characters and letters resulting from differences in language and currency formats. You can identify the layout for your keyboard by selecting the desired country or style from the *Keyboard Layout* submenu.

As with the *Language* option, you will be prompted to insert a Setup disk if you change this selection.

Changes to the *Keyboard Layout* are effective only within Windows. When you return to DOS, your keyboard will return to its usual configuration.

### MEASUREMENT SYSTEM

**Figure 41.** Many Windows applications involve linear measurements in their functions. The *Measurement* submenu lets you choose between the metric and English (Imperial) systems of measurement.

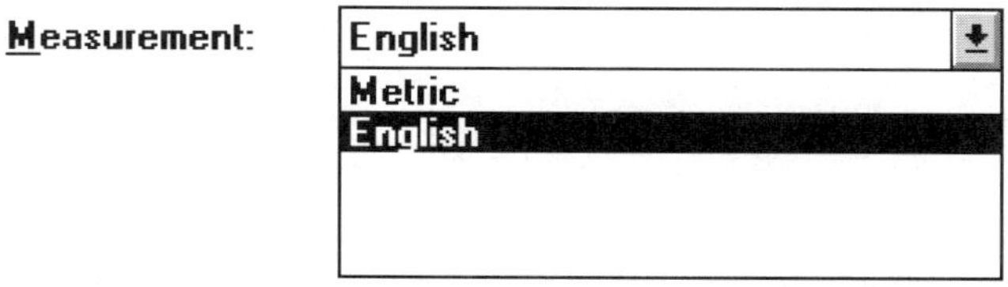


For some Windows applications, you can set this option within the program itself. Cancel the *International* dialog box to return to the screen.

## FONTS PROGRAM

**Figure 42(a).** Windows uses a variety of character styles, or fonts, in displaying and printing data. You may want to add to the available fonts or replace existing fonts with new ones. These functions are carried out through the Fonts program.

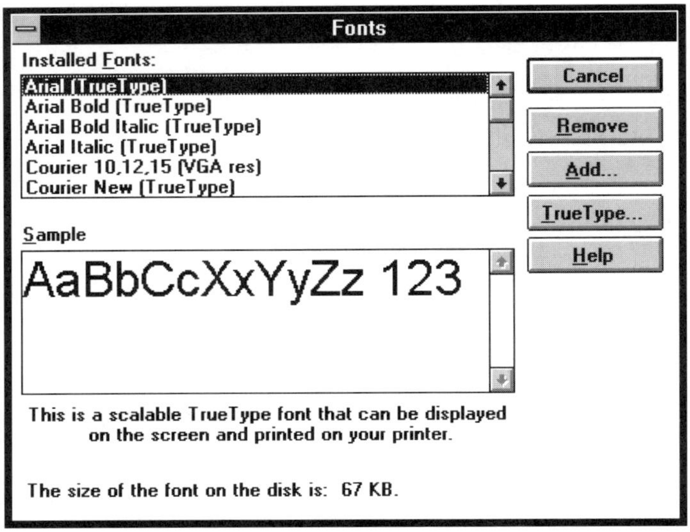


**Figure 42(b).** The *Fonts* dialog box contains a list box of the available fonts. By highlighting the name of a font, some sample characters will appear in the *Sample* box at the bottom of the dialog box.

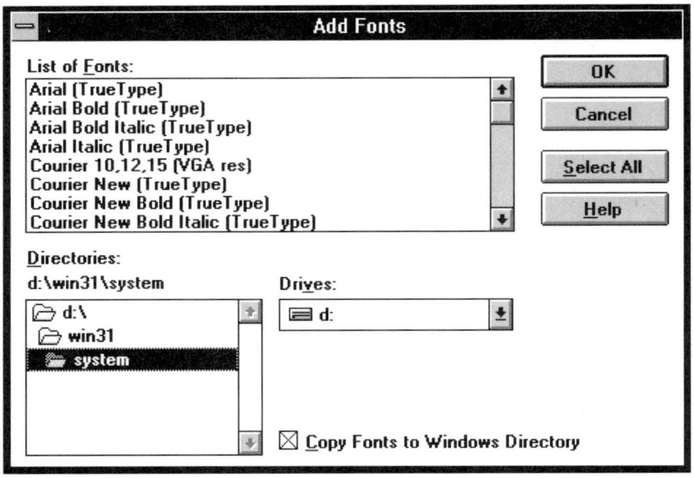


**Figure 43.** To add a font to the list, select *Add*. A file selection dialog box will appear from which you can select the font files you want to add to the Windows system.

Standard Windows fonts are contained in the *System* subdirectory, as shown. Fonts from other disks and directories are displayed by altering the *Directories* and *Drives* options.

**Figure 44.** To remove a highlighted font from the *Fonts* dialog box, click on the *Remove* button.

This displays the *Remove Font* dialog box. To remove the font, click on *Yes*, or *Yes to All* if more than one font is selected. This removes the font from the *Installed Fonts* list box and frees the memory being used. Do not remove MS Sans Serif because it is used in most Windows dialog boxes.

To remove the font completely, select the *Delete Font File From Disk* option in the *Remove Font* dialog box. Because this removes the font file from your hard disk, ensure that you have a backup of the font files before using this command. Cancel from the *Fonts* dialog box to return to the Control Panel.

## DATE/TIME PROGRAM

**Figure 45(a).** Your computer contains an internal clock and calendar that Windows consults in order to be aware of the date and time. The Date/Time program is used to set the date and time on your system.

**Figure 45(b).** The *Date & Time* dialog box displays the current date and time according to your computer system's internal clock and calendar.

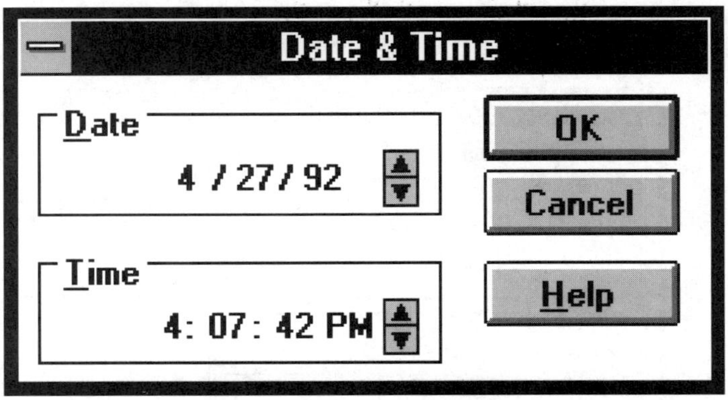


To change any of this information, highlight the appropriate value by clicking on it, and use the arrow buttons to raise or lower the value. Alternatively, you can simply highlight the item and type the new value directly. Click on *Cancel* to return.

# 386 Enhanced Settings

**Figure 46(a).** If your computer has an 80386 processor, you have what is usually referred to as a "three-eighty-six" system. On such systems (and higher processors), Windows can run in a special Enhanced mode, which allows it to use some of the advantages of these microprocessors.

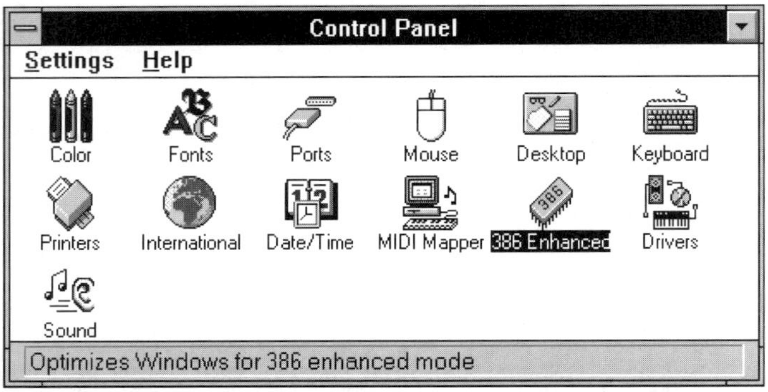


**Figure 46(b).** If Windows is capable of running in Enhanced mode, there is a 386 Enhanced program in the Control Panel window.

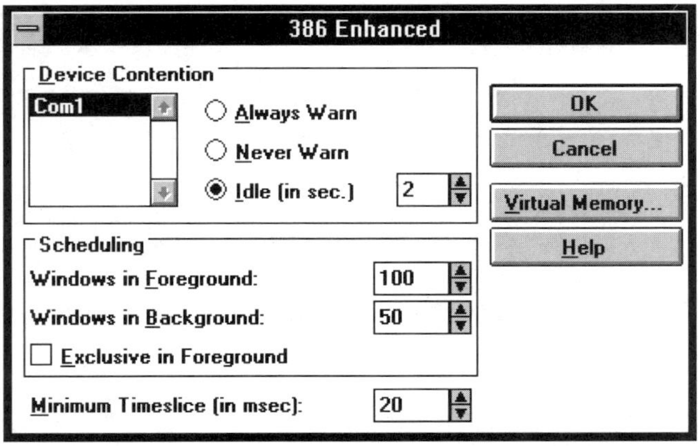


**Figure 47.** The 386 Enhanced program allows you to specify some of the special features that are only available with a three-eighty-six or higher system. When you select the 386 program from the Control Panel, the *386 Enhanced* dialog box appears.

## DEVICE CONTENTION

Because in Enhanced mode it is possible to run several applications simultaneously, provision must be made for situations in which more than one program tries to use a device at the same time. This is called device contention. The options listed below apply only when one of the applications concerned is a non-Windows application. When two Windows applications request access to a device, Windows handles their use of the device automatically, without these options.

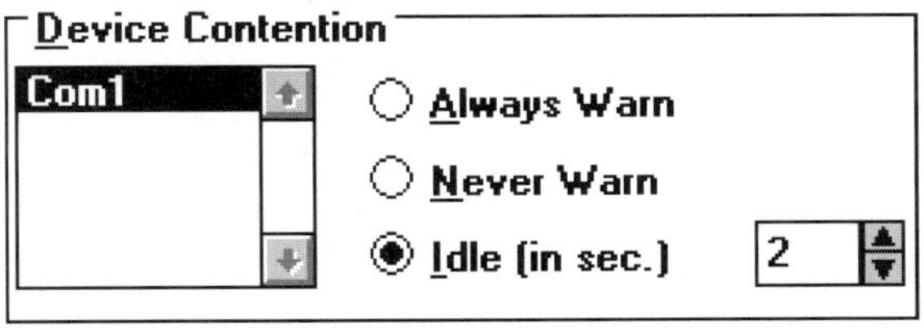


**Figure 48.** The *Device Contention* section of the *386 Enhanced* dialog box lets you determine what action is taken in the event of device contention.

Because each output port on your computer can be connected to a separate device, you can select *Device Contention* settings for each port.

For each port, highlight its name in the list and select the desired option from the set of radio buttons. In most cases, you should select the *Always Warn* option.

## SCHEDULING

When Windows is multitasking—running several applications at once—processing time is shared among all programs that are running. One application is always in the active window, the window that is selected and in the foreground of your screen display. In multitasking, the application in the active window, called the foreground application, is allocated processor time differently from the background applications.

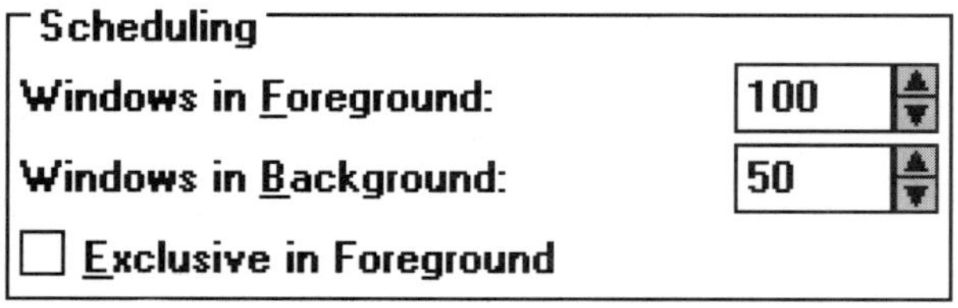


**Figure 49.** The scheduling option lets you set the level of priority that Windows applications are given when they are in the active window (*Windows in Foreground*) and when a non-Windows application is in the active window (*Windows in Background*).

The priority is set in the form of a number whose value may be between one and a thousand.

In addition to the priority numbers set in the 386 program, which apply to all Windows applications, each non-Windows application will have been assigned priority numbers as well in its PIF (see the discussion of the PIF Editor in Chapter 4). The amount of time it takes for the computer to process a particular application depends on that application's priority number as well as how many other applications are also running and their respective priority numbers.

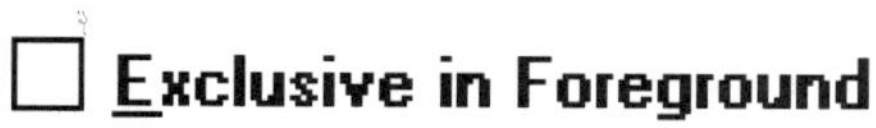


**Figure 50.** If you select the *Exclusive in Foreground* option, then all non-Windows applications will be suspended while a Windows application is in the active window.

## MINIMUM TIMESLICE

When Windows is multitasking, the computer is not really executing several programs simultaneously. In fact, the computer's processor will deal individually with each application but, by switching quickly between applications, it gives the impression that all are being executed at once.

**Figure 51.** The value for *Minimum Timeslice*, in the *386 Enhanced* dialog box represents, in milliseconds (thousandths of a second), how much time the processor will spend on a single function before moving on to the next one.

Every time the computer switches functions—at the end of each timeslice—some time is lost.

Larger values for the *Minimum Timeslice* will use the processor more efficiently but may cause the execution of applications to appear less smooth. Shorter timeslices make for less halting execution but overall execution will be slower, because more time will be lost in switching.

## VIRTUAL MEMORY

The *Virtual Memory* button in the *386 Enhanced* dialog box is used to set the characteristics of the Windows Swap file. As described in Chapter 1, the Swap file, located on the hard disk, holds information that Windows can access as though it were held in memory.

Using the Swap file increases the amount of memory available in excess of the true amount held in RAM on your computer system.

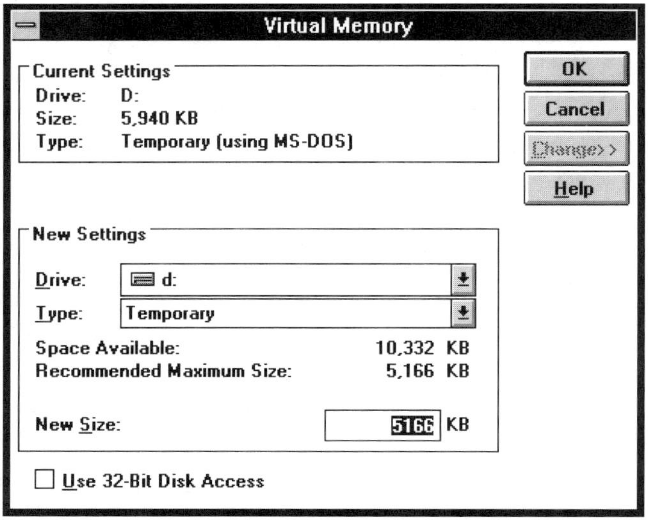


**Figure 52.** The *Virtual Memory* dialog box appears when the *Virtual Memory* button is pressed. Clicking on *Change* expands the dialog box so the settings can be changed. The *Current Settings* section of the dialog box shows the existing Swap file settings.

The *New Settings* section of the *Virtual Memory* dialog box allows you to set the drive that will hold the Swap file, whether the file is permanent or temporary, and the size of the Swap file.

When you click on *OK*, the new settings will be saved. You must restart Windows to implement the changes. Cancel from the *Virtual Memory* dialog box to return to the Control Panel.

## SOUND SETTINGS

### *DRIVERS*

**Figure 53(a).** The Drivers program enables you install drivers for external pieces of hardware such as sound cards and video players. A driver is essential if the hardware device being added is to communicate with Windows.

**Figure 53(b).** When you click on the *Add* button in the *Drivers* dialog box, the drivers that Windows can support are displayed. From this point, you select the appropriate driver for your piece of hardware and click on *OK*. It is essential to have your Windows program disks in order to install a new driver from this point.

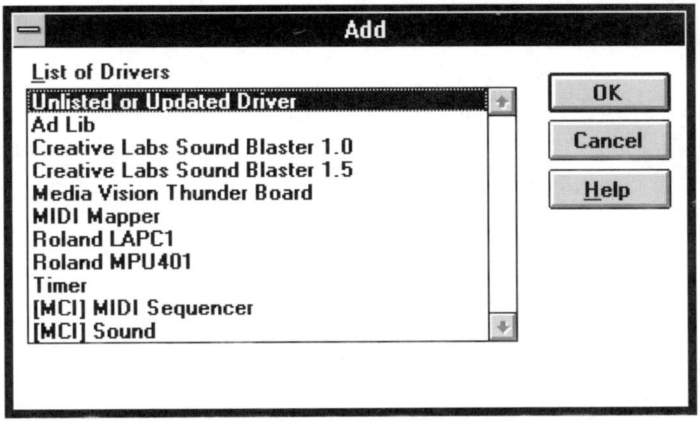


**Figure 54.** The drivers that are currently installed in Windows are listed in the *Installed Drivers* list box in the *Drivers* dialog box.

Cancel from this dialog box to return to the Control Panel.

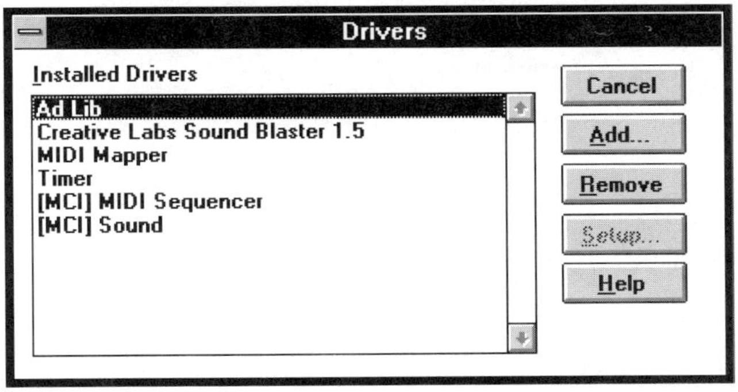


## SOUND PROGRAM

**Figure 55(a).** The Sound program lets you set Windows to play a particular sound at a given time.

**Figure 55(b).** You may have created your own sound using the *Sound Recorder* in the Accessories group and want it to play every time you close Windows. To do this, select *Windows Exit* from the *Events* list box and a sound file from the *Files* list box.

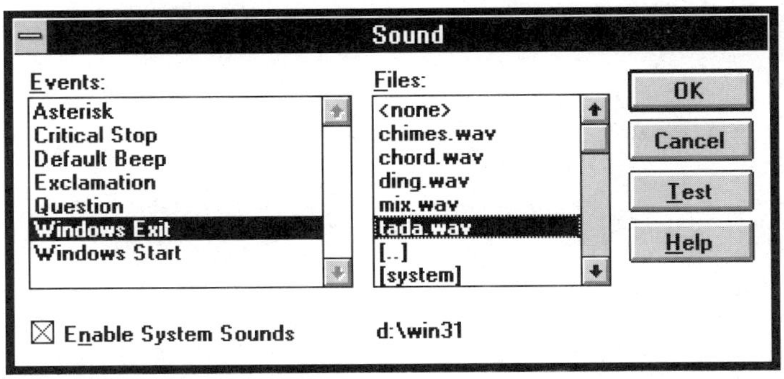

# THE FILE MANAGER

# 7

## SIMPLIFYING FILE MANAGEMENT

One of the principal functions of any operating system is to enable you to access and manipulate your disk files. In Windows, a special utility program, called the File Manager, allows you to do just that. The File Manager program item is located in the Main program group in the Program Manager. The icon for this program is in the shape of a filing cabinet, symbolizing the File Manager's function.

Using the File Manager, you can perform all the file manipulation commands to which you have access in DOS. The File Manager, however, lets you carry out these commands through the graphical system of menus and icons that characterizes the Windows environment.

Using this interactive system, most of the file commands in the File Manager are easier to use than their DOS equivalents. There are many functions accessible through the File Manager that are not available in DOS.

**Figure 1.** When you first execute the File Manager program, the File Manager window appears. Within the File Manager window, you will see the *Directory Tree* window. Within the File Manager window you will see a "directory tree"—a graphical representation of the subdirectories on the selected disk. The right section lists the files located in the subdirectory that is highlighted in the tree.

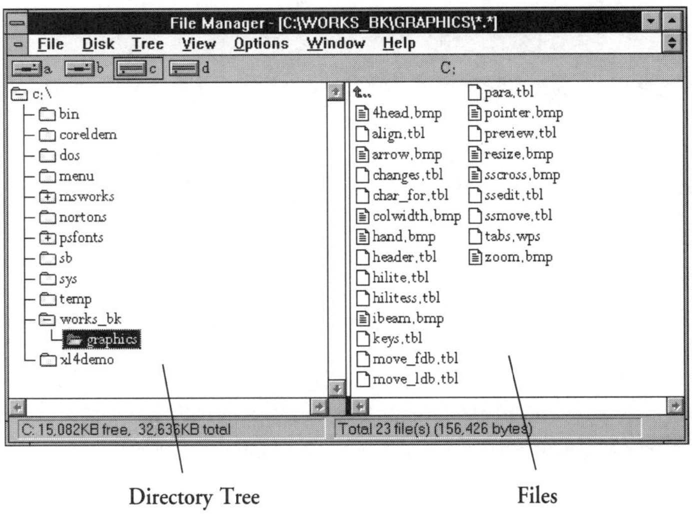

## DIRECTORY TREE

The *Directory Tree* window is a special window within the File Manager that displays the subdirectory structures of your disks.

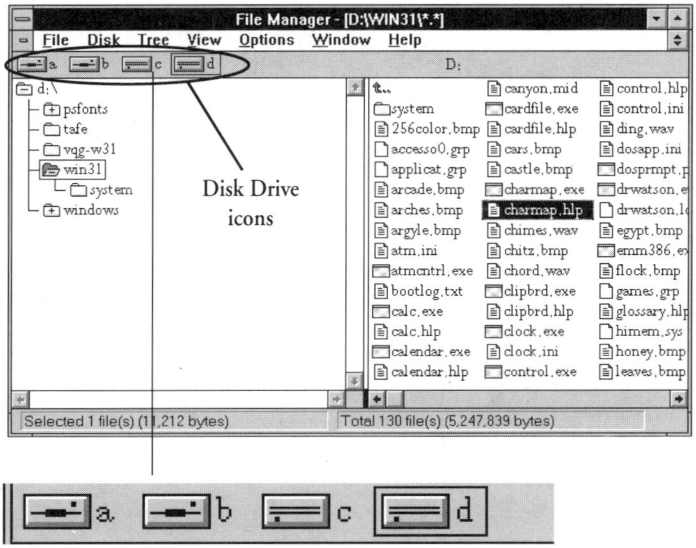


**Figure 2.** Immediately below the title bar of the *Directory Tree* window a set of icons represents the disk drives available on your system. In this sample there are two floppy drives (A: and B:) and two hard drives (C: and D:). Note the different icons for these two kinds of disk drive.

One of these disk drive icons will be highlighted. The information displayed in the lower portion of the Directory Tree window relates to the highlighted disk drive.

You can change the highlighted disk drive by clicking on the icon of your choice.

### *SUBDIRECTORY ICONS*

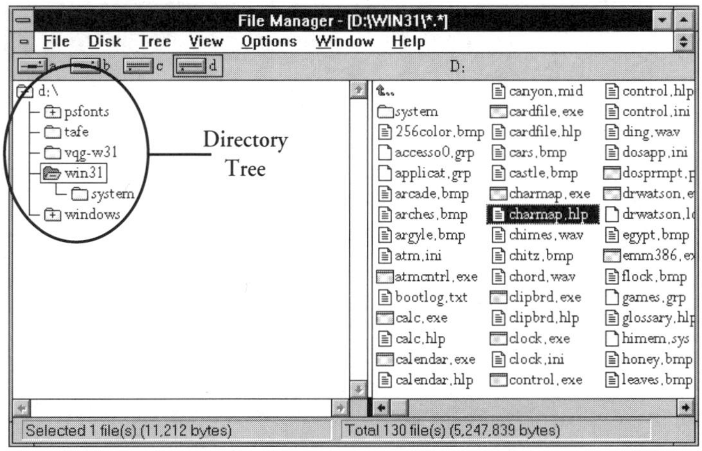


**Figure 3.** A Directory Tree is displayed below the disk drive icons. This is a graphical representation of the contents of the highlighted disk drive.

Each subdirectory is represented by an icon in the shape of a file folder with the subdirectory's name written beside it. If the *Indicate Expandable Branches* command is selected from the **Tree** menu—which is the default—the icon can take one of four forms.

**Figure 4.** The file folder icon by itself represents a simple subdirectory that does not contain any other subdirectories.

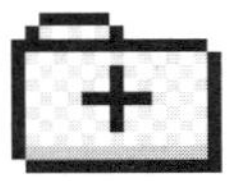

**Figure 5.** If the file folder icon has a + symbol in the center, it represents a directory that contains further subdirectories within it. These divisions are not currently being displayed. To expand the tree to display these subdirectories, double-click on the file folder icon. The hidden directory branches will be revealed and the icon will be replaced by a file folder with a - sign.

**Figure 6.** If the icon contains a – symbol, it represents a subdirectory, containing further subdirectory divisions, where those subdirectories are currently displayed. To contract the Directory Tree so as not to display these subdirectories, double-click on the file folder icon. The directory branches will disappear, and the icon will be replaced by a file folder with a + sign.

**Figure 7.** If a directory's icon takes the form of an open folder, the files contained within this subdirectory are currently being displayed in the right-hand side of the File Manager window.

## FILE ICONS

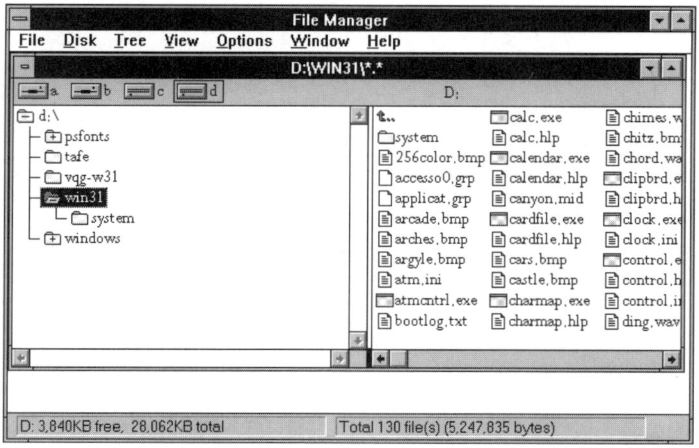


**Figure 8.** To list the files contained in any of these subdirectories, click on the subdirectory of your choice. The right side of the screen will display the files that are located in that subdirectory. The title bar will show the path of the selected subdirectory.

Each of the files in the selected subdirectory will be represented by a rectangular icon with the file's name appearing beside it. The icons, representing files, can take one of three forms.

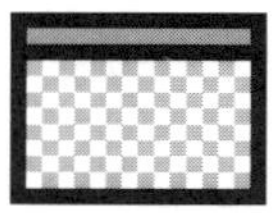

**Figure 9.** Program files, files with .COM, .EXE, or .PIF extensions, are represented by a rectangular icon with a bar across the top.

This icon is meant to resemble a window, because these program files represent separate applications that would each run in their own windows—though in the case of non-Windows applications, they might require the entire screen.

You can run one of these program files by double-clicking the mouse pointer on either the program's name or its icon.

**Figure 10.** Files that were created as data files, or as documents, by application programs are represented by an icon that resembles a text-filled sheet of paper. The File Manager uses the files' three-character extensions to determine if they were created by an application program and, if so, which one.

In Figure 8, for example, the files arcade.bmp and arches.bmp contain graphic images that were created using the Windows accessory program Paintbrush. The File Manager assumes that all files with a .bmp extension were created by Paintbrush.

If you double-click on one of these data file names, or their icons, the application program that created the file will be run, with the selected data file already opened.

**Figure 11.** All other files in your computer system, those that are not program files or recognized data files, are represented by an icon that resembles a blank sheet of paper.

When you are through viewing the files contained in a specific subdirectory, you can close the window containing the list of files by double-clicking in the window's Control Menu box.

## CHANGING THE DIRECTORY STRUCTURE

The File Manager has a menu bar from which you can select a wide range of file management commands. Most of these menu selections will be detailed in the next section of this chapter.

A few menu options deal directly with the structure of the Directory Tree and the subdirectories on your disks. These are covered below.

## ADDING SUBDIRECTORIES

**Figure 12.** Subdirectories can easily be added to any of your disks using the *Create Directory* command in the File Manager's **File** menu.

First, select the directory in which the new subdirectory is to be located—this is called the parent directory. Highlight the parent directory by clicking on its name in the Directory Tree. Then, select *Create Directory* from the **File** menu.

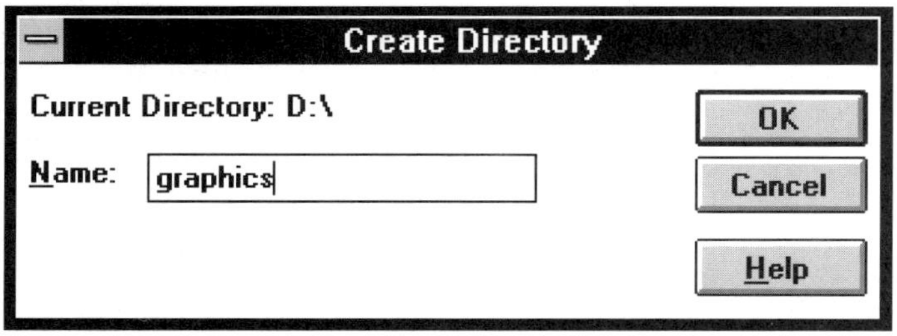


**Figure 13.** In the *Create Directory* window that appears, type the name for the new subdirectory that you are creating and select *OK*.

The Directory Tree will now contain your new subdirectory. If it is not visible in the display, you will have to expand the parent directory by double-clicking the file folder icon.

## REMOVING A SUBDIRECTORY

To remove a subdirectory from the Directory Tree, you must first highlight it in the Directory Tree window by clicking on its name.

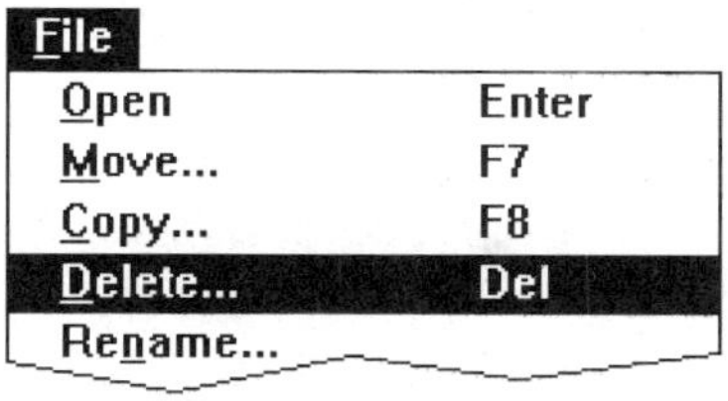


**Figure 14.** After highlighting the subdirectory to be deleted, select *Delete* from the **File** menu.

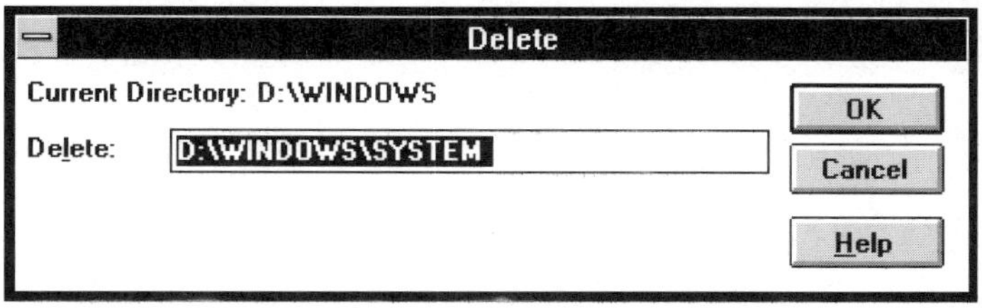


**Figure 15.** When you select *Delete*, this *Delete* dialog box appears. The subdirectory's name should already be written in the *Delete* section of the dialog box. If the information displayed is correct, select *OK*.

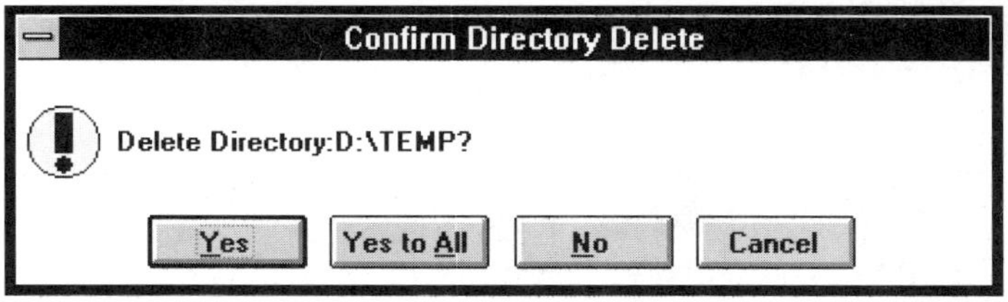


**Figure 16.** Before deleting your subdirectory, the File Manager will provide you with a warning dialog box to ensure that you intend the deletion. Select *Yes* to delete the subdirectory.

If there are any files in the subdirectory you are deleting, you will be shown a warning dialog box for each file before it is deleted. If you choose not to delete some of these files, the subdirectory will not be removed from the Directory Tree.

## File Manager Menu Bar

Through the commands available in its menu bar, the File Manager allows you to perform all the file-handling operations you would otherwise carry out from DOS. Because of the flexibility of this interactive system, operations that would require many commands, like the copying of multiple files, can be carried out in a few simple steps.

Some of the functions accessible through the menu bar can also be carried out with shortcuts that use the mouse and keyboard. Where such shortcuts are available, they will be outlined along with the menu option they replace.

## SELECTING FILES

Many of the File Manager's commands apply only to files that have been highlighted in a directory list window. There are several ways to highlight, or select, these files.

**Figure 17.** To highlight a single file, click the mouse pointer on the file's name or icon. The selected file will be highlighted, and all other files in the window will not be selected.

**Figure 18.** To highlight several files, hold down the Control key while clicking the file names. When the Control key is used, previously highlighted files do not become deselected when a new file is highlighted.

**Figure 19.** To quickly highlight a group of files that appear in sequence in their directory list window, highlight the first file in the list, hold down the Shift key, and click on the last file in the list. All files between the first and last file will be highlighted.

## *FILE MENU*

**Figure 20.** The commands in the **File** menu deal directly with the handling and manipulation of files in your computer system.

### OPEN COMMAND

The *Open* command has different meanings, depending on what type of item is highlighted in the File Manager's active window. In each of these cases, selecting the *Open* command is equivalent to double-clicking the highlighted item.

If the highlighted item is a subdirectory name, whether in the Directory Tree window or in a subdirectory's file list window, the *Open* command will open a file list window and display the files in the highlighted subdirectory.

If the highlighted item is a program file, the *Open* command will cause that program to be executed.

If you select the *Open* command when a data, or document, file is highlighted, the application that created the data file will be executed with the data file open.

**Figure 21.** Selecting the *Open* command for any file represented by a blank page icon will result in an error message. The File Manager cannot interpret the purpose of this third kind of file.

## MOVE AND COPY COMMANDS

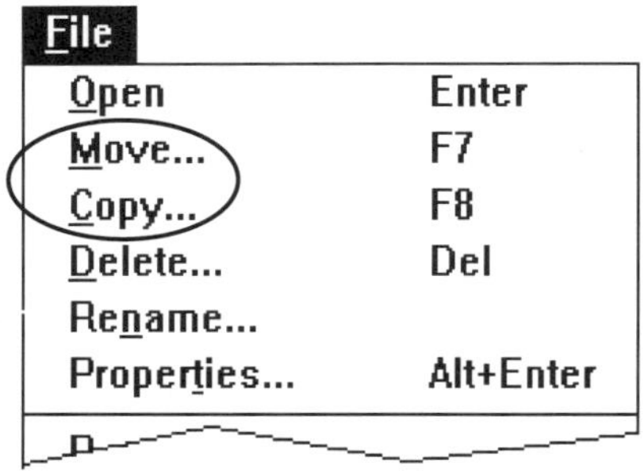


**Figure 22.** The *Move* and *Copy* commands allow you change the subdirectories in which files are located. With the *Move* command, the file is removed from its previous location and placed in the new one. Using the *Copy* command, the file is retained in its previous directory position, and a copy of that file is created in the new location.

Before selecting the command, highlight the file to be moved (or copied) in its directory list window.

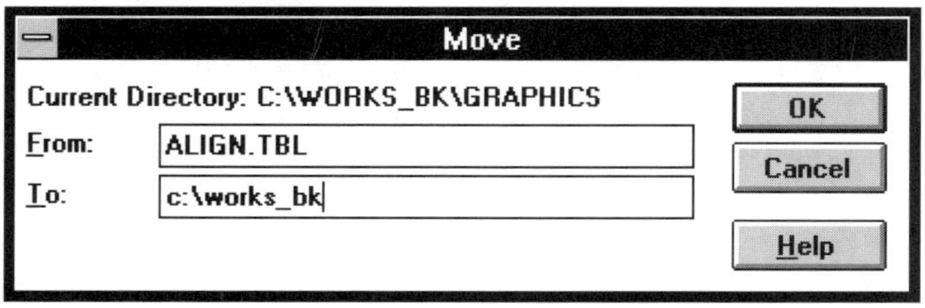


**Figure 23.** The *Move* (or *Copy*) dialog box contains two boxes into which you can type information. The file (or files) you have highlighted will already be entered in the *From* box. Type the destination drive name, subdirectory path, and the new file name—where this information differs from the old file specifications—in the *To* box.

While the command is carried out, the dialog box will display the name of the file that is being manipulated. If you select *Cancel* during this time, any files not yet moved (or copied) will not be acted on.

Files that have already been moved will remain in their new locations.

**Figure 24.** You can move files with the mouse by dragging the selected files from their directory list window to their new location. This location can be another directory list window, a subdirectory icon in the Directory Tree, or a disk drive icon at the top of the *Directory Tree* window.

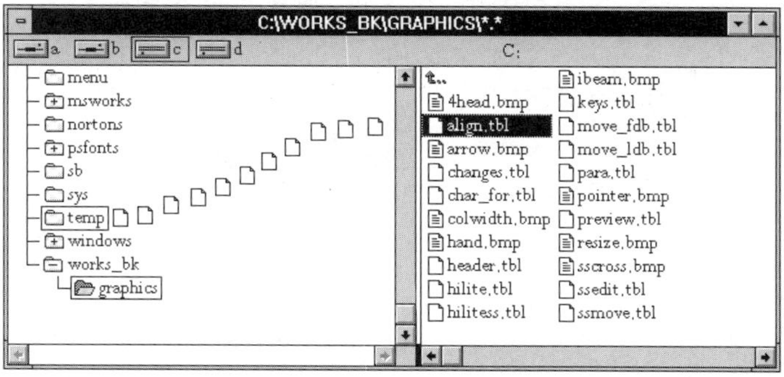


As you drag the highlighted files, the mouse pointer will take the form of a sheet of paper to represent a single file, or a stack of papers to represent several files.

If you are dragging files between subdirectories on the same disk, the result is a *Move* command. If you hold down the Control key while dragging the files, the result will be a *Copy*.

When dragging files between disks, the default is a *Copy* command. In this case, the Control key will change the action to a *Move*.

## DELETE COMMAND

**Figure 25.** The *Delete* command permits you to remove a file, or group of files, from their disk. Once *Delete* has been used on a file, it is permanently gone from your disk. Before selecting the *Delete* command, highlight the file, or files, that you want to remove.

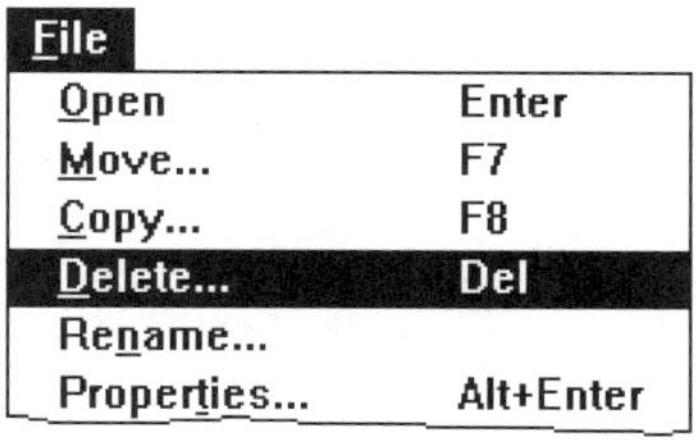


**Figure 26.** The *Delete* dialog box will appear with the selected files already listed in the *Delete* box. If this information is correct, click on *OK*.

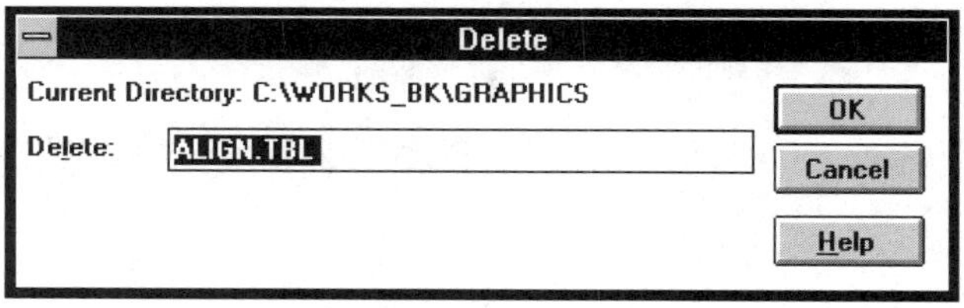

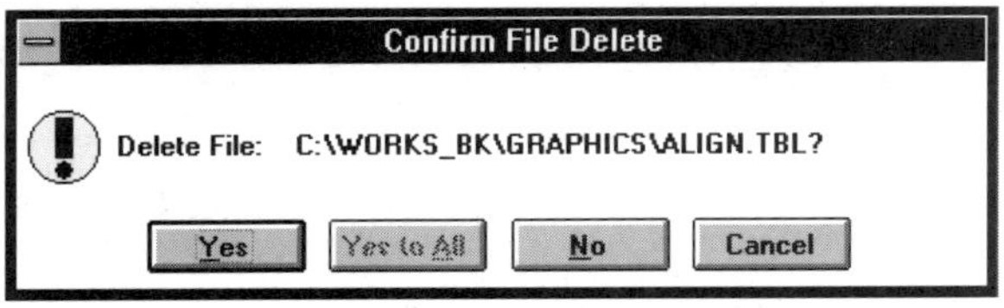


**Figure 27.** Because deletion is permanent, a warning dialog box will appear, allowing you to confirm the command.

As a shortcut to the Delete command, highlight the desired files and press the Delete key.

## RENAME COMMAND

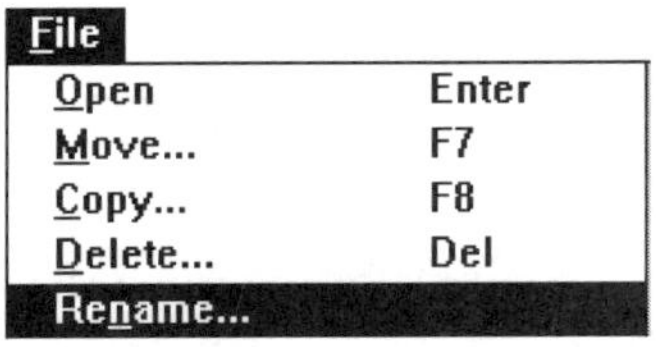


**Figure 28.** To change the name of a file on one of your disks, you must use the *Rename* command.

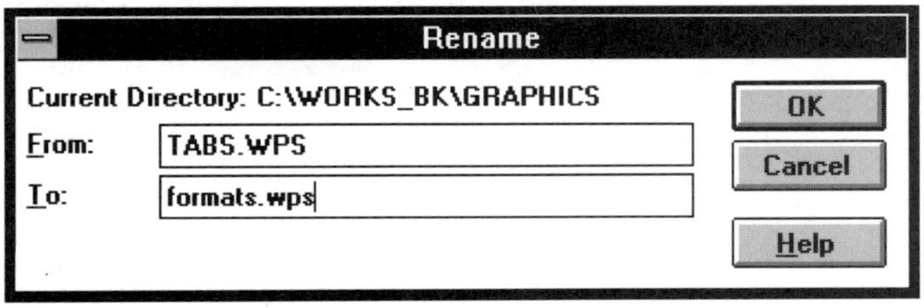


**Figure 29.** The *Rename* dialog box contains two boxes into which you can enter data. The *From* box will already contain the name of the highlighted file. In the *To* box, enter the new name for the file. If you have selected several files, be sure that the name you enter in the *To* box contains wildcard characters that will allow each new name to be different.

## PROPERTIES COMMAND

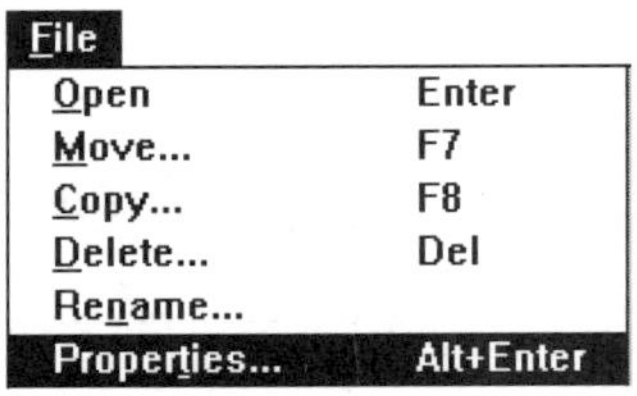


**Figure 30.** All DOS files possess four properties or attributes. It is not usually necessary to adjust these attributes, because they are set automatically. In the event that they do have to be changed, the *Properties* command is available.

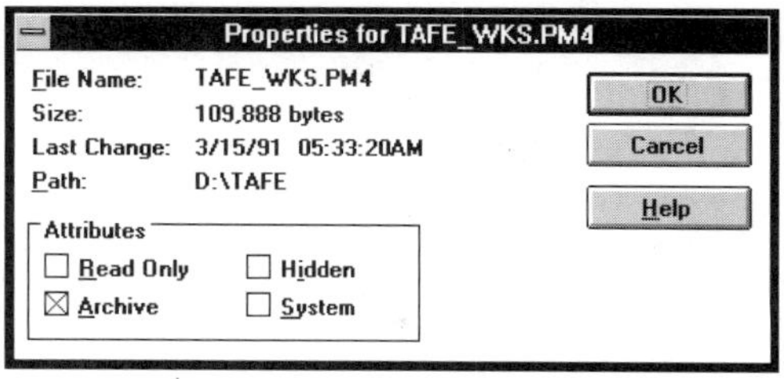


**Figure 31.** The *Properties* dialog box contains four check boxes—one for each attribute. Simply select the attributes that you want attached to the highlighted files.

## RUN COMMAND

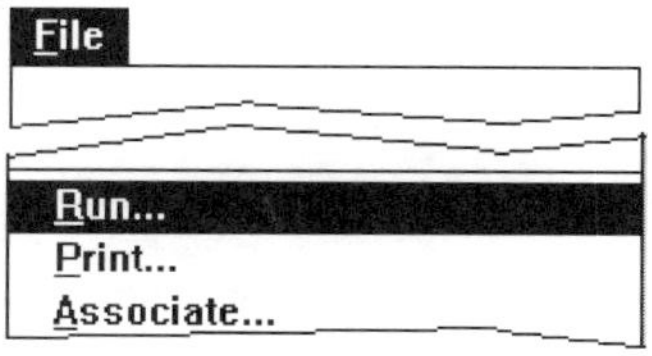


**Figure 32.** The *Run* command lets you execute a program file. This command has a similar effect to double-clicking on the program file's name in a directory list.

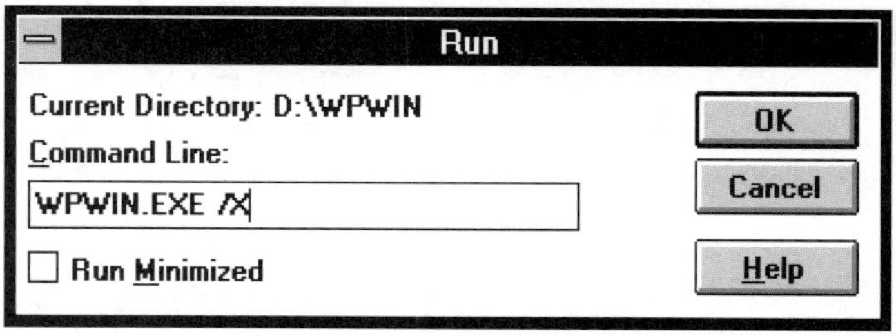


**Figure 33.** This *Run* dialog box appears when you select the *Run* command. Type the name of the program file you want to run.

Because the name is being keyed in, you can add any additional parameters to the command that you cannot add when using the mouse, or the *Open* command, to execute a program. In this example, the parameter /x has been added to the WPWIN.EXE command.

If the program file you are executing is located in the directory identified as the *Current Directory*, you do not need to type in the DOS path along with the file name.

## PRINT COMMAND

The *Print* command is selectable only when a directory list window is active and a file name is highlighted. This command allows you to print the contents of a file.

**Figure 34.** When the *Print* dialog box appears, the name of the highlighted file will already be displayed in the *Print* box. You can select another file by typing in its name, or accept the existing name by selecting *OK.*

## ASSOCIATE COMMAND

When you first run the File Manager, data files that have been created by any of the Windows accessory programs are automatically associated with the programs that created them. This association can be seen from the icons that represent these files. If you double-click, or *Open*, one of these files, the program that created the file will be executed and the file you selected will be opened within the application.

Using the *Associate* command, you can create this kind of relationship between other application programs and their data files. To use this command, you must first highlight one of the data files that you want to associate with a program file.

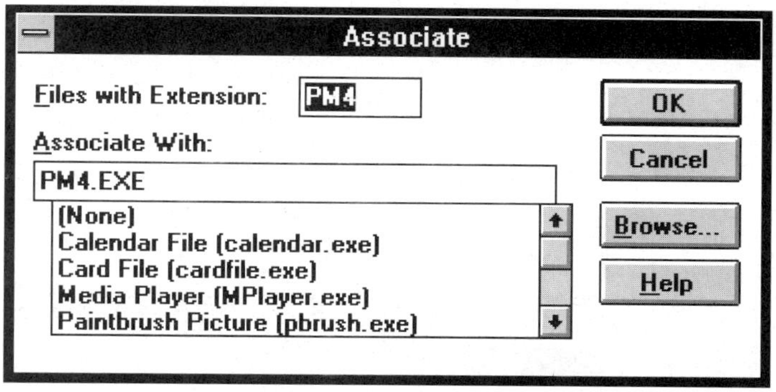


**Figure 35.** The *Associate* dialog box will appear when you select the *Associate* command from the **File** menu. From the list provided, select the name of the program file with which the data file is to be associated. If the program you require is not in the list, key its name and path directly into the *Associate With* text box.

All the data files with the same extension as the highlighted file will now be marked with the text-filled paper icon in the File Manager.

In this example, all files with the extension .PM4 are now associated with the program file PM4.EXE. Whenever you double-click or *Open* one of these files in the File Manager, the program file PM4.EXE (PageMaker Version 4.0) will be executed, and the selected file will be opened as a document in the program.

The extension list in the win.ini file will be updated so that .pm4 files will remain associated with PageMaker in the future.

## CREATE DIRECTORY COMMAND

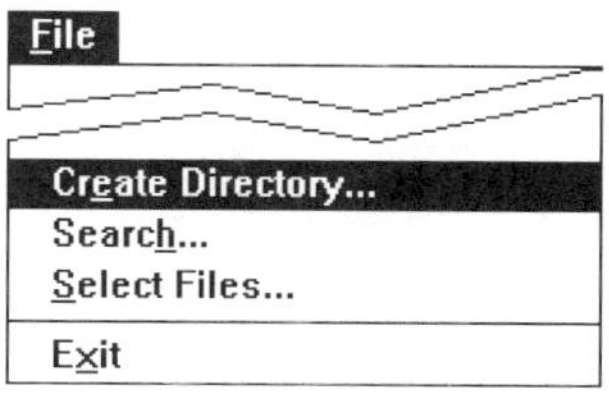


**Figure 36.** The *Create Directory* command creates a new subdirectory division within the subdirectory currently highlighted in the Directory Tree.

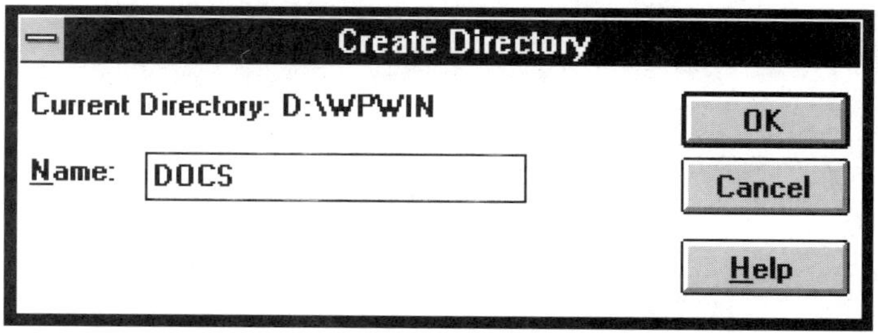


**Figure 37.** The *Create Directory* dialog box contains a *Name* text box in which you can type the name of the new subdirectory.

## SEARCH COMMAND

Sometimes you know the name of a file but cannot remember which subdirectory it is in. Rather than systematically searching through all your subdirectories, you can use the *Search* command to scan the selected disk for you.

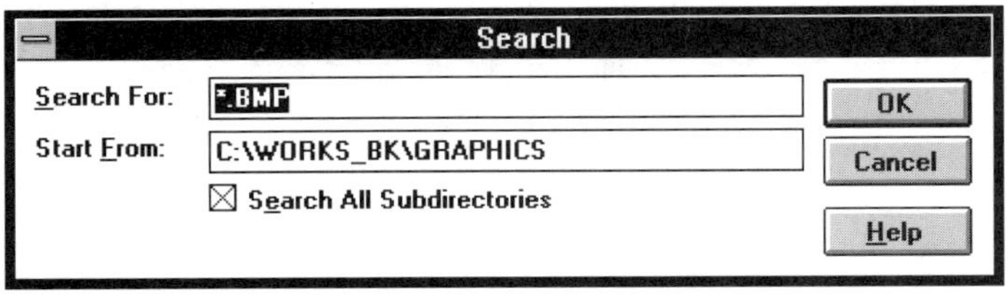


**Figure 38.** Type the name of the file that you are trying to find in the *Search For* dialog box, which appears when you select the *Search* command.

If you do not know the entire name of the file, you can type part of a name and use wild-card characters like the asterisk and question mark. The *Search* command will search for all files that match the name entered.

If you select the *Search All Subdirectories* option, the *Search* command will search all subdirectories on the selected disk. If this option is not selected, only the subdirectory highlighted in the Directory Tree, and any subdirectories below it, will be searched.

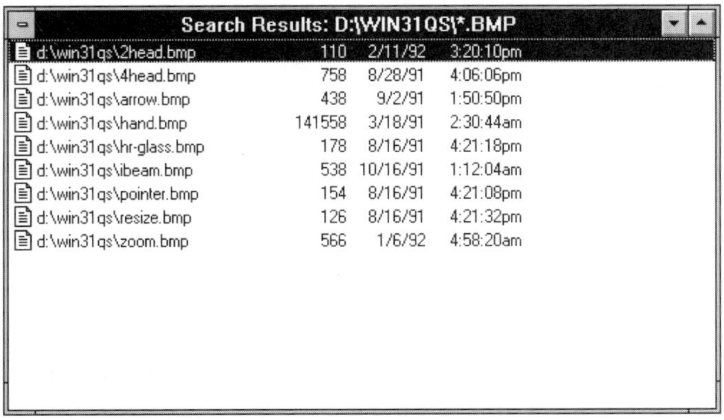


**Figure 39.** The *Search* command creates a new window, titled *Search Results*, listing all matching files and their path names. Double-clicking on these files has the same effect as it has in an ordinary directory list window.

## SELECT COMMAND

The *Select Files* command lets you highlight or "unhighlight" certain files in the active directory list window in a single command.

**Figure 40.** To select one file, key the name of that file into the *File(s)* text box and click on *Select*. Windows will mark the file, keeping the *Select Files* dialog box on the screen. You can then repeat the process using the name of another file you want to select. Click on *Close* to return to the File Manager, where Windows will select the marked files.

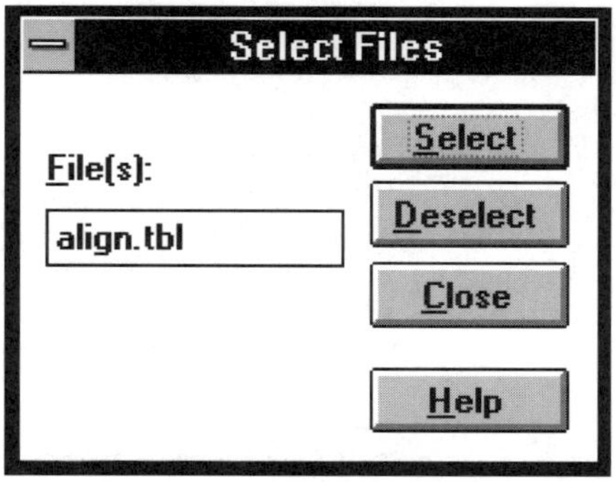


**Figure 41.** Wildcards can also be used to highlight specific files. When using wildcards, keep in mind that an asterisk (*) substitutes up to eight characters and a question mark (?) substitutes one character. For example, to highlight all files in a subdirectory, you would enter *.*.

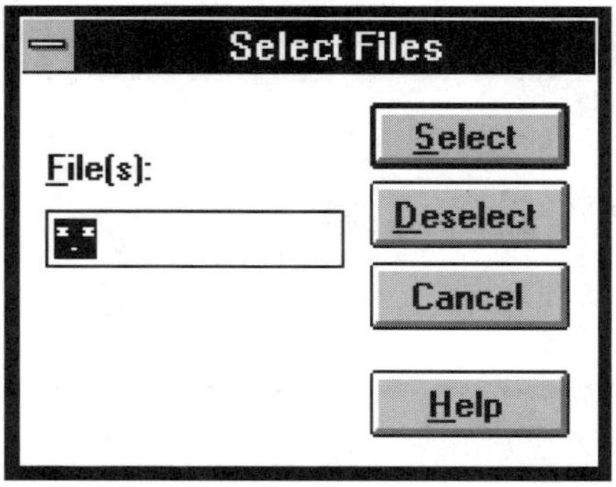


## EXIT COMMAND

**Figure 42.** The *Exit* command, in the **File** menu, terminates the running of the File Manager program and returns you to the Program Manager.

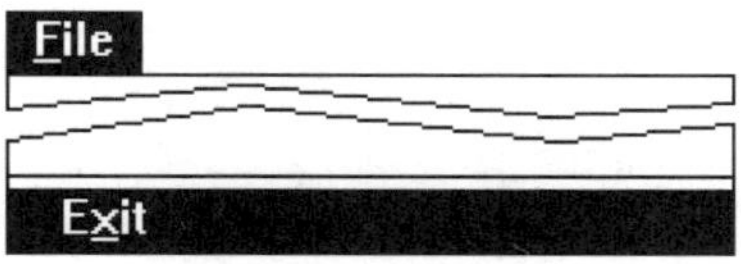

## DISK MENU

The **Disk** menu of the File Manager contains commands for dealing with the various disk drives that are part of your computer system.

### COPY DISK COMMAND

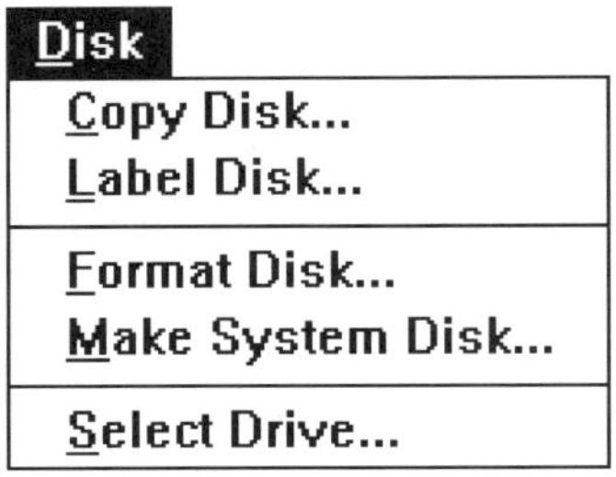


**Figure 43.** The *Copy Disk* command allows you to copy the entire contents of one floppy disk to another disk. Before selecting this command, you must highlight the directory tree icon of the floppy disk drive that contains the disk you want to copy.

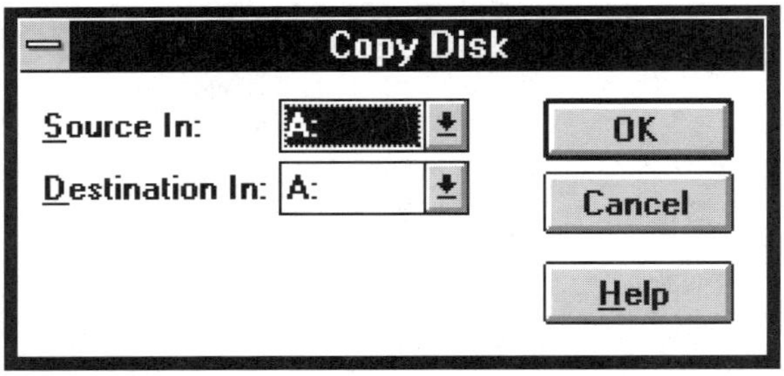


**Figure 44.** In the *Copy Disk* dialog box, enter the source and destination disk drives. If the destination disk drive is to be the same as the source drive, a dialog box will prompt you to change disks at the appropriate time.

### LABEL DISK COMMAND

The *Label Disk* command permits you to change the label, or name, that is part of every formatted disk's directory. In the File Manager, the selected disk's label is listed in the *Directory Tree* window below the disk drive icons.

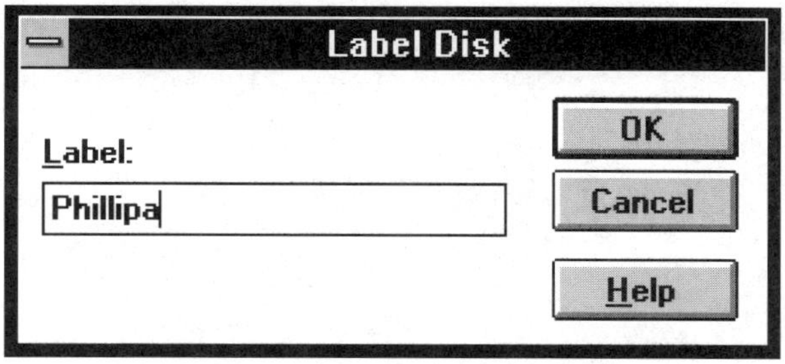


**Figure 45.** The *Label Disk* dialog box provides a text box in which you can type the new label for the selected disk. If the disk already has a label, the old label will be contained in this text box.

## FORMAT DISK COMMAND

The *Format Disk* command allows you to format a floppy disk without having to resort to the DOS FORMAT command.

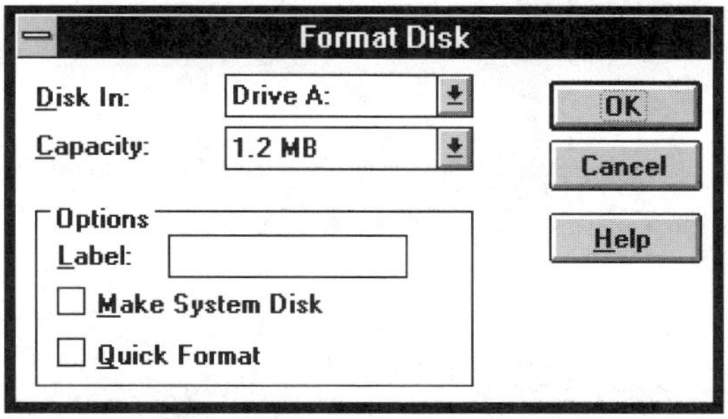


**Figure 46.** When you first select the *Format Disk* command, a dialog box will allow you to select the capacity at which the disk is to be formatted. Select the required capacity and enter a label for the formatted disk.

The *Quick Format* option formats a disk without checking it for bad sectors.

Any data, or other files, previously on the disk to be formatted will be lost during the format.

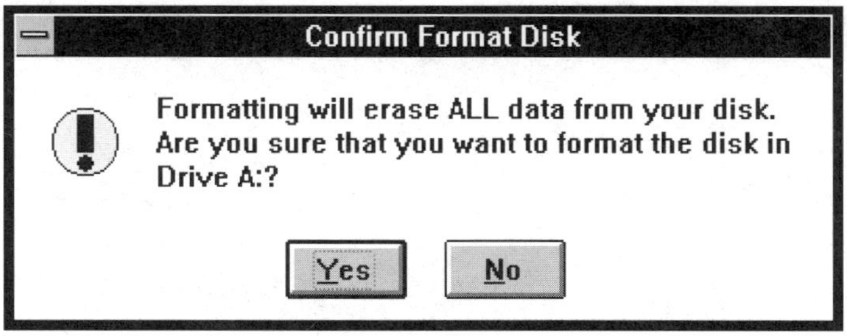


**Figure 47.** If you proceed with formatting, this second *Confirm Format Disk* dialog box will appear.

Windows uses this confirmation to ensure that the correct disk is in the disk drive before formatting begins.

If you select *Yes* the formatting procedure will begin, so be sure that the correct disk is inserted in the floppy drive.

### MAKE SYSTEM DISK COMMAND

The *Make System Disk* command copies the DOS system files onto a floppy disk. Disks that contain the DOS system files can be used as start-up disks on a DOS system.

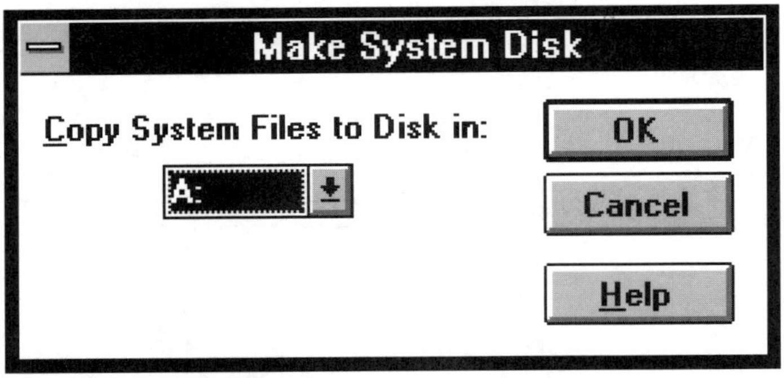


**Figure 48.** A warning dialog box will ensure that you intend to copy the files onto the selected disk. When you select *OK*, Windows copies the appropriate files.

### SELECT DISK COMMAND

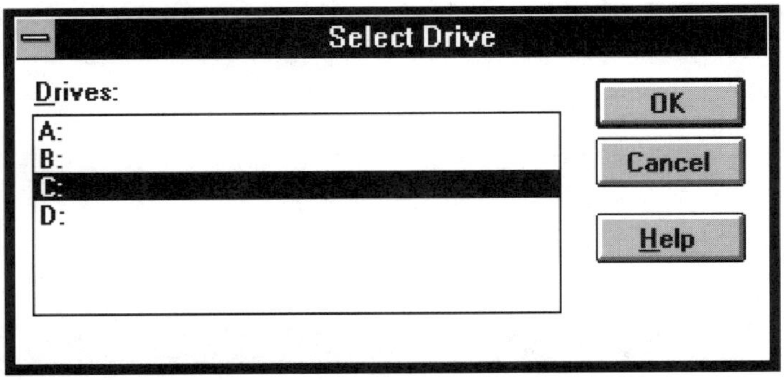


**Figure 49.** The *Select Drive* command is used as an alternative to clicking on the disk icons in the File Manager. Simply click on the disk you want to use and then on *OK*.

## TREE MENU

The **Tree** menu contains commands for modifying the display in the *Directory Tree* window.

### EXPAND ONE LEVEL COMMAND

**Figure 50.** The *Expand One Level* command displays the next level of subdirectories below the one that is currently highlighted. This command has the same effect as double-clicking on a file-folder icon that contains a + sign.

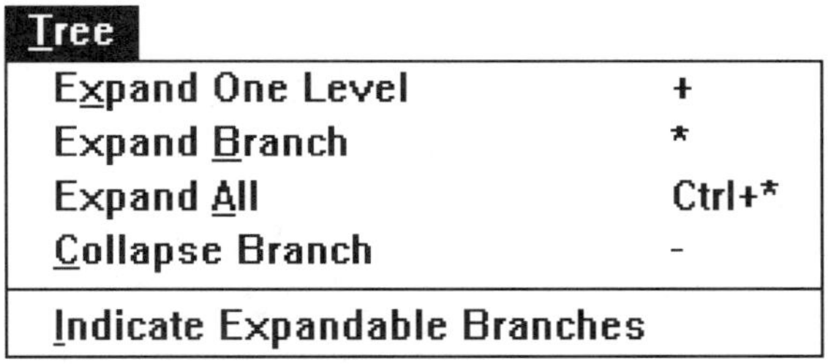


### EXPAND BRANCH COMMAND

**Figure 51.** The *Expand Branch* command causes all levels of subdirectories below the currently highlighted subdirectory to be displayed.

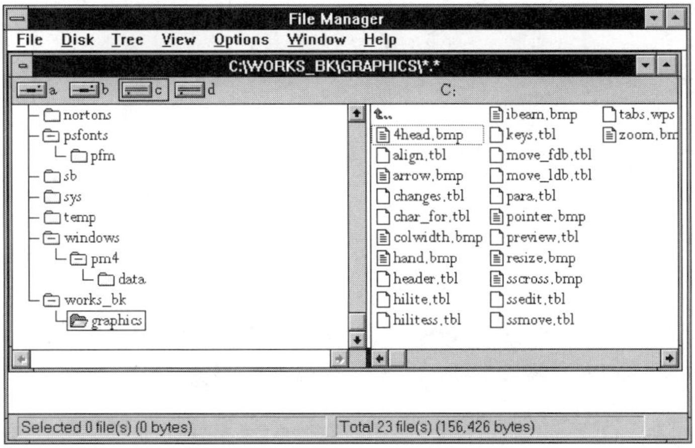


### EXPAND ALL COMMAND

The *Expand All* command expands all the subdirectories in the selected disk drive so that they are all displayed in the *Directory Tree* window.

### COLLAPSE BRANCH COMMAND

The *Collapse Branch* command collapses the highlighted branch of the Directory Tree so that its subdirectories are not displayed. This command is equivalent to double-clicking on a file-folder icon containing a - sign.

## VIEW MENU

**Figure 52.** The **View** menu contains commands that affect the way file information is displayed in directory list windows; the files themselves are unaffected by these commands.

### DIRECTORY WINDOW DISPLAYS

Using the first three options in the **View** menu, you can adjust the appearance of the active directory window.

The directory window usually appears as the example in Figure 53; a single window divided into two sections. By using the *Tree Only* and *Directory Only* options in the **View** menu, you can make the directory window display only one of these sections.

The line dividing the two sections of the directory window can be moved using the mouse. This feature allows you to adjust the relative sizes of the Directory Tree and directory list sections of the window.

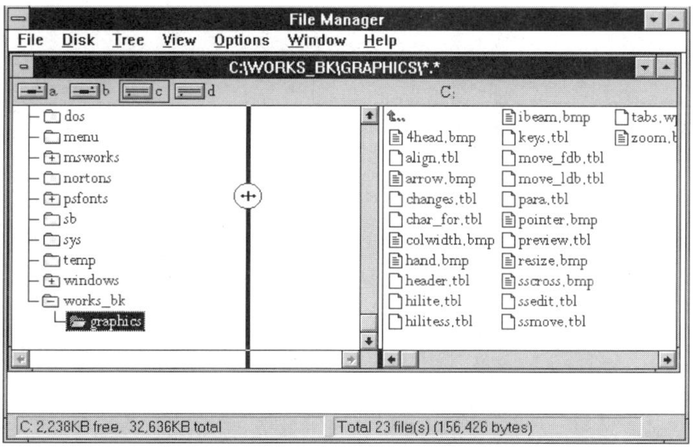


**Figure 53.** When the mouse pointer is over the dividing line, it takes the form of a double arrow icon, which can be dragged to the left or right to adjust the relative sizes of the window sections.

Selecting the *Split* command automatically places a dividing line on the screen. Move the mouse to the new location and click to set the new window sizes.

## FILE INFORMATION

The next three options in the **View** menu determine what information is displayed along with the names of the disk files. Only one of these three options can be selected at one time. The selected option is indicated by a check mark to its left.

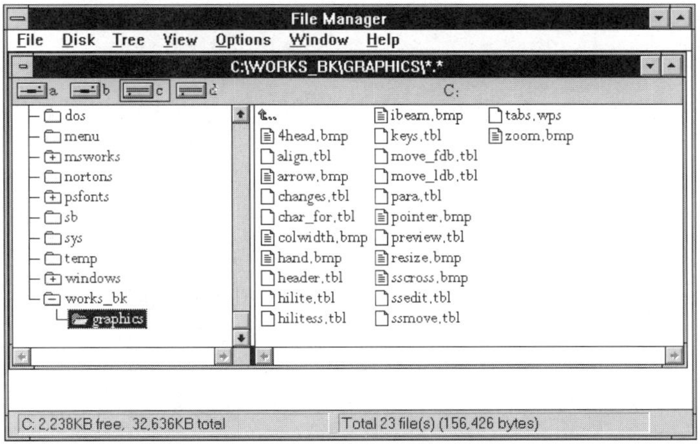


**Figure 54.** When the *Name* option is selected, only the name of the file is displayed alongside its icon in directory list windows. Using this option, the files can be listed in several columns. More files can be displayed in the same space than with the other display options.

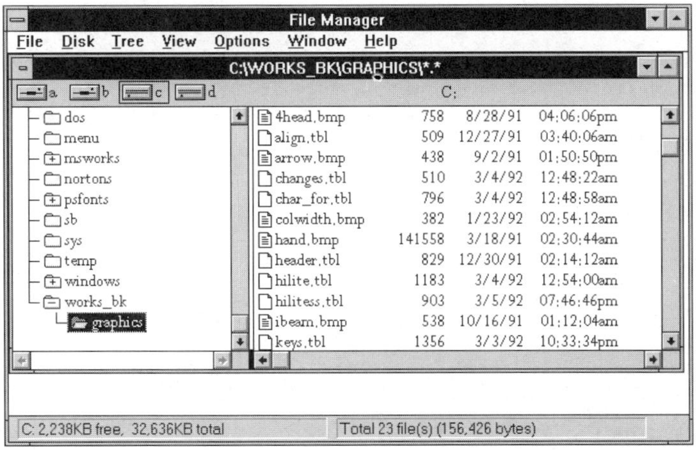


**Figure 55.** The *All File Details* selection causes the file names to be displayed, along with four additional pieces of information about the file. These are the date of the last modification, the time of the last modification, the size of the file in bytes, and the DOS file attributes.

Because of the extra information, only one column of files can be displayed.

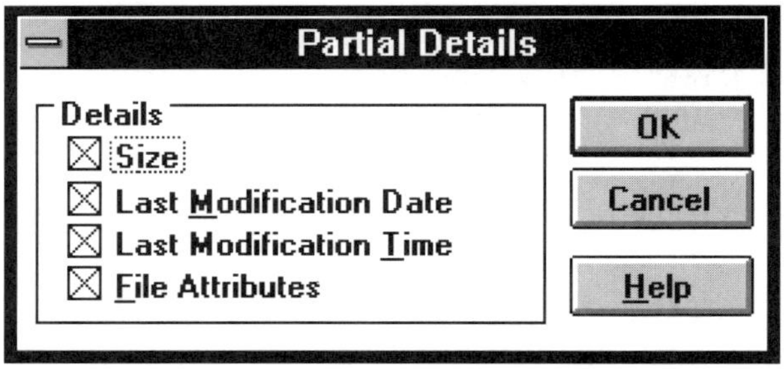


**Figure 56.** *The Partial Details* selection lets you decide which details are displayed.

## SORT ORDER

The next three **View** menu options let you set the order in which the files are displayed in their directory list windows. Again, only one of these three commands can be selected at a time; the selected option is marked with a check mark.

The *Sort by Name* option lists the files alphabetically in their directory list windows. This is the usual setting for this set of options. Most of the examples in this chapter were made with the *Sort by Name* option selected.

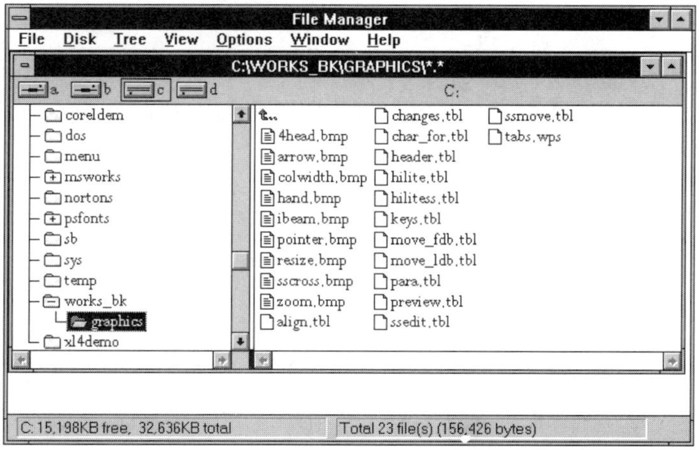


**Figure 57.** The *Sort by Type* option causes the files to be listed in the alphabetical order of their extensions so that all files of the same type appear together.

Within groups of files that have the same extension, the files are sorted alphabetically by name.

The *Sort by Size* and *Sort by Date* options order the files on the basis of their size and date, respectively.

### BY FILE TYPE COMMAND

The *By File Type* command permits you to determine which files will be displayed in the directory lists. Usually all files except hidden files are displayed. You can change this setting using the *By File Type* command.

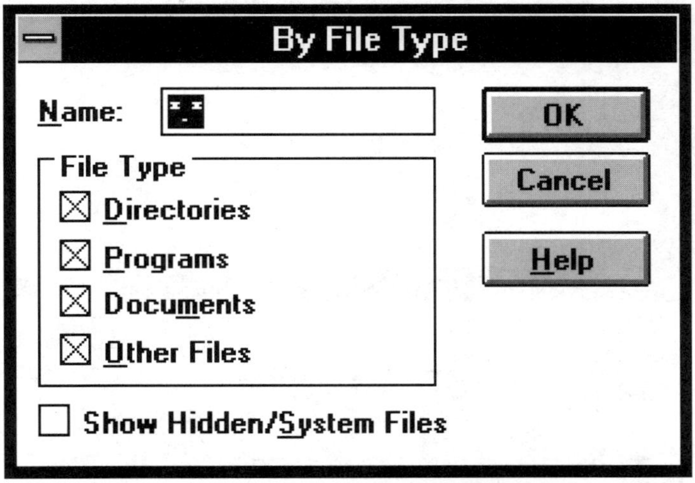


**Figure 58.** The *By File Type* dialog box contains a *Name* text box where you can type the name of the files you want displayed. You can use the asterisk and question mark wildcards to specify a range of files.

The *File Type* box contains a set of check boxes from which you can select the types of files to include in the listings.

## *OPTIONS MENU*

The **Options** menu contains some miscellaneous settings that affect various parts of the File Manager program.

### CONFIRMATION COMMAND

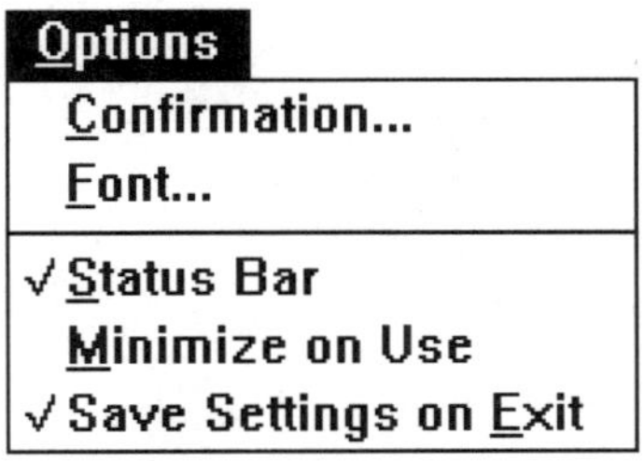


**Figure 59.** You will have noticed that many operations carried out in the File Manager, including copying, moving, and deleting files, are preceded by warning dialog boxes that confirm the procedure before it is performed. The *Confirmation* command lets you disable these warnings on some, or all, of these operations.

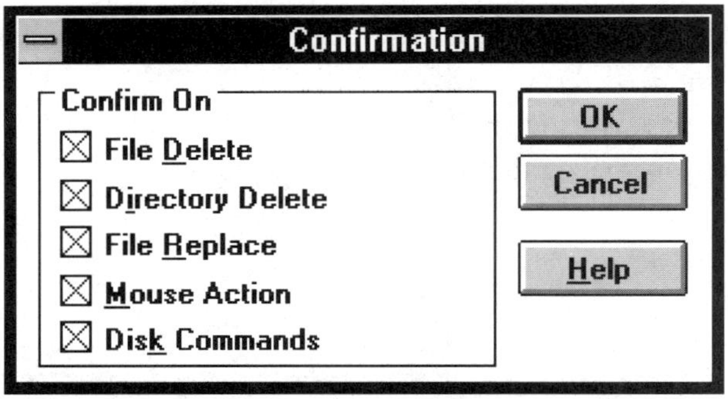


**Figure 60.** The *Confirmation* dialog box provides a set of check boxes listing the various procedures that can require confirmation. Select those operations where you want to receive a warning and deselect those procedures where confirmation is unnecessary.

## FONT COMMAND

The information displayed in the File Manager can be represented using any of the fonts available to the Windows program.

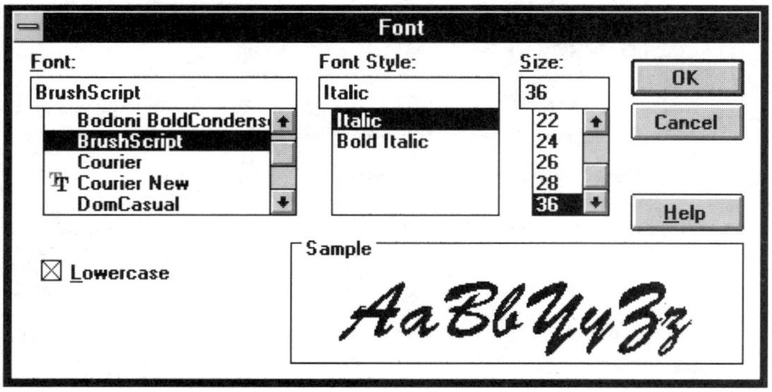


**Figure 61.** The *Font* command invokes the *Font* dialog box, which allows you to select the font style and size of the information displayed in the File Manager.

The *Lowercase* option, if selected, will display all subdirectory and file names in lowercase. You may find this format easier to read than uppercase text.

## MISCELLANEOUS OPTIONS

The remaining three selections in the **Options** menu are indicated with a check mark if they have been selected.

The status bar is located at the bottom of the File Manager window. It displays information about the currently selected items. If you deselect the *Status Bar* option in the **Options** menu, the status bar will not be displayed.

If the *Minimize on Use* command in the **Options** menu is selected, the File Manager will automatically be minimized to an icon if a program file is executed.

If the *Save Settings on Exit* command is selected, changes made in the File Manager will be retained for the next time File Manager is opened. If it is not selected, the File Manager will revert back to the original display before these changes were made.

## WINDOW MENU

**Figure 62.** The commands in the **Window** menu are designed to help you navigate through and manipulate the various windows that can be open in the File Manager.

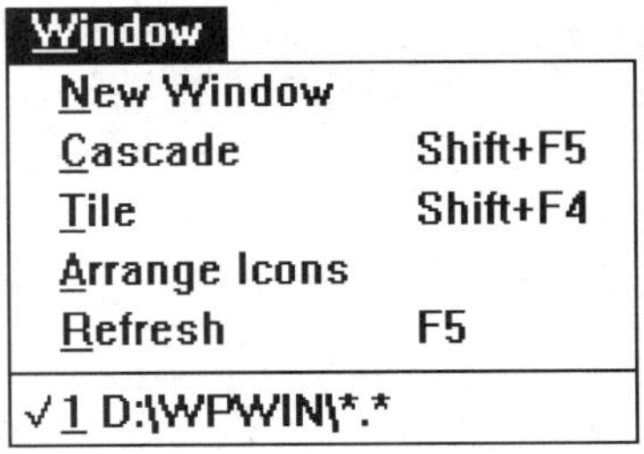


### NEW WINDOW COMMAND

**Figure 63.** Many directory windows can be open at once in the File Manager. The *New Window* command activates a new directory window in the foreground of the File Manager window.

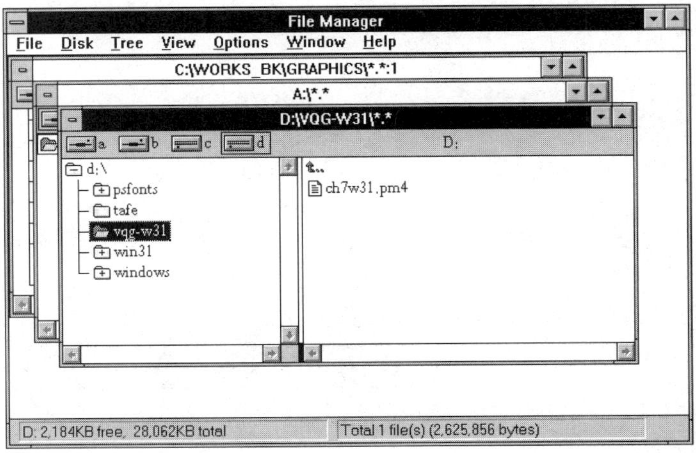

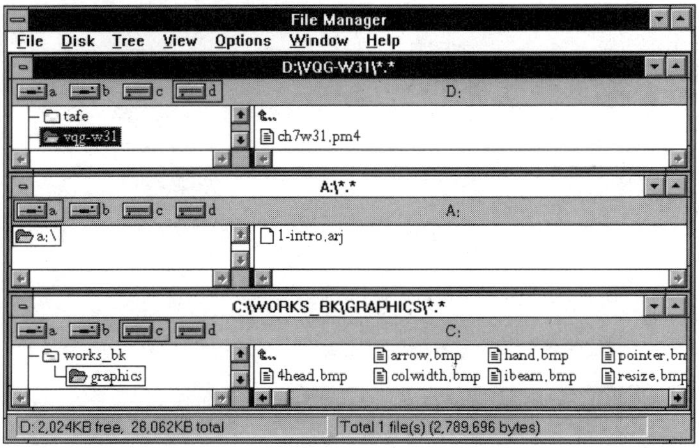


## CASCADE AND TILE COMMANDS

**Figure 64.** The *Cascade* and *Tile* commands let you arrange the open windows in the File Manager. You can arrange the windows in either an overlapping (*Cascade*) or a side-by-side (*Tile*) pattern (shown).

## REFRESH COMMAND

The *Refresh* command instructs the File Manager to read the current disk and rewrite the windows that are displayed on the screen.

Use this command to update the File Manager display if you have changed the floppy disk in one of your drives or if another application has changed the contents of one of your disks.

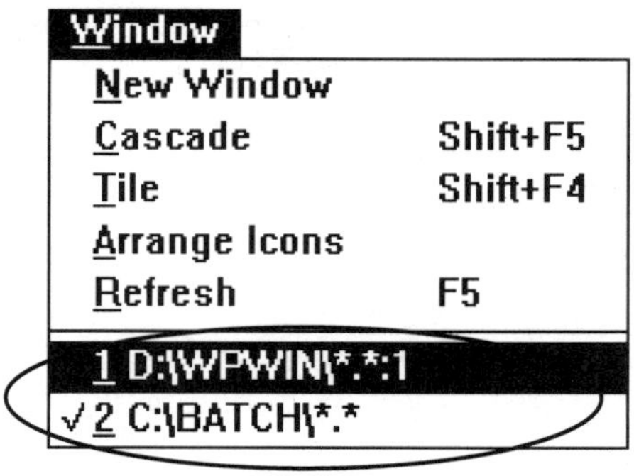


## SELECTING THE ACTIVE WINDOW

**Figure 65.** The bottom portion of the **Window** menu lists all the windows that are currently open in the File Manager. The active window is indicated with a check mark.

To make one of the other windows the active window, click on that window's name in this list. The selected window will come to the foreground in the File Manager window, while its name in the **Window** menu will be marked.

## HELP MENU

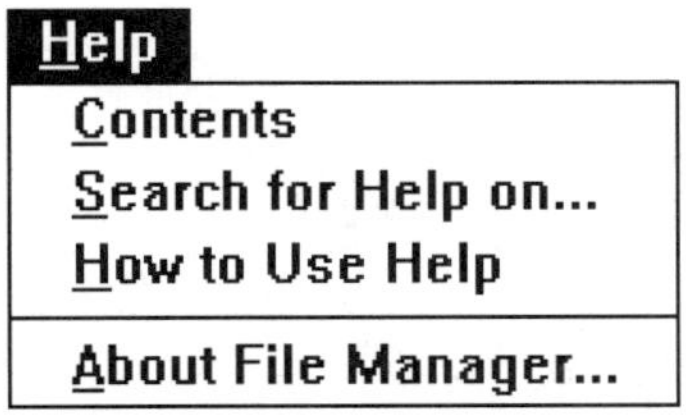


**Figure 66.** The File Manager also has a **Help** menu from which you can obtain Help information about the various File Manager functions. See the discussion of the Program Manager's Help facility (in Chapter 3) for an outline of the Help facility's operation.

# APPENDIX A. DIALOG BOXES

A

## PROGRAM MANAGER

### FILE MENU

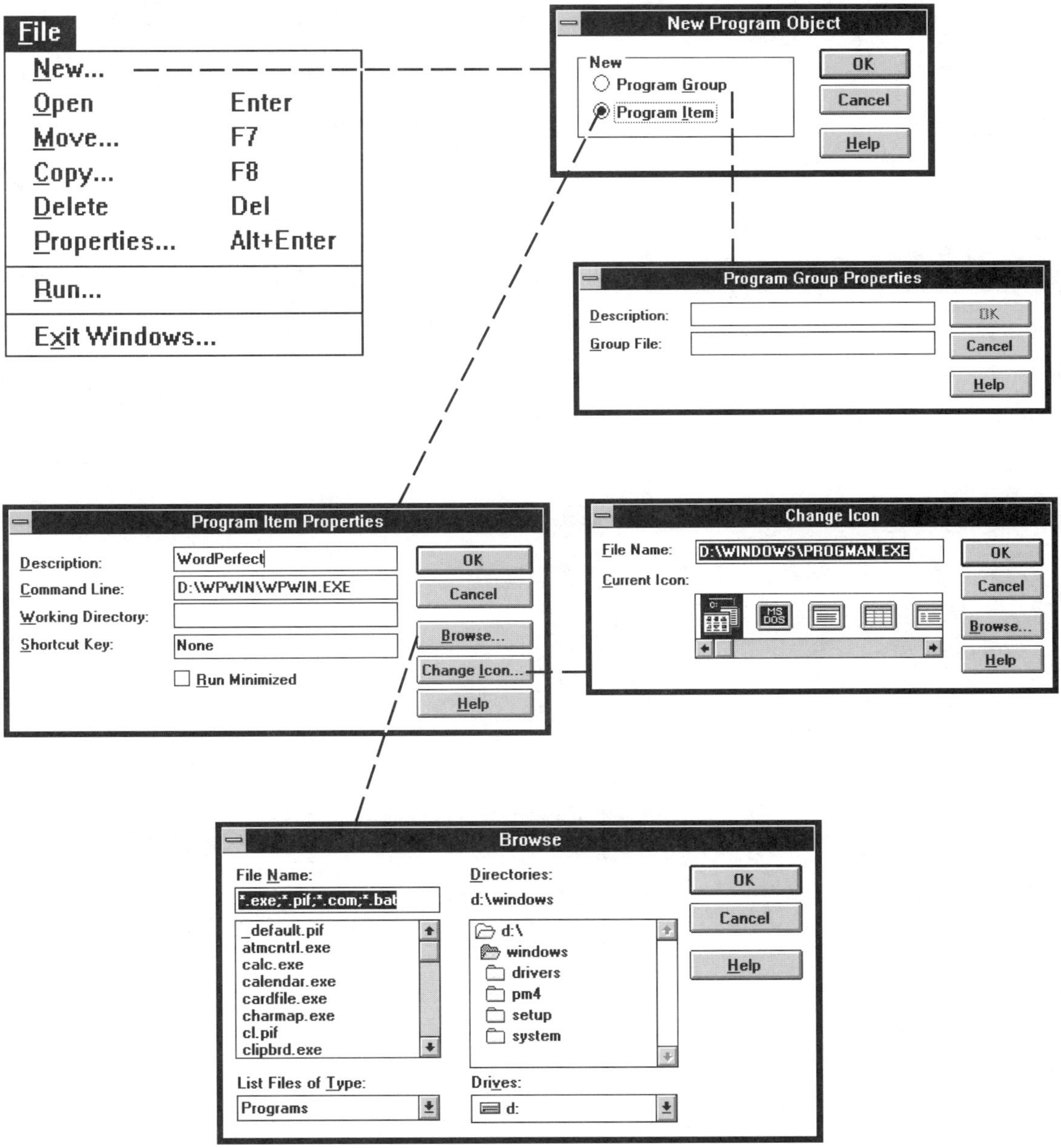

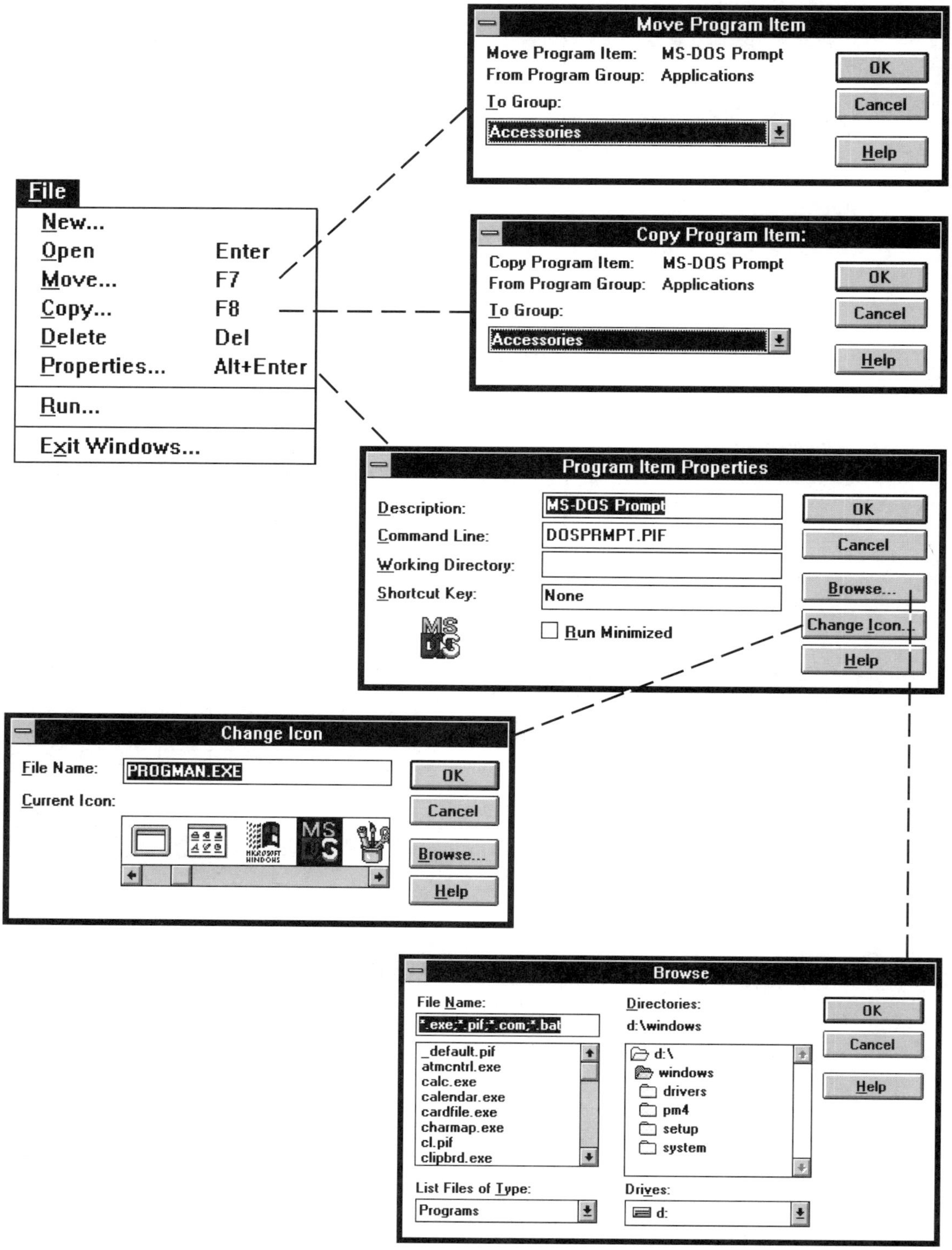
Move Program Item
Move Program Item: MS-DOS Prompt
From Program Group: Applications
To Group:
Accessories
OK
Cancel
Help
File
New...
Open Enter
Move... F7
Copy... F8
Delete Del
Properties... Alt+Enter
Run...
Exit Windows...
Copy Program Item:
Copy Program Item: MS-DOS Prompt
From Program Group: Applications
To Group:
Accessories
OK
Cancel
Help
Program Item Properties
Description: MS-DOS Prompt
Command Line: DOSPRMPT.PIF
Working Directory:
Shortcut Key: None
Run Minimized
OK
Cancel
Browse...
Change Icon...
Help
Change Icon
File Name: PROGMAN.EXE
Current Icon:
OK
Cancel
Browse...
Help
Browse
File Name:
*.exe;*.pif;*.com;*.bat
_default.pif
atmcntrl.exe
calc.exe
calendar.exe
cardfile.exe
charmap.exe
cl.pif
clipbrd.exe
Directories:
d:\windows
d:\
windows
drivers
pm4
setup
system
OK
Cancel
Help
List Files of Type:
Programs
Drives:
d:

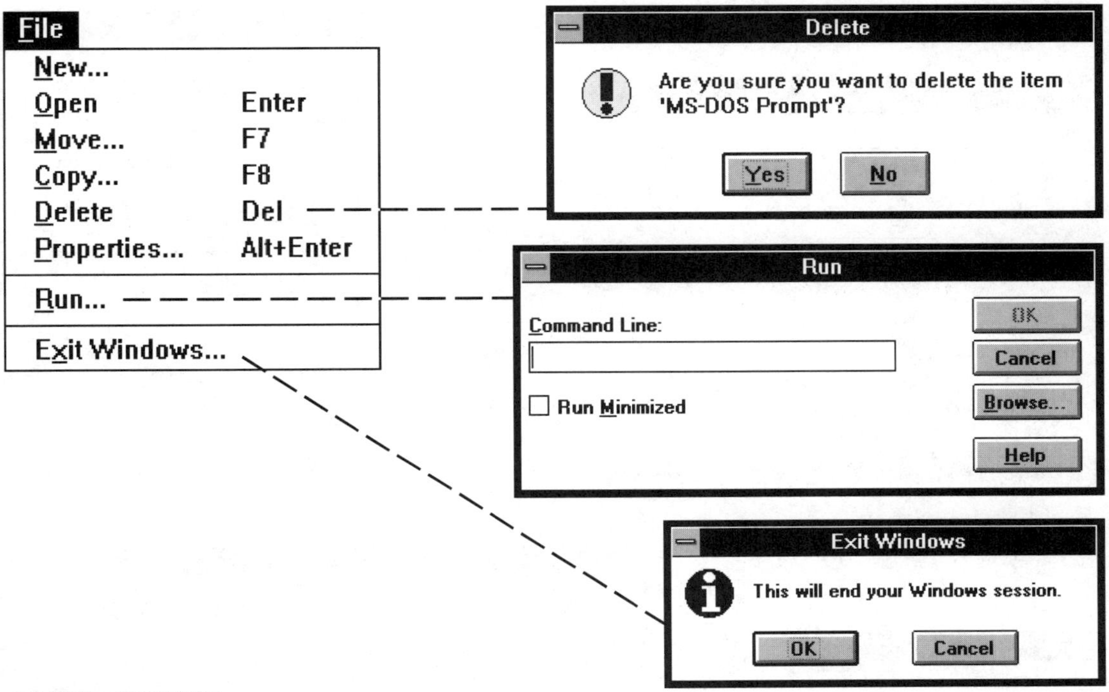
File
New...
Open Enter
Move... F7
Copy... F8
Delete Del
Properties... Alt+Enter
Run...
Exit Windows...
Delete
Are you sure you want to delete the item 'MS-DOS Prompt'?
Yes
No
Run
Command Line:
Run Minimized
OK
Cancel
Browse...
Help
Exit Windows
This will end your Windows session.
OK
Cancel

## OTHER MENUS

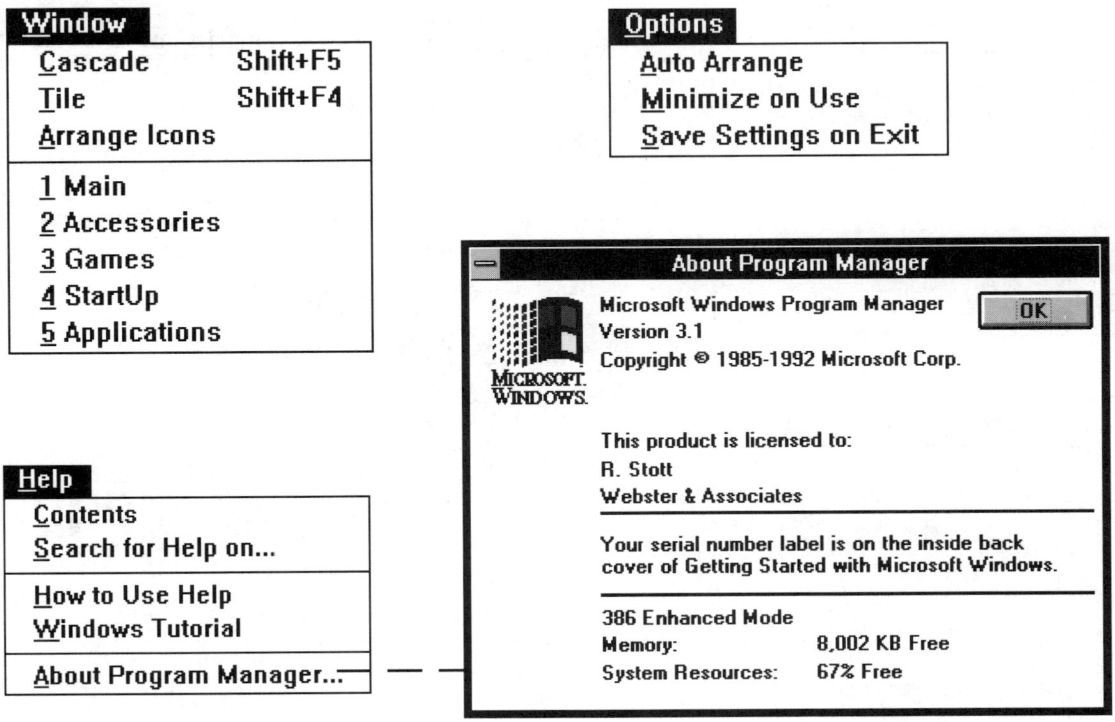
Window
Cascade Shift+F5
Tile Shift+F4
Arrange Icons
1 Main
2 Accessories
3 Games
4 StartUp
5 Applications
Options
Auto Arrange
Minimize on Use
Save Settings on Exit
Help
Contents
Search for Help on...
How to Use Help
Windows Tutorial
About Program Manager...
About Program Manager
Microsoft Windows Program Manager
Version 3.1
Copyright © 1985-1992 Microsoft Corp.
OK
MICROSOFT. WINDOWS.
This product is licensed to:
R. Stott
Webster & Associates
Your serial number label is on the inside back cover of Getting Started with Microsoft Windows.
386 Enhanced Mode
Memory: 8,002 KB Free
System Resources: 67% Free

# Control Panel

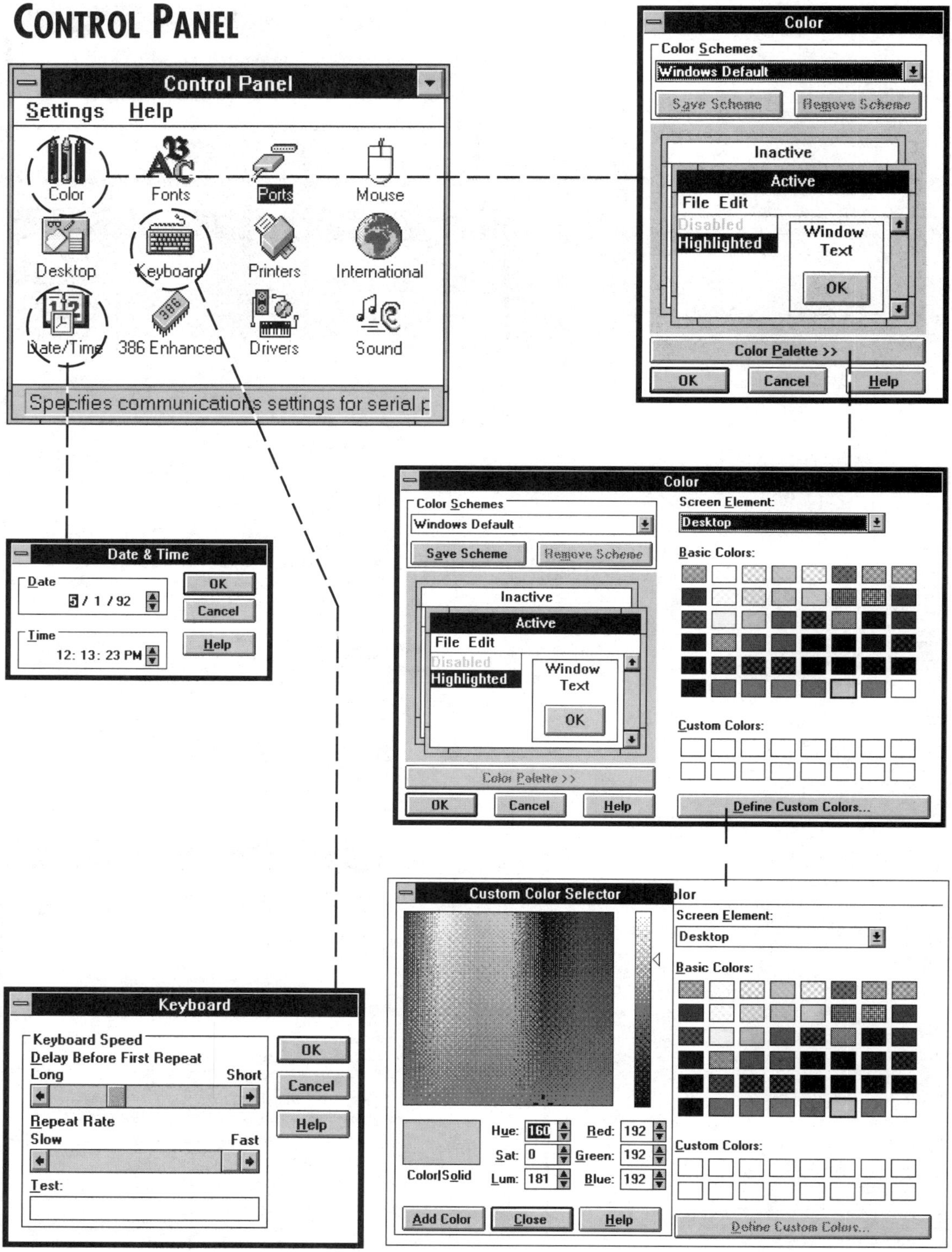

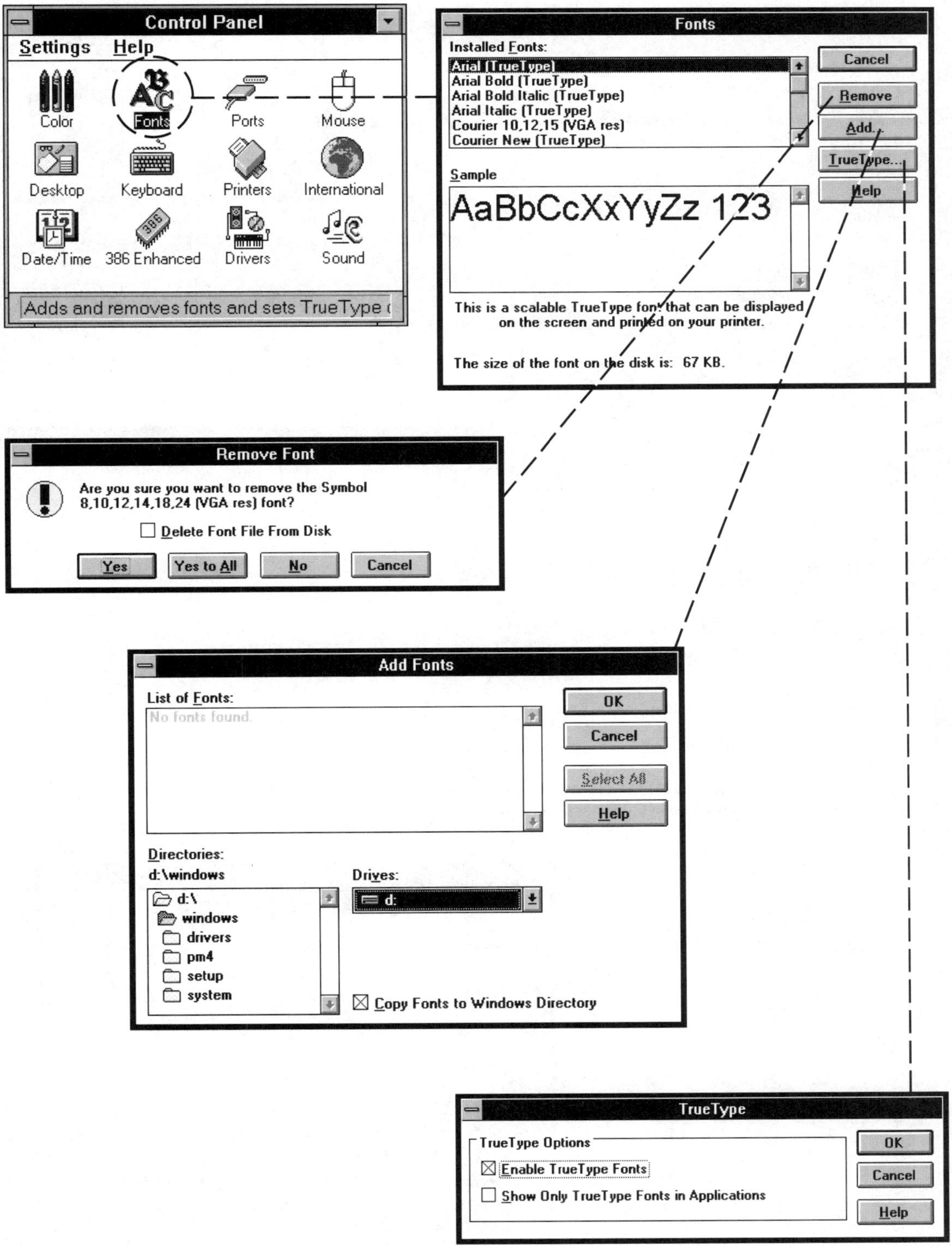
Control Panel
Settings Help
Color
Fonts
Ports
Mouse
Desktop
Keyboard
Printers
International
Date/Time
386 Enhanced
Drivers
Sound
Adds and removes fonts and sets TrueType
Fonts
Installed Fonts:
Arial (TrueType)
Arial Bold (TrueType)
Arial Bold Italic (TrueType)
Arial Italic (TrueType)
Courier 10,12,15 (VGA res)
Courier New (TrueType)
Cancel
Remove
Add...
TrueType...
Help
Sample
AaBbCcXxYyZz 123
This is a scalable TrueType font that can be displayed on the screen and printed on your printer.
The size of the font on the disk is: 67 KB.
Remove Font
Are you sure you want to remove the Symbol 8,10,12,14,18,24 (VGA res) font?
Delete Font File From Disk
Yes
Yes to All
No
Cancel
Add Fonts
List of Fonts:
No fonts found.
OK
Cancel
Select All
Help
Directories:
d:\windows
d:\
windows
drivers
pm4
setup
system
Drives:
d:
Copy Fonts to Windows Directory
TrueType
TrueType Options
Enable TrueType Fonts
Show Only TrueType Fonts in Applications
OK
Cancel
Help

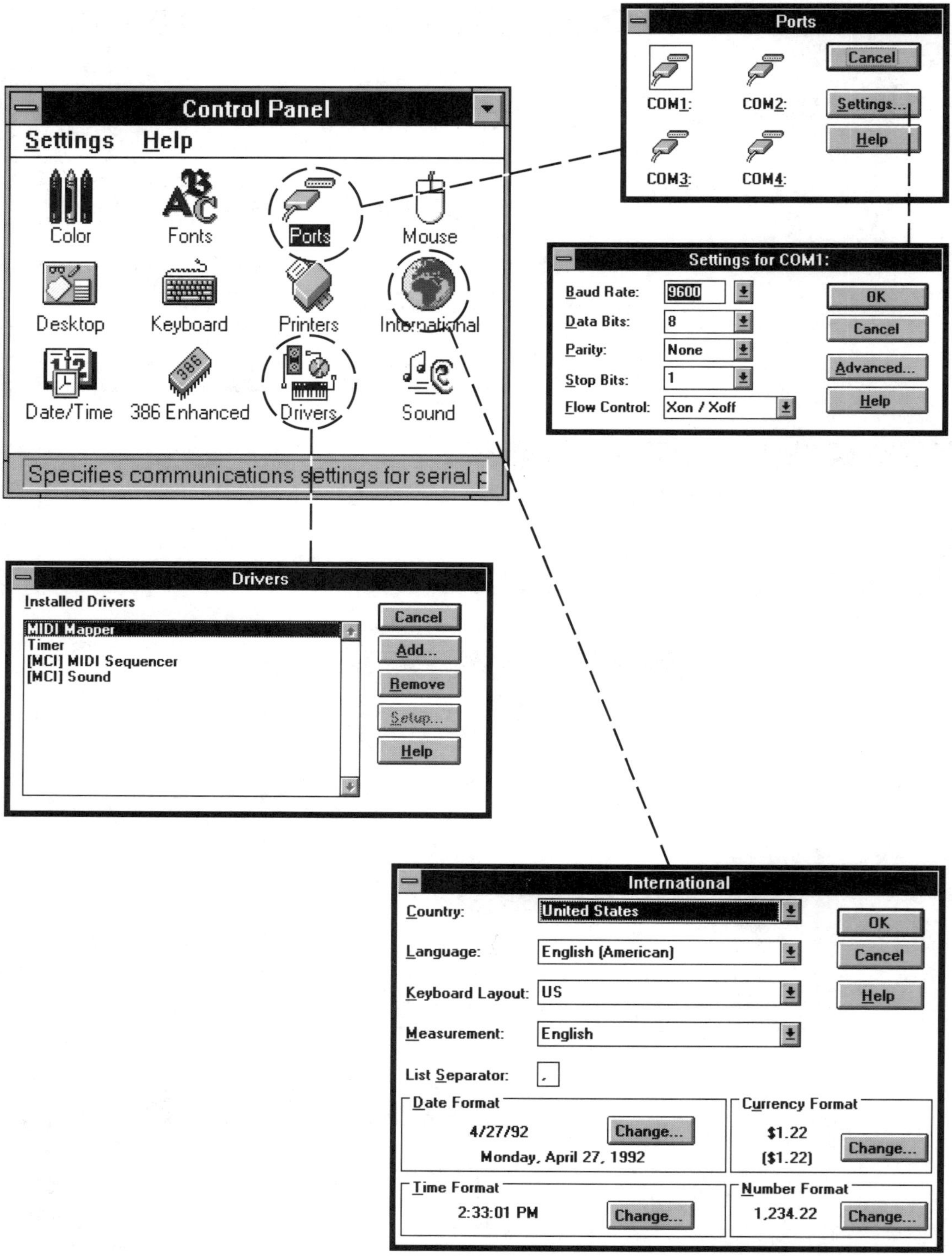
Control Panel
Settings Help
Color
Fonts
Ports
Mouse
Desktop
Keyboard
Printers
International
Date/Time
386 Enhanced
Drivers
Sound
Specifies communications settings for serial p
Ports
COM1:
COM2:
COM3:
COM4:
Cancel
Settings...
Help
Settings for COM1:
Baud Rate: 9600
Data Bits: 8
Parity: None
Stop Bits: 1
Flow Control: Xon / Xoff
OK
Cancel
Advanced...
Help
Drivers
Installed Drivers
MIDI Mapper
Timer
[MCI] MIDI Sequencer
[MCI] Sound
Cancel
Add...
Remove
Setup...
Help
International
Country: United States
Language: English (American)
Keyboard Layout: US
Measurement: English
List Separator: ,
OK
Cancel
Help
Date Format
4/27/92
Monday, April 27, 1992
Change...
Currency Format
$1.22
($1.22)
Change...
Time Format
2:33:01 PM
Change...
Number Format
1,234.22
Change...

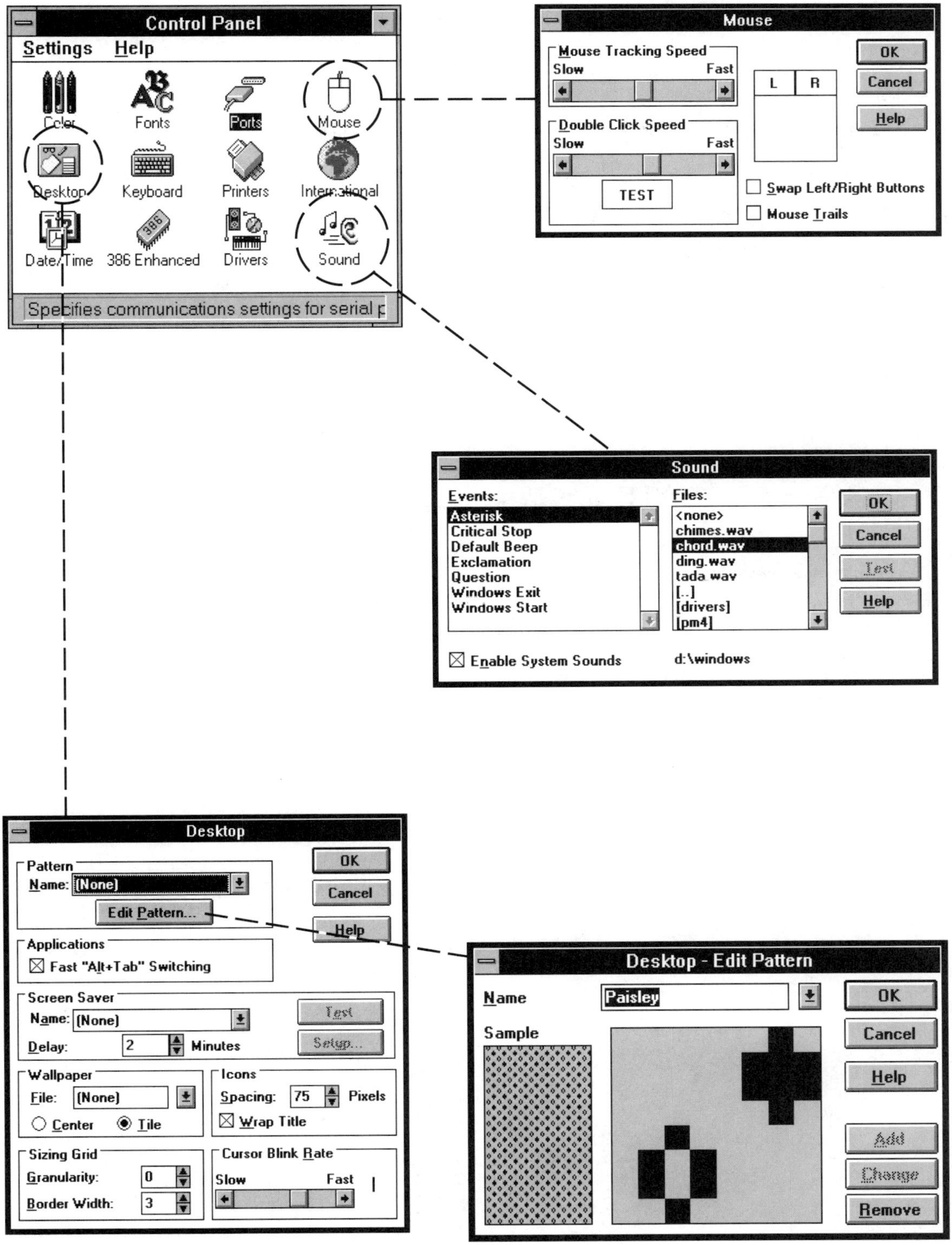
Control Panel
Settings
Help
Color
Fonts
Ports
Mouse
Desktop
Keyboard
Printers
International
Date/Time
386 Enhanced
Drivers
Sound
Specifies communications settings for serial p
Mouse
Mouse Tracking Speed
Slow
Fast
Double Click Speed
Slow
Fast
TEST
L
R
OK
Cancel
Help
Swap Left/Right Buttons
Mouse Trails
Sound
Events:
Asterisk
Critical Stop
Default Beep
Exclamation
Question
Windows Exit
Windows Start
Files:
<none>
chimes.wav
chord.wav
ding.wav
tada.wav
[..]
[drivers]
[pm4]
OK
Cancel
Test
Help
Enable System Sounds
d:\windows
Desktop
Pattern
Name: (None)
Edit Pattern...
OK
Cancel
Help
Applications
Fast "Alt+Tab" Switching
Screen Saver
Name: (None)
Delay: 2 Minutes
Test
Setup...
Wallpaper
File: (None)
Center
Tile
Icons
Spacing: 75 Pixels
Wrap Title
Sizing Grid
Granularity: 0
Border Width: 3
Cursor Blink Rate
Slow
Fast
Desktop - Edit Pattern
Name
Paisley
Sample
OK
Cancel
Help
Add
Change
Remove

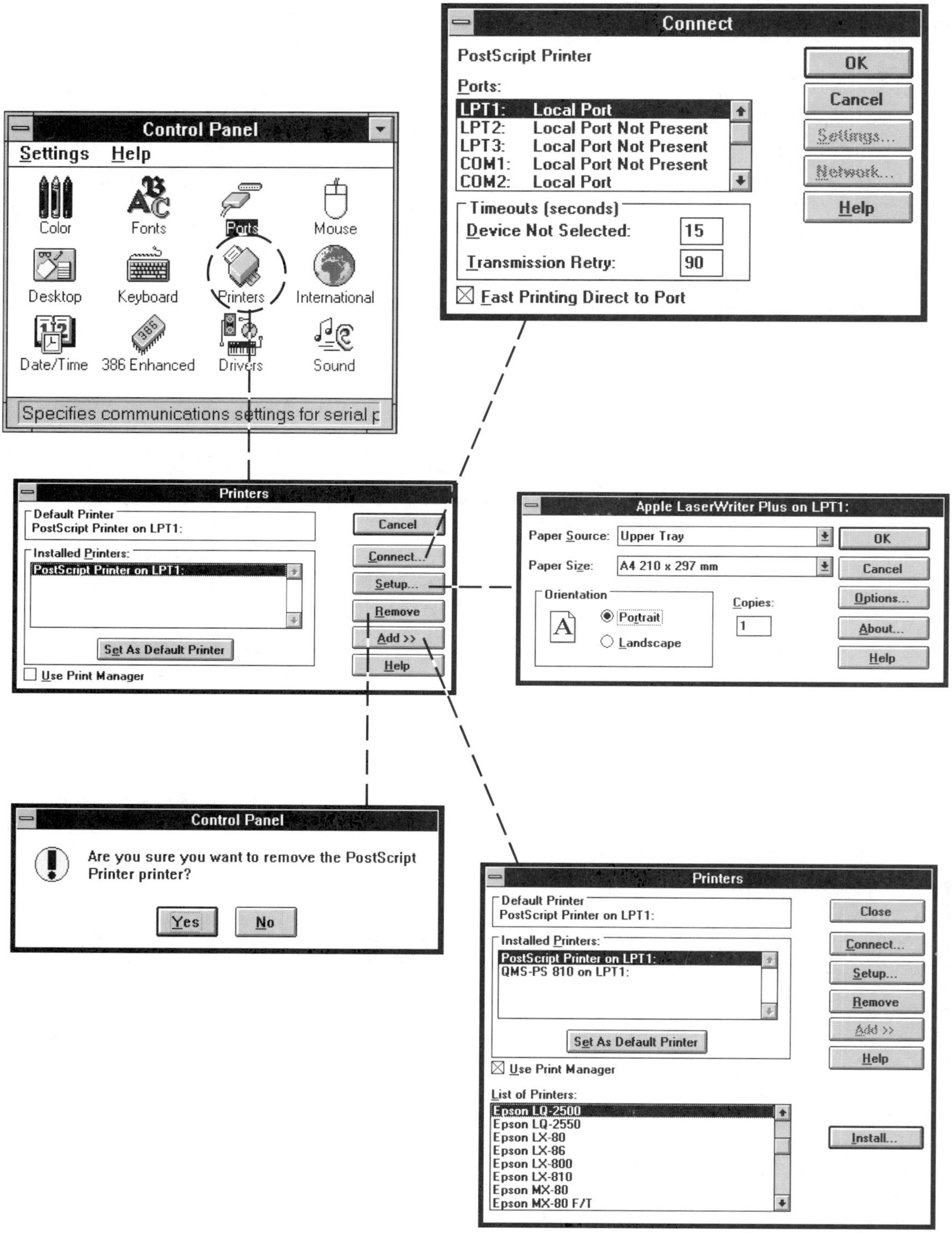
Connect
PostScript Printer
Ports:
LPT1: Local Port
LPT2: Local Port Not Present
LPT3: Local Port Not Present
COM1: Local Port Not Present
COM2: Local Port
Timeouts (seconds)
Device Not Selected: 15
Transmission Retry: 90
Fast Printing Direct to Port
OK
Cancel
Settings...
Network...
Help
Control Panel
Settings Help
Color
Fonts
Ports
Mouse
Desktop
Keyboard
Printers
International
Date/Time
386 Enhanced
Drivers
Sound
Specifies communications settings for serial p
Printers
Default Printer
PostScript Printer on LPT1:
Installed Printers:
PostScript Printer on LPT1:
Set As Default Printer
Use Print Manager
Cancel
Connect...
Setup...
Remove
Add >>
Help
Apple LaserWriter Plus on LPT1:
Paper Source: Upper Tray
Paper Size: A4 210 x 297 mm
Orientation
Portrait
Landscape
Copies:
1
OK
Cancel
Options...
About...
Help
Control Panel
Are you sure you want to remove the PostScript Printer printer?
Yes
No
Printers
Default Printer
PostScript Printer on LPT1:
Installed Printers:
PostScript Printer on LPT1:
QMS-PS 810 on LPT1:
Set As Default Printer
Use Print Manager
List of Printers:
Epson LQ-2500
Epson LQ-2550
Epson LX-80
Epson LX-86
Epson LX-800
Epson LX-810
Epson MX-80
Epson MX-80 F/T
Close
Connect...
Setup...
Remove
Add >>
Help
Install...

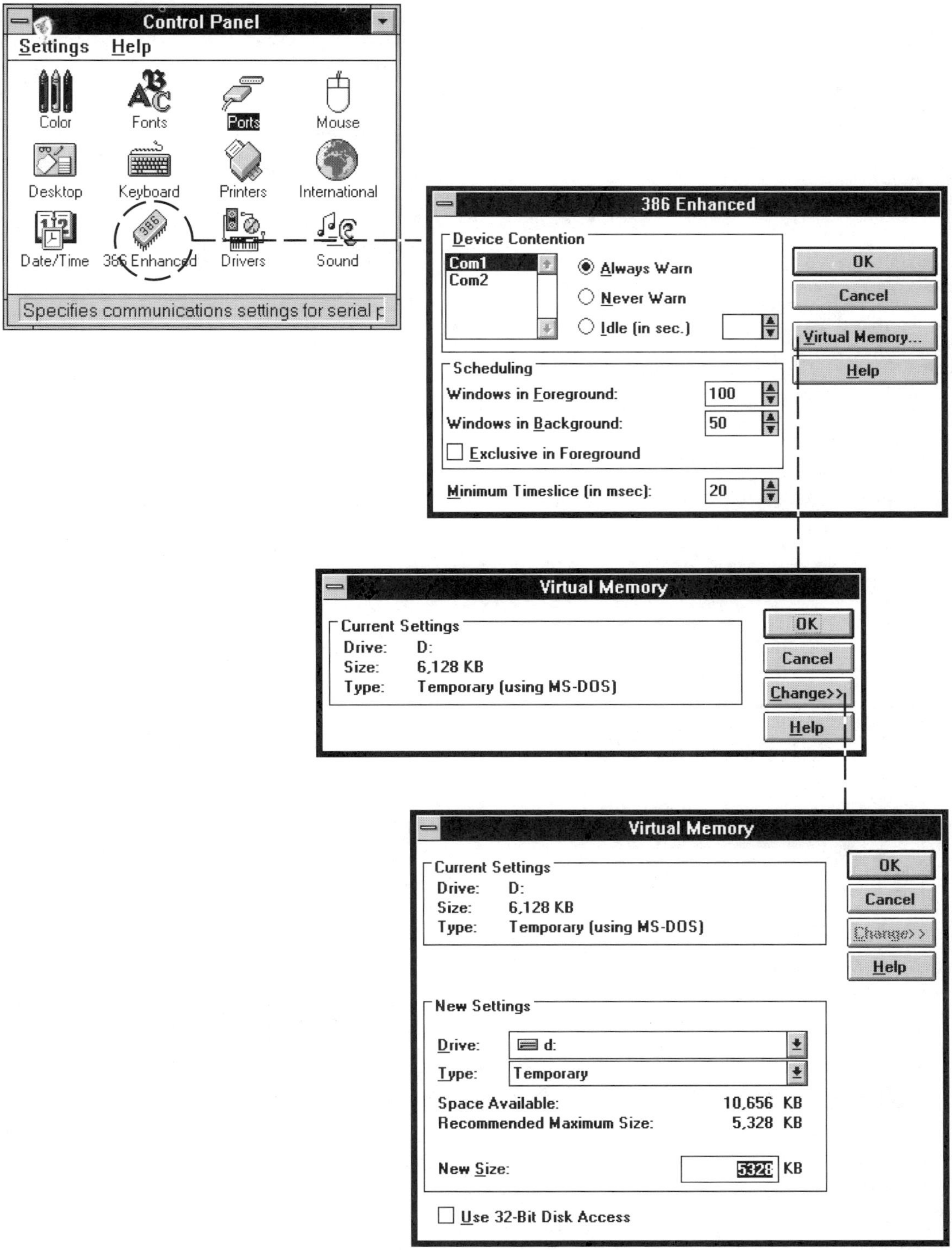
Control Panel
Settings Help
Color
Fonts
Ports
Mouse
Desktop
Keyboard
Printers
International
Date/Time
386 Enhanced
Drivers
Sound
Specifies communications settings for serial p
386 Enhanced
Device Contention
Com1
Com2
Always Warn
Never Warn
Idle (in sec.)
OK
Cancel
Virtual Memory...
Help
Scheduling
Windows in Foreground: 100
Windows in Background: 50
Exclusive in Foreground
Minimum Timeslice (in msec): 20
Virtual Memory
Current Settings
Drive: D:
Size: 6,128 KB
Type: Temporary (using MS-DOS)
OK
Cancel
Change>>
Help
Virtual Memory
Current Settings
Drive: D:
Size: 6,128 KB
Type: Temporary (using MS-DOS)
OK
Cancel
Change>>
Help
New Settings
Drive: d:
Type: Temporary
Space Available: 10,656 KB
Recommended Maximum Size: 5,328 KB
New Size: 5328 KB
Use 32-Bit Disk Access

# FILE MANAGER

## *FILE MENU*

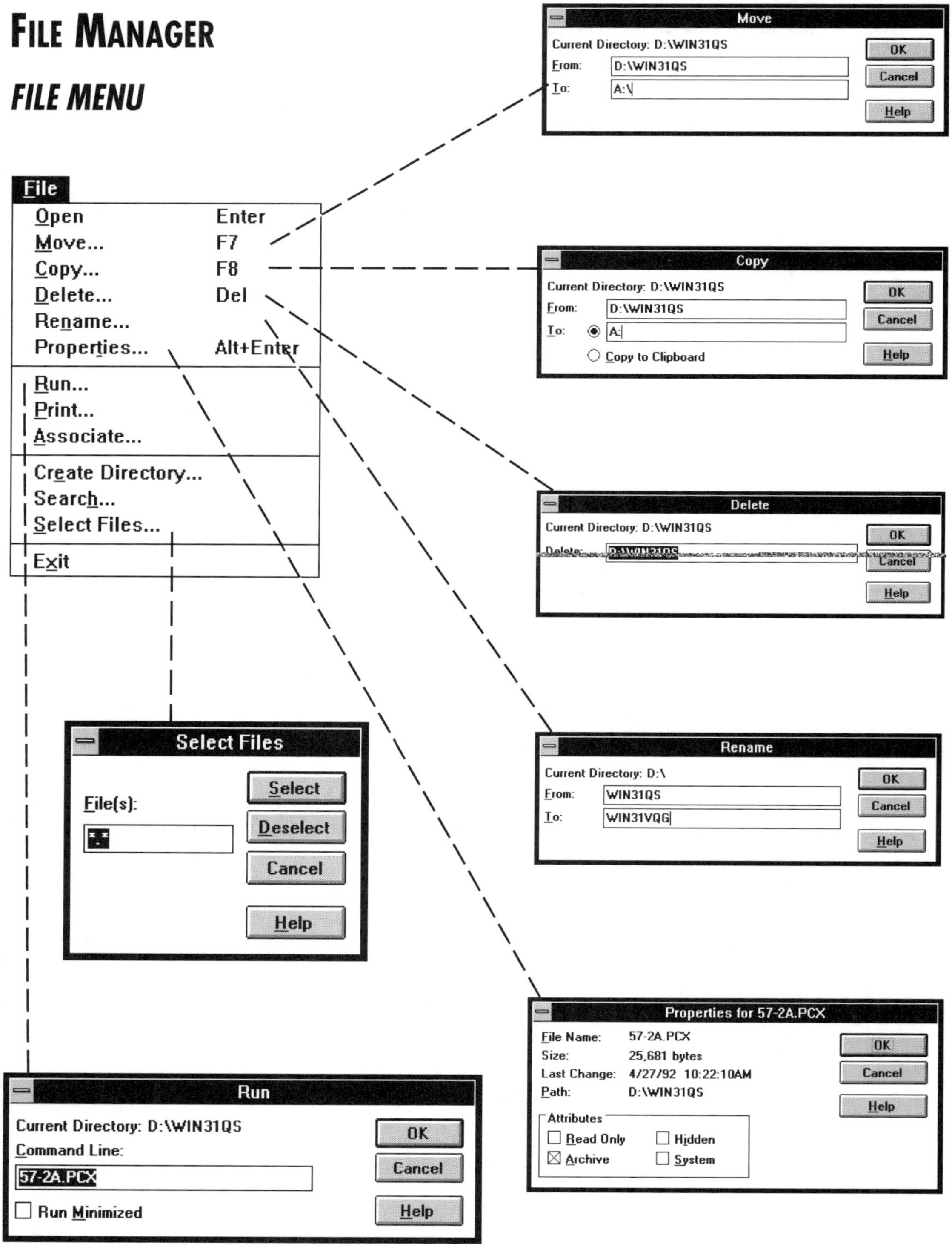

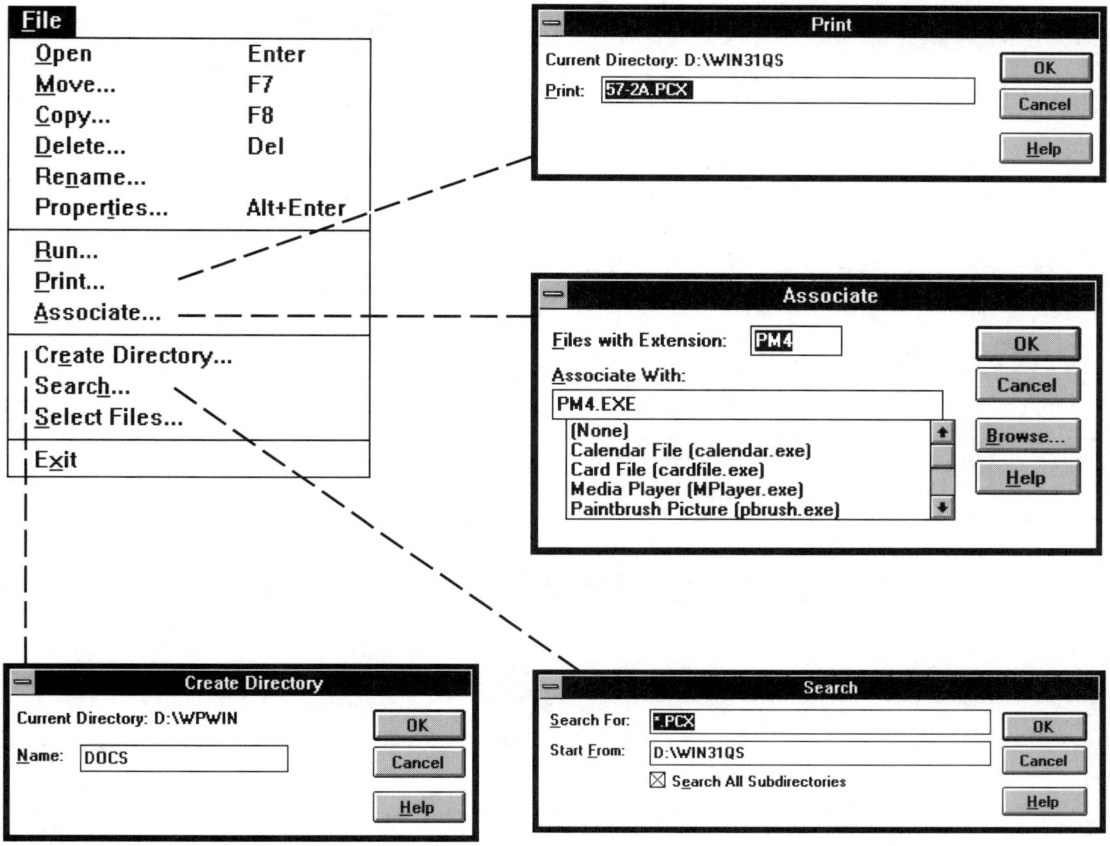
File
Open Enter
Move... F7
Copy... F8
Delete... Del
Rename...
Properties... Alt+Enter
Run...
Print...
Associate...
Create Directory...
Search...
Select Files...
Exit
Print
Current Directory: D:\WIN31QS
Print: 57-2A.PCX
OK
Cancel
Help
Associate
Files with Extension: PM4
Associate With:
PM4.EXE
(None)
Calendar File (calendar.exe)
Card File (cardfile.exe)
Media Player (MPlayer.exe)
Paintbrush Picture (pbrush.exe)
OK
Cancel
Browse...
Help
Create Directory
Current Directory: D:\WPWIN
Name: DOCS
OK
Cancel
Help
Search
Search For: *.PCX
Start From: D:\WIN31QS
Search All Subdirectories
OK
Cancel
Help

## OTHER MENUS

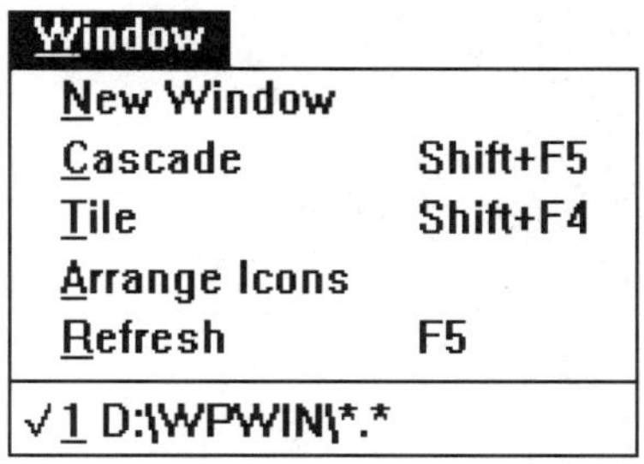
Window
New Window
Cascade Shift+F5
Tile Shift+F4
Arrange Icons
Refresh F5
√1 D:\WPWIN*.*

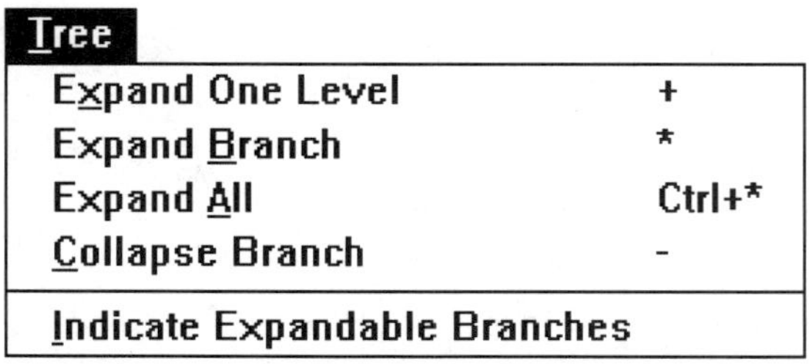
Tree
Expand One Level +
Expand Branch *
Expand All Ctrl+*
Collapse Branch -
Indicate Expandable Branches

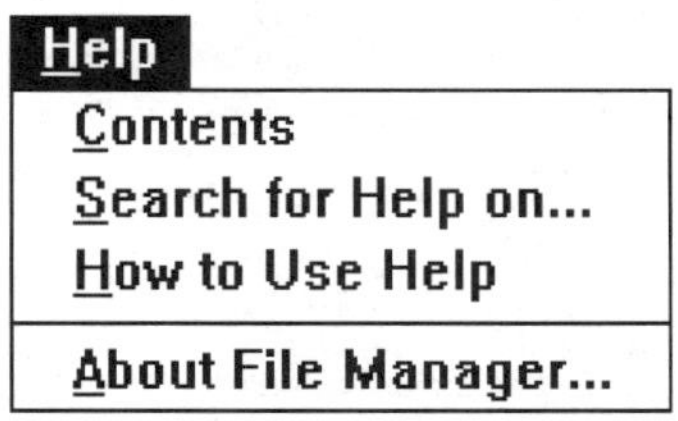
Help
Contents
Search for Help on...
How to Use Help
About File Manager...

## DISK MENU

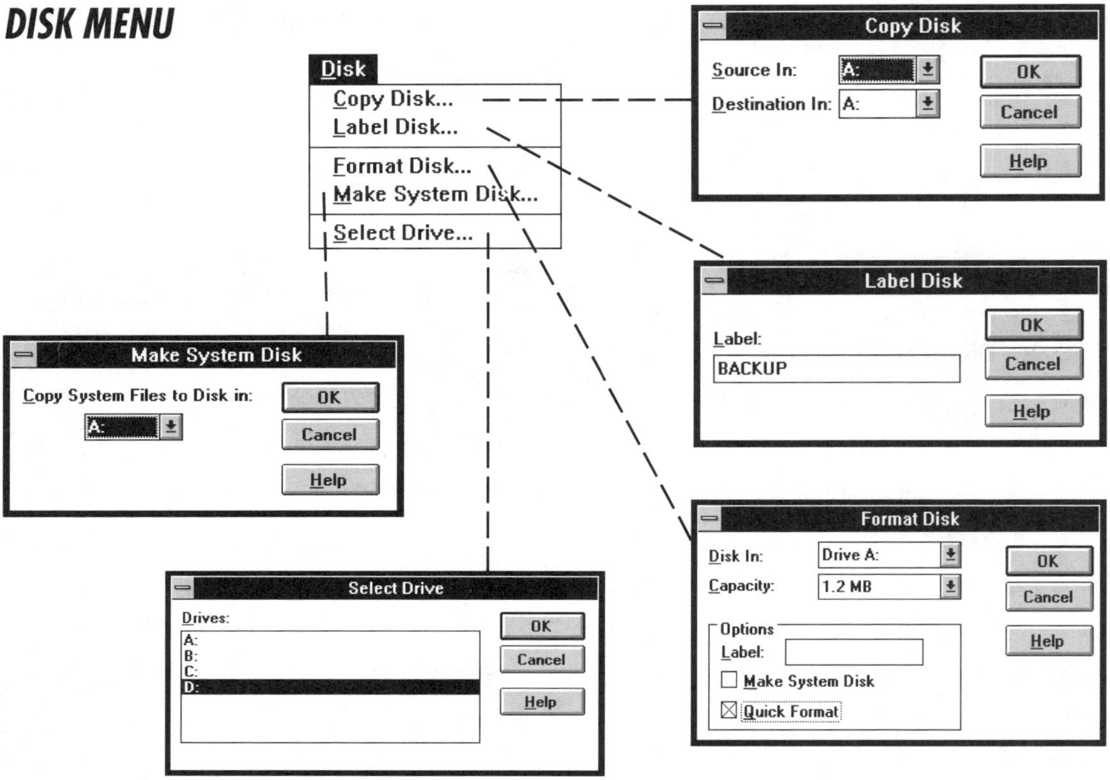


## VIEW MENU

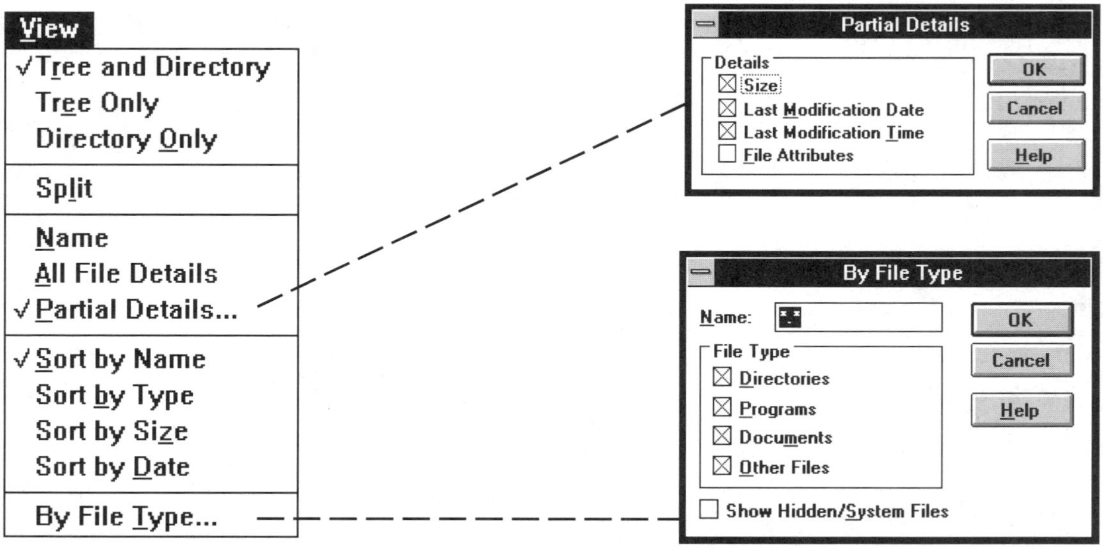

# OPTIONS MENU

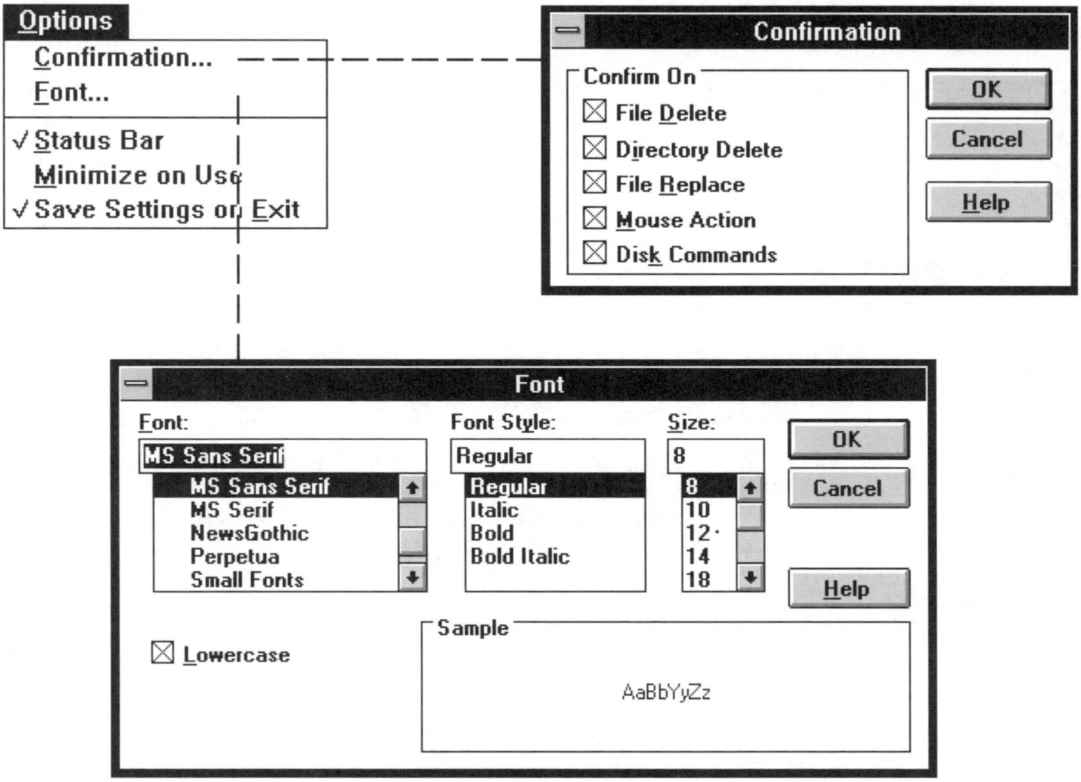

# PRINT MANAGER

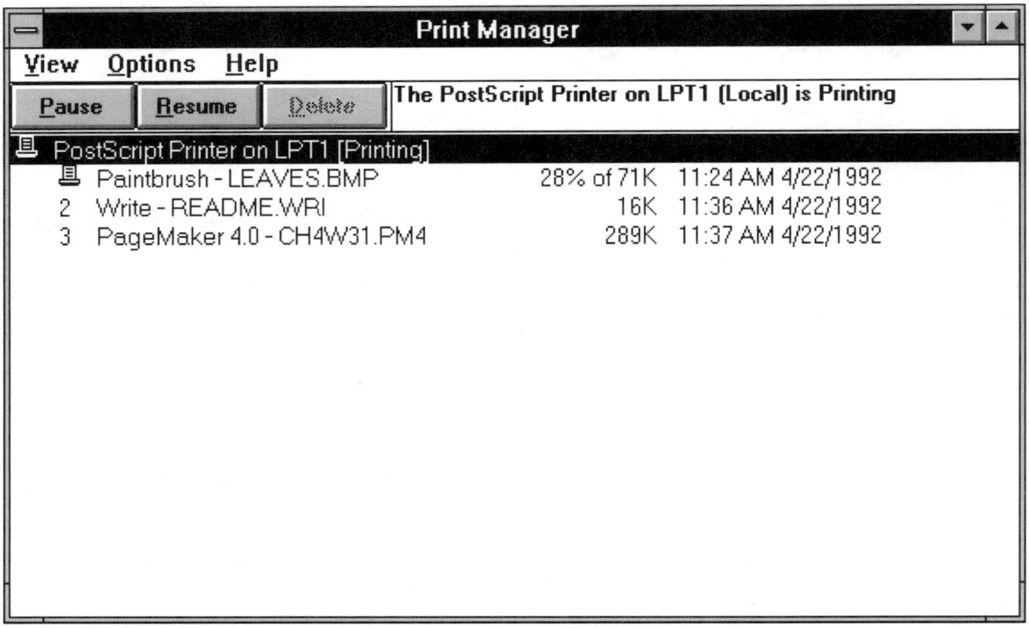


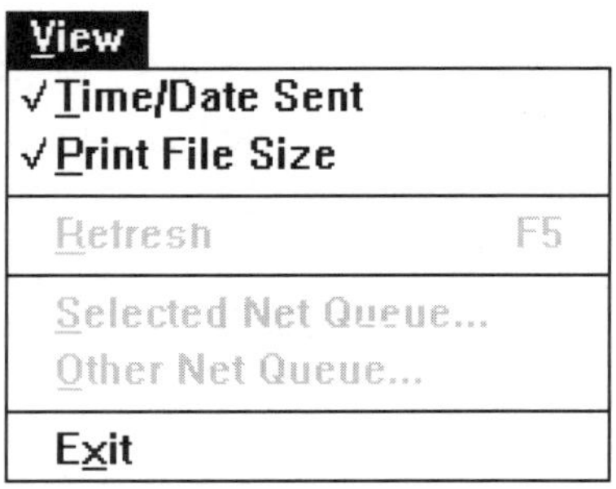


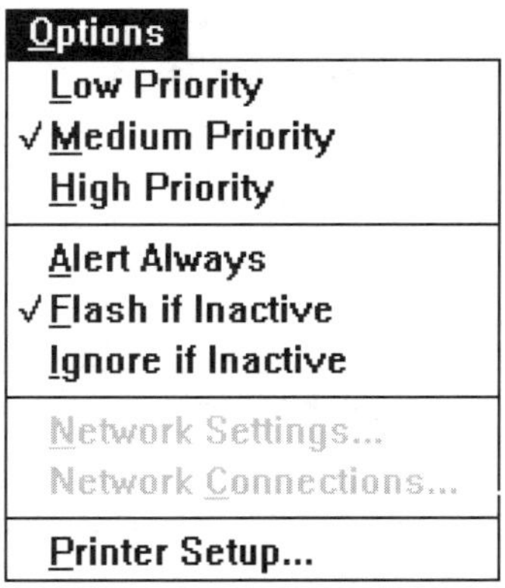


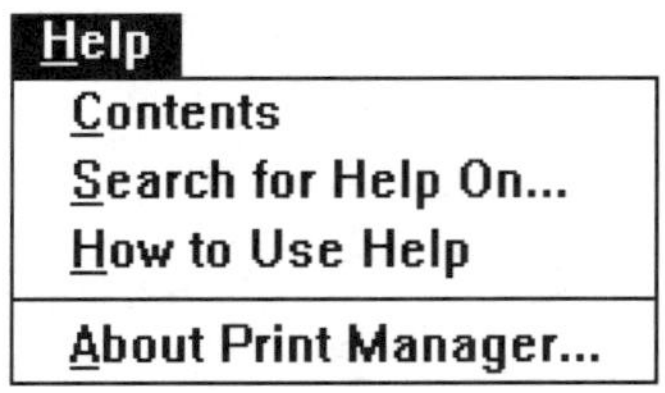

# Windows Setup

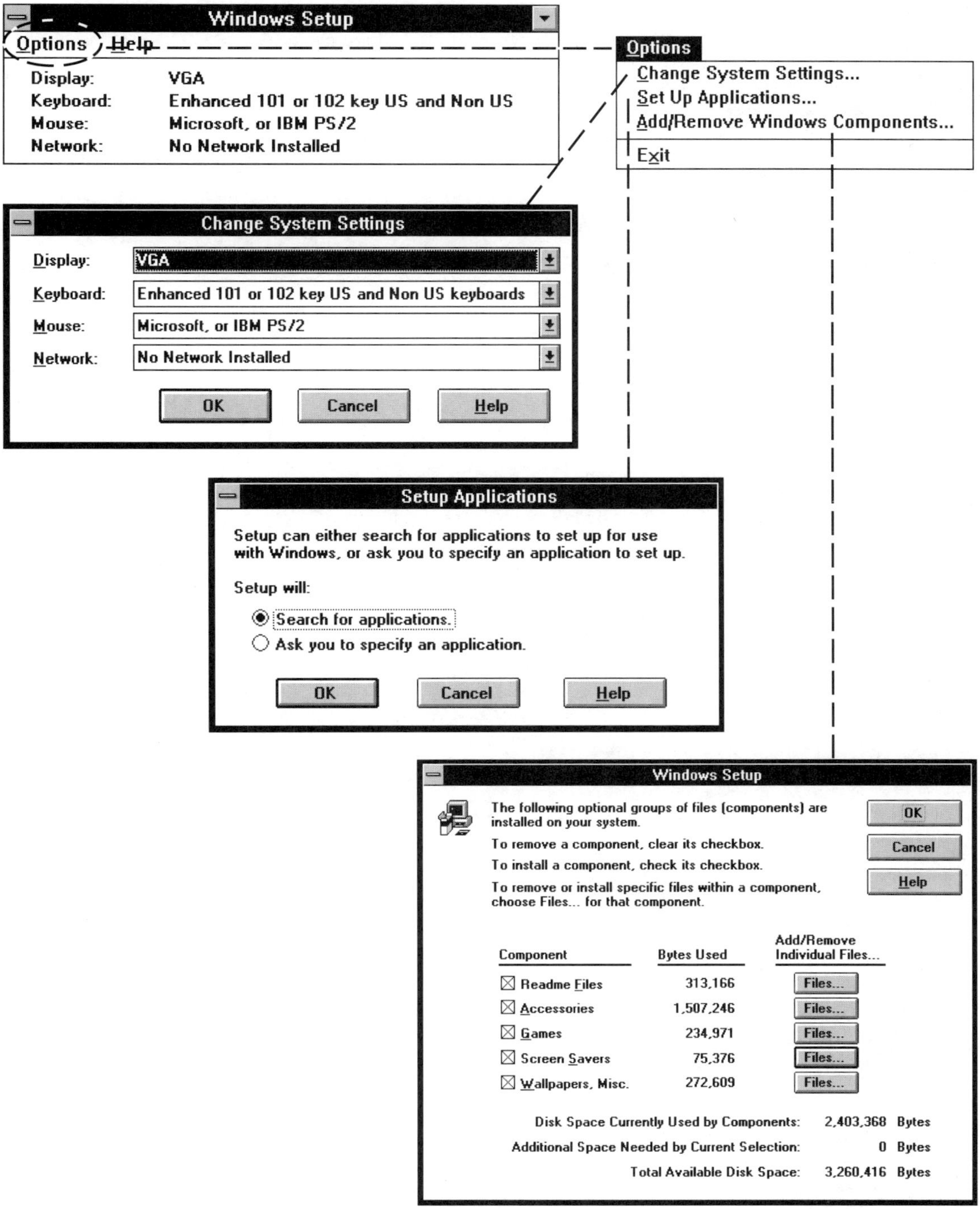

# INDEX

## R



## S



## T



## U



## V



## W